W9-CAG-676

AP® ENGLISH LANGUAGE AND COMPOSITION
ALL ACCESS®

Susan Bureau
Alvirne High School
Hudson, New Hampshire

Stacey A. Kiggins, M.A.
Edison High School
Alexandria, Virginia

Katherine A. Nesselrode
Mandarin High School
Jacksonville, Florida

Kristi R. McGauley, M.Ed.
Mandarin High School
Jacksonville, Florida

Edited by
John Allen
BBE Associates
Oklahoma City, Oklahoma

Research & Education Association
Visit our website: www.rea.com

Research & Education Association
61 Ethel Road West
Piscataway, New Jersey 08854
E-mail: info@rea.com

AP® ENGLISH LANGUAGE AND COMPOSITION ALL ACCESS®

Published 2017

Copyright © 2013 by Research & Education Association, Inc.
All rights reserved. No part of this book may be reproduced in any
form without permission of the publisher.

Printed in the United States of America

Library of Congress Control Number 2012949600

ISBN-13: 978-0-7386-1083-2
ISBN-10: 0-7386-1083-6

Cover image: © iStockphoto.com/CEFutcher

Contents

Chapter 1: Welcome to REA's All Access for AP English Language and Composition

Chapter 2: Strategies for the Exam

Chapter 3: Approaching the Multiple-Choice Questions: The Passages

Chapter 4: Approaching the Multiple-Choice Questions: Rhetorical Strategies

Chapter 5: Approaching the Multiple-Choice Questions: Grammar, Usage, and Style — 67

Chapter 6: Approaching the Multiple-Choice Questions: Documenting Sources — 89

Chapter 7: Approaching the Multiple-Choice Questions: Analyzing a Passage — 95

Chapter 8: Approaching the Essay Questions: Writing an Essay   107

Chapter 9: Approaching the Essay Questions: Grammar, Punctuation, and Spelling   123

Chapter 10: Approaching the Essay Questions: Rhetorical Modes   155

Chapter 11: Approaching the Essay Questions: The Style-Analysis Essay 171

Chapter 12: Approaching the Essay Questions: The Persuasive Essay 181

Chapter 13: Approaching the Essay Questions: The Synthesis Essay 189

Chapter 14: Approaching the Essay Questions: Strategy and Preparation 197

About Our Authors

Susan Bureau is the English Department Head at Alvirne High School in Hudson, New Hampshire, where she has taught AP English Language and Composition for the past nine years. She has a B.A. in English from The University of New Hampshire.

Stacey A. Kiggins received her B.A. degree in Secondary English Education from the University of North Carolina at Greensboro, and her M.A. degree in Initiatives in Educational Transformation, from George Mason University, Virginia. She is the English department chair at Thomas A. Edison High School in Alexandria, Virginia. She has taught a variety of English disciplines, including: Advanced Placement Language and Composition, International Baccalaureate English, and Speech and Debate. Ms. Kiggins is the coach of a nationally recognized speech and debate team, and was the 2010 Virginia Association of Communications Arts and Sciences Speech Teacher of the Year.

Kristi McGauley is currently in her thirteenth year of teaching English. She joined Mandarin High School in November of 2005. Before arriving at MHS, she taught for seven years in a private school. Ms. McGauley graduated with a B.A. in English from Clearwater Christian College and earned her M.Ed. in Secondary English Education at the University of North Florida. She is chair of the school's literacy team.

Katherine A. Nesselrode graduated from the University of Tampa with a Bachelor of Arts in English. She was Nationally Board Certified in 2008. She has been teaching English for 22 years, currently at Mandarin High School in Jacksonville, Florida. She has taught high school English for 17 years and taught middle school English for the first five years of her teaching career.

John Allen has more than 25 years of experience in test preparation. The owner of test-prep developer BBE Associates, Ltd., Allen received his B.A. degree from the University of Oklahoma in 1979. He has collaborated on several textbooks in the field of English-language arts.

About REA

Founded in 1959, Research & Education Association (REA) is dedicated to publishing the finest and most effective educational materials—including study guides and test preps—for students of all ages.

Today, REA's wide-ranging catalog is a leading resource for students, teachers, and other professionals. Visit *www.rea.com* to see a complete listing of all our titles.

Acknowledgments

In addition to our authors, we would like to thank Larry B. Kling, Vice President, Editorial, for supervising development; Pam Weston, Publisher, for setting the quality standards for production integrity and managing the publication to completion; John Cording, Vice President, Technology, for coordinating the design and development of the online REA Study Center; Diane Goldschmidt, Managing Editor, for coordinating development of this edition.

Welcome to REA's All Access for AP English Language and Composition

A new, more effective way to prepare for your AP exam.

There are many different ways to prepare for an AP exam. What's best for you depends on how much time you have to study and how comfortable you are with the subject matter. To score your highest, you need a system that can be customized to fit you: your schedule, your learning style, and your current level of knowledge.

This book, and the free online tools that come with it, will help you personalize your AP prep by testing your understanding, pinpointing your weaknesses, and delivering flashcard study materials unique to you.

Let's get started and see how this system works.

How to Use REA's AP All Access

The REA AP All Access system allows you to create a personalized study plan through three simple steps: targeted review of exam content, assessment of your knowledge, and focused study in the topics where you need the most help.

Here's how it works:

Review the Book	Study the topics tested on the AP exam and learn proven strategies that will help you tackle any question you may see on test day.
Test Yourself & Get Feedback	As you review the book, test yourself. Score reports from your free online tests and quizzes give you a fast way to pinpoint what you really know and what you should spend more time studying.
Improve Your Score	Armed with your score reports, you can personalize your study plan. Review the parts of the book where you are weakest, and use the REA Study Center to create your own unique e-flashcards, adding to the 100 free cards included with this book.

Finding Your Strengths and Weaknesses: The REA Study Center

The best way to personalize your study plan and truly focus on the topics where you need the most help is to get frequent feedback on what you know and what you don't. At the online REA Study Center, you can access three types of assessment: topic-level quizzes, mini-tests, and a full-length practice test. Each of these tools provides true-to-format questions and delivers a detailed score report that follows the topics set by the College Board.

Topic-Level Quizzes

Short online quizzes are available throughout the review and are designed to test your immediate grasp of the topics just covered.

Mini-Tests

Two online mini-tests cover what you've studied in each half of the book. These tests are like the actual AP exam, only shorter, and will help you evaluate your overall understanding of the subject.

Full-Length Practice Test

After you've finished reviewing the book, take our full-length exam to practice under test-day conditions. Available both in this book and online, this practice test gives you the most complete picture of your strengths and weaknesses. We strongly recommend that you take the online version of the exam for the added benefits of timed testing, automatic scoring, and a detailed score report.

Improving Your Score: e-Flashcards

With your score reports from our online quizzes and practice test, you'll be able to see exactly which topics you need to review. Use this information to create your own flashcards for the areas where you still need additional review. And, because you will create these flashcards through the online REA Study Center, you'll be able to access them from any computer or smartphone.

Not quite sure what to put on your flashcards? Start with the 100 free cards included when you buy this book.

After the Full-Length Practice Test: *Crash Course*

After finishing this book and taking our full-length practice exam, pick up REA's *Crash Course for AP English Language and Composition*. Use your most recent score reports to identify any areas where you are still weak, and turn to the *Crash Course* for a rapid review presented in a concise outline style.

REA's Suggested 8-Week AP Study Plan

Depending on how much time you have until test day, you can expand or condense our eight-week study plan as you see fit.

To score your highest, use our suggested study plan and customize it to fit your schedule, targeting the areas where you need the most review.

	Review 1-2 hours	Quiz 15 minutes	e-Flashcards Anytime, anywhere	Mini-Test 30 minutes	Full-Length Practice Test 3 hours
Week 1	Chapters 1-4	Quiz 1	Access your e-flashcards from your computer or smartphone whenever you have a few extra minutes to study. Start with the 100 free cards included when you buy this book. Personalize your prep by creating your own cards for topics where you need extra study.		
Week 2	Chapters 5-6	Quiz 2			
Week 3	Chapter 7	Quiz 3		Mini-Test 1 (The Mid-Term)	
Week 4	Chapter 8	Quiz 4			
Week 5	Chapters 9-11	Quiz 5			
Week 6	Chapters 12-14	Quiz 6			
Week 7	Review Chapter 2 Strategies			Mini-Test 2 (The Final)	
Week 8					Full-Length Practice Exam (Just like test day)

Need even more review? Pick up a copy of REA's *Crash Course for AP English Language and Composition*, a rapid review presented in a concise outline style. Get more information about the *Crash Course* series at *www.rea.com*.

Test-Day Checklist

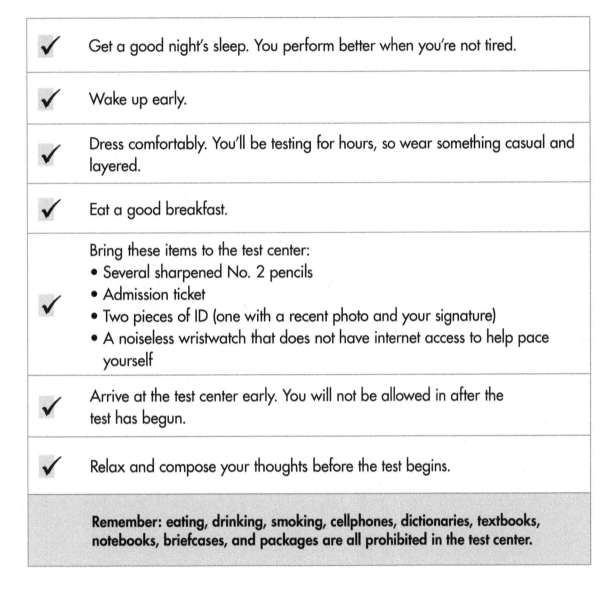

✓	Get a good night's sleep. You perform better when you're not tired.
✓	Wake up early.
✓	Dress comfortably. You'll be testing for hours, so wear something casual and layered.
✓	Eat a good breakfast.
✓	Bring these items to the test center: • Several sharpened No. 2 pencils • Admission ticket • Two pieces of ID (one with a recent photo and your signature) • A noiseless wristwatch that does not have internet access to help pace yourself
✓	Arrive at the test center early. You will not be allowed in after the test has begun.
✓	Relax and compose your thoughts before the test begins.

Remember: eating, drinking, smoking, cellphones, dictionaries, textbooks, notebooks, briefcases, and packages are all prohibited in the test center.

Strategies for the Exam

What Will I See on the AP English Language and Composition Exam?

One May morning, you stroll confidently into the school library where you're scheduled to take the AP English Language and Composition exam. You know your stuff: you paid attention in class, followed your textbook, took plenty of notes, and reviewed your coursework by reading a special test prep guide. You can write for different purposes using standard written English, analyze and synthesize a variety of sources, and cite sources using professional conventions. So, how will you show your knowledge on the test?

The Multiple-Choice Section

First off, you'll complete a lengthy multiple-choice section that mainly tests your ability to analyze the rhetoric of prose passages. This section will require you to answer 55 multiple-choice questions in just 60 minutes. Here are the major areas covered on the AP English Language and Composition exam:

- author's purpose and audience
- rhetorical modes of writing
- grammar and mechanics
- structure and organization
- development
- footnotes and sources

So, being able to identify the satirical purpose of a passage from Jonathan Swift's "A Modest Proposal" will not do you much good unless you can also explain the rhetorical effects he uses to achieve his "reasonable" tone, the point of the analogies or metaphors he employs, and the way that he develops his theme. It sounds like a lot, but by *working quickly and methodically* you'll have plenty of time to address this section effectively. We'll look at this in greater depth later in this chapter.

The Free-Response Section

After time is called on the multiple-choice section, you'll get a short break before diving into the free-response, or essay, section. This section requires you to produce three written responses in 120 minutes. Like the multiple-choice section, the free-response portion of the exam expects you to be able to *apply your own knowledge to analyze and synthesize primary and secondary sources,* in addition to being able to introduce a complex central idea and develop it with appropriate evidence, concise explanations, and clear transitions.

What's the Score?

Although the scoring process for the AP exam may seem quite complex, it boils down to two simple components: your multiple-choice score plus your free-response scores. The multiple-choice section accounts for 45 percent of your overall score, and is generated by awarding one point toward your "raw score" for each question you answer correctly. The free-response section accounts for 55 percent of your total score. In this section, each question counts equally toward your final score. Trained graders read students' written responses and assign points according to grading rubrics. The number of points you accrue out of the total possible will form your score on the free-response section.

The College Board scores your AP exam on a scale of 1 to 5. Although individual colleges and universities determine what credit or advanced placement, if any, is awarded to students at each score level, these are the assessments typically associated with each numeric score:

5 Extremely well qualified

4 Well qualified

3 Qualified

2 Possibly qualified

1 No recommendation

Section I: Strategies for the Multiple-Choice Section of the Exam

Because the AP exam is a standardized test, each version of the test from year to year must share many similarities in order to be fair. That means that you can always expect certain things to be true about your English Language and Composition exam.

Which of the following phrases accurately describes a multiple-choice question on the AP English Language and Composition exam?

(A) always has five choices

(B) requires analysis of the rhetoric and structure of a nonfiction prose passage

(C) may ask you to find a wrong idea or group related concepts

Did you pick "all of the above?" Good job!

(D) more likely to test interpretation and application of author's purpose and effects than concrete details

(E) all of the above*

What does this mean for your study plan? You should focus on author's purpose and how various rhetorical tools and methods can be applied to achieve certain effects. Think about different types of text structure, such as cause-effect and comparison-contrast. You should also review details of grammatical structure, such as parallelism or subordination. Keep in mind, too, how different compositional elements can interact; an author's purpose may provide an explanation for the rhetorical strategies in use and vice versa. This means that you should consider the connections among concepts such as subject matter, tone, structure, vocabulary, and grammar. This will help prepare you for questions that ask you to use Roman numerals to consider aspects of a passage in isolation and in combination. Let's examine a typical Roman-numeral item:

The passage in Hamlet that begins "To be or not to be" is best described as which of the following?

---

*Of course, on the actual AP English Language and Composition exam, you won't see any choices featuring "all of the above" or "none of the above." Do, however, watch for "except" questions. We'll cover this kind of item a bit later in this section.

I. a soliloquy

II. a call to arms

III. a meditation on suicide

(A)   I only

(B)   II only

(C)   III only

(D)   I and III only

(E)   I, II, and III

The question is tricky because (A) and (C) are both partly correct, but neither is the *best* answer. (B) and (E) are not correct because they both include II, and the passage is *not* a call to arms. The best answer is (D) because the passage is a soliloquy (a speech to oneself) that is also a meditation on suicide.

Types of Questions

You've already seen a list of the general content areas that you'll encounter on the AP English Language and Composition exam. But how do those different areas translate into questions?

Question Type	Sample Question Stems
Author's purpose and audience	The author's primary concern in this passage is to _____.
	Which of the following sentences from the passage represent the author's main point?
	The author uses _____ to appeal to the audience's _____ (emotions, sense of justice, patriotism, etc.).
	If one were to take the author's advice, one should _____.
Rhetorical modes of writing	The tone of the passage can best be described as _____ (often the answers include two words, i.e., supercilious and scornful, reverent and respectful, etc.).
	The shift in point of view has the effect of _____.
	The author's reference to _____ serves primarily to _____.
	The third paragraph of the passage is unified by metaphors of _____.
	The author uses the word _____ to suggest that _____.

(continued)

(continued)

Question Type	Sample Question Stems
Grammar and mechanics	The subject of the verb _____ is which of the following? Which of the following is grammatically parallel to _____?
Structure and organization	The structure of lines 00-00 can best be described as _____. In relation to the rest of the passage, the _____ paragraph serves to _____. The description of _____ helps to unify the passage by _____. Which of the following best describes the relationship between the first and second paragraphs?
Development	The passage is developed through _____ (a series of examples, an extended comparison, an analogy, etc.). The pattern of exposition in this passage is best described as _____. The examples in the passage are meant to illustrate _____.
Footnotes and sources	Which of the following is an accurate reading of footnote 3? What is the author's source for the assertion that_____?

Throughout this book you will find tips on the features and strategies you can use to answer different types of questions.

Achieving Multiple-Choice Success

It's true that you don't have a lot of time to finish this section of the AP exam. But it's also true that you don't need to get every question right to get a great score. Answering just two-thirds of the questions correctly — along with a good showing on the free-response section — can earn you a score of 4 or 5. That means that not only do you not have to answer every question right, you don't even need to answer every question at all. By *working quickly and methodically*, however, you'll have all the time you'll need. Plan to spend about 40 seconds on each multiple-choice question. You may find it helpful to use a timer or stopwatch as you answer one question a few times to help you get a handle on how long 40 seconds feels in a testing situation. If timing is hard for you, set a timer for ten minutes each time you take one of the 15-question online quizzes that accompany this book to help you practice working at speed. Let's look at some other strategies for answering multiple-choice items.

Process of Elimination

You've probably used this strategy, intentionally or unintentionally, throughout your entire test-taking career. The process of elimination requires you read each answer choice and consider whether it is the best response to the question given. Because the AP exam typically asks you to find the best answer rather than the only answer, it's almost always advantageous to read each answer choice. More than one choice may have some grain of truth to it, but only one — the right answer — will be the most correct. Let's examine a multiple-choice question and use the process-of-elimination approach:

In the third paragraph, when the author says, "I am surprised that the senator's nose didn't grow like Pinocchio's when he insisted flatly that he was anxious to compromise," he is employing which figure of speech?

(A)   hyperbole

(B)   allusion

(C)   onomatopoeia

(D)   personification

(E)   euphemism

> Consider each answer choice and eliminate those that are clearly wrong, such as *onomatopoeia* and *euphemism*. Remember that *personification* means to give human characteristics to a nonhuman creature or object, so this is also incorrect. Remember that Pinocchio is a character in a children's tale — a literary character. Does *hyperbole* or *allusion* mean a reference to a literary character or situation? (*Allusion* does indeed mean this.) If necessary, take your best guess. You've got a fifty percent chance of being right.

Students often find the most difficult question types on the AP exam to be those that ask you to find a statement that is not true or to identify an exception among otherwise similar things. To answer these questions correctly, you must be sure to carefully read and consider each answer choice, keeping in mind that four of them will be correct and just one wrong. Sometimes, you can find the right answer by picking out the one that just does not fit with the other choices. If four answer choices relate to the way Emerson uses botanical imagery in a passage from his essay "Compensation," for example, the correct answer choice may well be the one that addresses an image that has nothing to with plants. Let's look at a multiple-choice question of this type.

In the "Gettysburg Address," Lincoln's purposes include all the following EXCEPT

(A) ~~connect the Union's war objectives to the nation's founding.~~

(B) ~~honor the Union soldiers who died in the battle of Gettysburg.~~

(C) ~~affirm the Union's determination to prevail against the Confederate armies.~~

(D) declare that slavery had to be abolished from the North American continent.

(E) ~~inspire the Union's soldiers to win the war for the sake of those who had given their lives for the Union cause.~~

> To answer a NOT or EXCEPT question correctly, test each option by asking yourself: *Is this choice true? Does this correctly state a purpose Lincoln had in writing the Gettysburg Address?* Notice that all the answers except (D) correctly name a purpose connected to the Union war effort and Union soldiers. You may wish to physically cross off answer choices as you eliminate them.

Predicting

Although using the process of elimination certainly helps you consider each answer choice thoroughly, testing each and every answer can be a slow process. To help answer the most questions in the limited time given AP test takers, you may find it helpful to instead try predicting the right answer before you read the answer choices. For example, you know that the answer to the math problem 2 + 2 will always be four. If you saw this multiple-choice item on a math test, you wouldn't need to systematically test each response, but could go straight to the right answer. You can apply a similar technique to even complex items on the AP exam. Brainstorm your own answer to the question before reading the answer choices. Then, pick the answer choice closest to the one you brainstormed. Let's look at how this technique could work on a common type of question on the AP English Language and Composition exam.

When the authors refer to Lenin's limited endorsement of capitalism in his 1921 New Economic Policy speech to distract from their true preference for socialism, they are using which rhetorical fallacy?

(A) red herring

(B) scare tactics

(C) hasty generalization

(D) slippery slope

(E) straw man argument

> You might remember from your studies that a fallacious argument that seeks to distract or shift attention away from the main issue by introducing an irrelevant idea is called a "red herring." You can predict that this is the correct answer, since the question uses the word "distract." Then, scan the answer choices to find the correct one.

What should you do if you don't see your prediction among the answer choices? Your prediction should have helped you narrow down the choices. You may wish to apply the process of elimination to the remaining options to further home in on the right answer. Then, you can use your knowledge of rhetorical tools and practices to make a good guess.

Learning to predict takes some practice. You're probably used to immediately reading all of the answer choices for a question, but in order to predict well, you usually need to avoid doing this. Remember, the test maker doesn't want to make the right answers too obvious, so the wrong answers are intended to sound like appealing choices. You may find it helpful to cover the answer choices to a question as you practice predicting. This will help make sure that you don't sneak a peek at the choices too soon. Let's examine another question to practice predicting in this way. Read the following paragraph and question and predict an answer.

> Paris is a beautiful city, perhaps the most beautiful on earth. Long, broad avenues are lined with seventeenth and eighteenth century apartments, office buildings, and cafés. Flowers give the city a rich and varied look. The bridges and the river lend an air of lightness and grace to the whole urban landscape.

In this paragraph, the word "rich" most nearly means

(A) wealthy

(B) polluted

(C) prismatic

(D) dull

(E) affluent

> Think about how the word "rich" is used in this paragraph. It obviously doesn't refer to material wealth, but to visual richness, as in color and variety. From this analysis, you can predict that the answer will have to do with these qualities. Now, scan the answer choices to find the right one.

By thinking about the context and predicting the answer before reading the choices, you have not been tempted by the options that sound plausible but are wrong. For example, choices (A) and (E) are both synonyms for a common meaning of "rich," and thus seem like plausible picks for the right answer. However, the correct answer is (C), prismatic, with its connotation of a rich variety of colors.

Avoiding Common Errors

Remember, while you should try to answer every question on the exam, the main goal is to answer questions correctly. Take care to work at a pace that allows you to avoid these common mistakes:

- Missing key words that change the meaning of a question, such as *not*, *except*, or *least*. You might want to circle these words in your test booklet so you're tuned into them when answering the question.

- Overthinking an item and spending too much time agonizing over the correct response.

- Changing your answer but incompletely erasing your first choice.

Some More Advice

Let's quickly review what you've learned about answering multiple-choice questions effectively on the AP exam. Using these techniques on practice tests will help you become comfortable with them before diving into the real exam, so be sure to apply these ideas as you work through this book.

- Focus on learning the strategies and techniques of writing and mechanics so you can effectively analyze any passage.

- You have just about 40 seconds to complete each multiple-choice question. Pacing yourself during practice tests and exercises can help you get used to these time constraints.

- Because there is no guessing penalty, remember that making an educated guess is to your benefit. Remember to use the process of elimination to narrow your choices. You might just guess the correct answer and get another point!

- Instead of spending valuable time pondering narrow distinctions or questioning your first answer, trust yourself to make good guesses most of the time.

- Read the question and think of what your answer would be before reading the answer choices.

- Expect the unexpected. You will see questions that ask you to analyze a piece of writing in various ways, such as identifying an irrelevant idea, focusing on a small point of grammatical structure, or making a broad generalization.

Section II: Strategies for the Free-Response Section of the Exam

The AP English Language and Composition exam always contains a free-response section that includes a **synthesis essay** and two essay questions. You will have 15 minutes to read the sources for the synthesis essay and 120 minutes to write the synthesis essay and answer the essay questions. Generally, you will encounter one **rhetorical analysis** or **language analysis essay question**, and one **argument essay question**. The first type of essay question requires you to analyze a passage for its author's use of rhetorical strategies. The second requires you to make a cogent, well-reasoned argument about some point in a passage of writing.

Taking on the Synthesis Essay

The synthesis essay question will present you with an essay prompt along with several sources, including one visual source such as a photograph, painting, or chart. Before you can begin writing, you must spend 15 minutes reviewing the sources. You might want to take notes on them. Synthesis essay questions rarely present you with sources already familiar to you, so you will need to use what you know about the topic in order to interpret the sources. Let's take a look at a typical synthesis essay question.

(Suggested reading time — 15 minutes)

(Suggested writing time — 40 minutes)

Obviously, a parent has an enormous impact on a child's life. However, experts differ on just how a parent influences a child, and how that influence affects the child's development. What aspects of a child's life are most impacted by a parent? Or is the impact of a parent overstated in some ways?

Carefully read the following six sources, including the introductory information for each source. Then synthesize information from at least three of the sources and incorporate it into a coherent, well-developed essay that defends, challenges, or qualifies the claim that a parent influences the physical and emotional development of a child.

Make sure that your argument is central; use the sources to illustrate and support your reasoning. Avoid merely summarizing the sources. Indicate clearly which sources you are drawing from, whether through direct quotation, paraphrase, or summary. You may cite sources as Source A, Source B, etc., or by using the descriptions in parentheses.

Source A (Maslow)

Source B (National Institute of Mental Health)

Source C (Eisenberg)

Source D (Hastings)

Source E (Cartoon)

Source F (Child Stats)

Source G (President George W. Bush)

This list features the usual types of sources that you will see in a synthesis essay question. Following are the sources themselves, including six text passages and one image. Remember, you will have 15 minutes at the beginning of the time allotted for the synthesis essay during which you are required to read and consider the sources. Use this time wisely by thoroughly examining the documents and taking notes, if necessary. Now read the sources themselves.

Source A

Maslow, Abraham. "A Theory of Human Motivation." *Psychological Review* 50.4 (1943): 370–96. Motional-literacy-education.com. Mark Zimmerman, 2002. Web. 13 Oct. 2010.

The following passage is excerpted from a book by Abraham Maslow, a classical psychologist who was best known for his research on human needs.

[An] indication of the child's need for safety is his preference for some kind of undisrupted routine or rhythm. He seems to want a predictable, orderly world. For instance, injustice, unfairness, or inconsistency in the parents seems to make a child feel anxious and unsafe. This attitude may be not so much because of the injustice per se or any particular pains involved, but rather because this treatment threatens to make the world look unreliable, or unsafe, or unpredictable. Young children seem to thrive better under a system which has at least a skeletal outline of rigidity, in which there is a schedule of a kind, some sort of routine, something that can be counted upon, not only for the present but also far into the future. Perhaps one could express this more accurately by saying that the child needs an organized world rather than an unorganized or unstructured one.

The central role of the parents and the normal family setup are indisputable. Quarreling, physical assault, separation, divorce or death within the family may be particularly terrifying. Also parental outbursts of rage or threats of punishment directed to the child, calling him names, speaking to him harshly, shaking him, handling him roughly, or actual physical punishment sometimes elicit such total panic and terror in the child that we must assume more is involved than the physical pain alone. While it is true that in some children this terror may represent also a fear of loss of parental love, it can also occur in completely rejected children, who seem to cling to the hating parents more for sheer safety and protection than because of hope of love.

Source B

"Child and Adolescent Violence Research at the NIH." *NIMH · Home.* 2000. Web. 16 Oct. 2010.< http://www.nimh.nih.gov.>

The following passage is excerpted from a National Institute of Mental Health overview that summarizes research into the causes, diagnosis, prevention, and treatment of child and adolescent violence.

The research on risk for aggressive, antisocial, and violent behavior includes multiple aspects and stages of life, beginning with interactions in the family. Such forces as weak bonding, ineffective parenting (poor monitoring, ineffective, excessively harsh, or inconsistent discipline, inadequate supervision), exposure to violence in the home, and a climate that supports aggression and violence puts children at risk for being violent later in life. . . .

. . . When antisocial behavior emerges later in childhood or adolescence, it is suspected that genetic factors contribute less, and such youths tend to engage in delinquent behavior primarily because of peer influences and lapses in parenting. The nature of the child's social environment regulates the degree to which heritable early predisposition results in later antisocial behavior. Highly adaptive parenting is likely to help children who may have a predisposition to antisocial behavior. . . .

Research has demonstrated that youths who engage in high levels of antisocial behavior are much more likely than other youths to have a biological parent who also engages in antisocial behavior. This association is believed to reflect both the genetic transmission of predisposing temperament and the maladaptive parenting of antisocial parents.

The importance of some aspects of parenting may vary at different ages. For example, inadequate supervision apparently plays a stronger role in late childhood and adolescence than in early childhood. There is evidence from many studies that parental use of physical punishment may play a direct role in the development of antisocial behavior in their children. In longitudinal studies, higher levels of parental supervision during childhood have been found to predict less antisocial behavior during adolescence. Other researchers have observed that parents often do not define antisocial behavior as something that should be discouraged, including such acts as youths bullying or hitting other children or engaging in "minor" delinquent acts such as shoplifting.

Research examining the mental health outcomes of child abuse and neglect has demonstrated that childhood victimization places children at increased risk for delinquency, adult criminality, and violent criminal behavior. Findings from early research on trauma suggest that traumatic stress can result in failure of systems essential to a person's management of stress response, arousal, memory, and personal identity that can affect functioning long after acute exposure to the trauma has ended. One might expect that the consequences of trauma can be even more profound and long lasting when they influence the physiology, behavior, and mental life of a developing child or adolescent.

Source C

Eisenberg, Leon. "What's Happening to American Families? ERIC Digest." *ERICDigests.org.* 1991. Web. 16 Oct. 2010.

The following passage is excerpted from an article that focuses on changes in the structure and role of the American family.

Few issues vex Americans more than what has happened to the role of the family in caring for children. Almost one in four of the nation's youngsters under 18 lives with only one parent, almost always the mother. If the youngster is black, the ratio rises to one in two. The divorce ratio has tripled and the percentage of out-of-wedlock births among teenage women has doubled over the past 15 years.

Caring for infants is not just a dilemma for female-headed households. Whether or not the family is intact, more than half of all mothers with a preschool child are in the labor force, 50 percent more than the proportion employed out of the home a decade ago. The Labor Department reports that the number of women holding two or more jobs has increased five-fold since 1970.

What we need, we hear on all sides, is a return to the good old days when parents were responsible for their kids and kids obeyed their parents. We long for a return to an age when fundamental values were shared by all. If there WAS such an age, can we go back to it? No one doubts that today's family is harassed and overburdened. The question is: could what seemed to work then work now?

In the aftermath of the Industrial Revolution, the American family has been stripped of two of its traditional social functions: serving as a unit for economic production and as a school for the vocational training of children. The first function has been usurped by commercial firms, the second by the state. Two functions remain: first, the physical and emotional gratification of the family's adult members, and second, the socialization of the children into community mores and the promotion of their development. . . .

. . . [E]conomist Victor Fuchs has calculated that between 1960 and 1986, the opportunity for children to spend time with parents declined by 10 hours per week for the average white child, and 12 hours for the black child. The principal reason is the increase in the proportion of mothers holding paid jobs; not far behind is the increase in one-parent households. Fathers in intact families could offset the loss in hours of mothering by doing more fathering; there is little evidence that they do so. . . .

Parents of the past learned by modeling themselves not only on their parents, but on uncles, aunts, and grandparents at home or nearby. As they grew up, they learned how to care for younger siblings because they were expected to. The isolated nuclear family and the sharp sequestration of age groups in today's society combine to deprive today's children of these experiences.

. . . As society continues to evolve, so will the family. As the family changes, we will need to continue to monitor the state of our children.

Source D

Hastings, P. D., K. E. McShane, R. Parker, and F. Ladha. "Parents' Influence on Kids' Behavior: Not Much: Cognitive Daily." *Journal of Genetic Psychology* 168.2 (2007): 177–200. Science-Blogs. Dan Munger, 20 May 2008. Web. 16 Oct. 2010.

The following is an excerpt from research findings indicating the influence or lack thereof that parents have on their children.

How do you raise "good kids"? It's one of the questions that plagues parents even before their kids are born. Although everyone's child can't be above average, we all want our kids to be nice to others, to "get along" in the world. But kids don't necessarily cooperate. How do we keep them from becoming delinquents, convicts, or worse?

Unfortunately a lot of the research suggests that parents don't actually have much influence on their kids' behavior – peers, other environmental factors, and genetics seem to have a larger impact. Yet as parents, we can't simply throw up our hands and give up. We exert whatever small influence we do have, and hope it doesn't backfire.

Some studies have suggested that mothers have a disproportionate influence on kids, and that an authoritative parenting style leads to the best results (more prosocial children, who get along with others better). But according to a research team led by Paul Hastings, many of these studies are flawed because they don't measure masculine prosocial behaviors – the actions more likely to be seen in boys than girls. Girls, they say, tend to be more helpful, sympathetic, and passionate, while boys are more friendly, engaged, and assertive (without being aggressive). All these behaviors are really prosocial.

Hastings and his colleagues had the parents of 133 two- to five-year-olds read several stories about interactions between children and asked how they would respond to the situation if their child had been involved in the situation. The parents also filled in a survey to determine how authoritative their parenting style was.

From five to nine months later, the children themselves were observed playing in a group. After playing for 40 minutes, the experimenter gave them a new toy drum and observed how well they interacted with the new toy. Did they take turns? Did they make sure everyone had a chance to play? In addition, the kids' preschool teachers answered a questionnaire about each child's prosocial behavior.

Was there a relationship between the parents' earlier responses and the children's behavior later?

Giving behaviors are those stereotypically considered feminine: giving a toy to another child, accepting an invitation to play, and offering a different activity. "Attributions" corresponds to parents stating that prosocial behaviors were part of their child's disposition. For mothers, there was a significant positive correlation between attribution and girls' later giving behavior. Mothers who discussed positive behavior with their sons had sons who later exhibited giving. Finally, mothers' indirect praise of their daughters (to teachers, for example) was also correlated significantly with later giving behavior. None of the fathers' strategies correlated significantly with giving.

Source E

Baldwin, Mike. "Parental Influence Cartoon Illustration Blowup." *CartoonStock - Cartoon Pictures, Political Cartoons, Animations.* Web. 16 Oct. 2010.

"Your father kicked in the screen and threw the set out the window. He feels violence on TV is a bad influence."

Source F

"America's Children: Key National Indicators of Well-Being." *Childstats.gov*. 2000. Web. 16 Oct. 2010.

The following information is excerpted from a publication that addresses the relationship between a mother's level of education and a child's proficiency upon entry to kindergarten.

As children enter kindergarten for the first time, they demonstrate a diverse range of cognitive knowledge, social skills, and approaches to learning. This indicator highlights their proficiency in several key skills needed to develop the ability to read. How well children read eventually affects how they learn and ultimately influences their chances for school success. Social skills and positive approaches to learning are also related to success in school and are equally important at this age. The depth and breadth of children's knowledge and skills are related to both developmental and experiential factors. These include child characteristics such as age, gender, and cognitive and sensory limitations and characteristics of the child's home environment and preschool experience. Mother's education is the background variable that is consistently related to children's knowledge and skills.

Source G

"White House. Parents' *Day Presidential Proclamation*. 25 July 2003. Web. 16 Oct. 2010.

The following is excerpted from a press release issued in July 2003 by the White House for President George W. Bush.

Children are a daily reminder of the blessings and responsibilities of life and a source of joy, pride, and fulfillment. Parents, stepparents, adoptive parents, and foster parents have the important responsibility of providing for, protecting, nurturing, teaching, and loving their children. On Parents' Day, we honor America's mothers and fathers and celebrate the values that bind families from one generation to the next and help define us as a Nation.

As a child's first teachers, parents are the most influential and effective instructors in a child's life. Through their words, actions, and sacrifices, parents are living examples for children. Young boys and girls watch their parents closely and imitate their behavior. Parents play a critical role in instilling responsibility, integrity, and other life lessons that shape the lives of America's future leaders.

My Administration is committed to supporting our Nation's families. We are working with faith-based and community organizations to promote healthy marriages, responsible parenting, and education. And we are committed to fully funding and supporting the Promoting Safe and Stable Families Program, which helps strengthen family bonds, promote adoption, and provide help for vulnerable children across our country.

Volunteer service is one way parents can spend time with their children while encouraging them to learn the value of helping others. . . . Parenting is one of the most rewarding and challenging endeavors in life. On this special day, we recognize the hard work and compassion of America's parents and celebrate the mothers and fathers who are positive role models for their children. I encourage parents to spend more time reading, talking, and volunteering with their children. I also urge parents to share the joys and wisdom of parenthood with new families in their communities and those planning families for the future.

NOW, THEREFORE, I, GEORGE W. BUSH, President of the United States of America, by virtue of the authority vested in me by the Constitution and laws of the United States and consistent with Public Law 103–362, as amended, do hereby proclaim Sunday, July 27, 2003, as Parents' Day. I encourage all Americans to express their respect and appreciation to parents everywhere for their contributions to their children, families, communities, and our Nation. I also call upon citizens to observe this day with appropriate programs, ceremonies, and activities.

IN WITNESS WHEREOF, I have hereunto set my hand this twenty-fifth day of July, in the year of our Lord two thousand three, and of the Independence of the United States of America the two hundred and twenty-eighth.

Step One: Reading and Evaluating the Sources

Use the beginning 15-minute period to read all the sources, reserving judgment until you have completed all of them. This is important for a couple of reasons. First, you may not know enough about the topic to have an informed opinion, so you will need the sources to develop one. Second, the available sources might not be the ones that support the position you want to take. Given your limited time to think and respond to the essay question, it is probably best to choose the sources that will help you make a focused response, regardless if it is an exact reflection of your true opinions or beliefs. Nevertheless, the sources included are generally diverse enough to support a variety of responses.

Remember that the prompt asked you to use *at least* three of the sources in developing your essay. If you want to use more, that's fine. Also, try to acknowledge the sources that contradict your opinion or position. Higher-scoring responses often reflect the complexity of the issue by including some discussion of opposing viewpoints. Just remember to state firmly why you disagree with these viewpoints. You don't want to sound unfocused and indecisive.

If you wish, take notes and mark up the sources as you consider them. Circle key ideas or points that you wish to include in your essay. Also, jot down a personal experience or an example from literature or history that would complement a source.

Step Two: Developing an Outline

The test maker recommends that students plan to spend 40 minutes in addition to the reading period to plan and write the synthesis essay. Even though time is relatively short, you should dedicate 5 minutes to developing a simple outline to guide your writing. That's because creating a simple outline will allow you to organize your thoughts, brainstorm good examples, and reject ideas that don't really work once you think about them. Your outline should include a thesis statement and the main points you wish to include in your essay. To help organize your essay, you may wish to divide your ideas up paragraph by paragraph, or list them in the order in which you plan to discuss them. In your outline, add references to the specific sources you wish to include in your response to help you remember what you've read. Make your outline short, to the point, and complete, including ideas for a conclusion. By following the outline, your response will be focused and logical.

Perhaps the most important part of your outline is your thesis statement. If possible, your thesis statement should be a clear, direct response to the question posed in the essay prompt. Including a relevant and well-supported thesis is the single most important step you can take to achieving a good score on the synthesis essay — or indeed on any essay question. A well-written essay with no thesis will score much lower than an average-quality essay that accomplishes its goal of supporting an argument or position. To help you generate a suitable thesis, restate the question or prompt with your answer in a complete sentence. For example, a good thesis for the example question might be, *The ways that a parent influences a child's life are numerous and profound, although they can also be both positive and negative.*

Step Three: Writing a Response

Once you've written a good outline, stick to it! As you write your response, you'll find that most of the hard work is already done, and you can focus on expressing your ideas clearly, concisely, and completely. Remember, too, that the essay scorers know what information has been provided in the sources. Don't waste time and effort quoting the contents of the documents extensively. Refer to your sources in the way prescribed in the directions. Be sure to include all of the major ideas from your outline and to stick to the topic. You'll have plenty of time to complete your essay if you don't get distracted and follow your plan.

As you're writing your response, keep in mind what the AP Readers will see when they sit down to consider your essay weeks from now. Expressing your ideas clearly and succinctly will help them best understand your point and ensure that you get the best possible score. Remember, this is an academic essay, so write in a formal style, with no slang, abbreviations, or other kinds of casual language. You should also limit your use of the first-person singular, unless you are including a brief example from your own experience. Using your clearest handwriting will also do wonders for your overall score; free-response graders are used to reading poor handwriting, but that doesn't mean they can decipher every hasty scribble that you make. Printing your response instead of writing it in cursive is another option, as well as skipping lines between lines of writing.

Another good way to help AP Readers understand the point of your response is to state your thesis clearly and succinctly in the opening of your essay. This will highlight your focus from the start and let scorers know what they're looking for through the rest of the essay. Restating your thesis and main ideas at the end of the essay is another good practice.

Step Four: Revising Your Response

Even the best writers make mistakes, especially when writing quickly: skipping or repeating words, misspelling names of people or places, neglecting to include an important point from an outline are all common errors when rushed. Reserving a few minutes at the end of your writing period will allow you to review your responses quickly and make any necessary corrections. Adding skipped words or including forgotten information are the two most important edits you can make to your writing, because these will clarify your ideas and help your score.

A Sample Synthesis Essay Response

After you've read and considered the sources, outlined and planned your response, and written and revised your essay, what will you have? A thoughtful response likely to earn you a good score, that's what. Review the sample response below to help you understand what a well-planned, thoughtful synthesis essay should contain.

We all have many influences in our lives, and those influences may change as we grow and develop. However, parents almost always play a major role in a person's life. The influences of a parent in a child's life are numerous, and they can be both positive and negative.

Parents affect our performance at school. Schools expect all students to get along with one another; however, children whose parents are antisocial are not likely to possess adequate skills to meet those expectations (Source B) since children almost always imitate their parent's behavior (Source G). Additionally, a parent's level of education may affect a child's academic performance. The ChildStats website correlates mothers' education level with young children's proficiency in the skills they need even at the kindergarten level (Source F). One can speculate from these figures that the less-educated mother may simply not have the knowledge to help her children learn what they need to know, but other factors (e.g., home environment may also be involved. Children who come from unhappy homes are not likely to care much about doing well at school — and may not be able to perform well even if they do care.

Parents influence the way we look at the world and what we expect in life. Maslow pointed out that children expect and need some type of predictable schedule (Source A). When parents fail to provide an orderly routine, the child may learn to perceive the world as chaotic and unpredictable, even as an adult. Orderliness and predictability encompass parental supervision and rules. Those who lack parental supervision are probably not going to feel as successful or secure about themselves because they will feel uncertain about what may happen.

Parents influence the type of person an individual becomes. President George W. Bush reminded Americans of "the values that bind families from one generation to the next" (Source G). However, these values are not always positive. Little good can come from having weak or abusive parents. As Source B indicates, the child who has a weak bond with parents and suffers abuse may become violent as an adult. And physical abuse as we grow up may cause us to feel life-long rejection. Children learn more from what a parent does than what he or she says (Source E). Obviously, the way our parents treat us affects our self-image, and our self-image plays a key role in the type of individuals we become.

In his press release, President Bush referred to children as "a source of joy, pride, and fulfillment" (Source G). His viewpoint is idealistic and sometimes unrealistic. Although parents are undoubtedly major influences in our lives, not every parent welcomes the responsibility of raising a child; in that case, the child may not be successful in school, and he or she may grow up to be insecure and have low self-esteem. In contrast, the individual who is fortunate enough to have educated, warm, and caring parents is likely to be success-oriented and secure.

Taking on the Essays

You've conquered the synthesis essay, and now you're ready for the next stage of the free-response section: the standard essays. In the remainder of this section of the exam, you'll respond to two additional essay questions. As with the synthesis essay, your success on these essays will hinge on your ability to write a cohesive, thesis-based essay.

Most of the standard essay questions require you to read a single brief passage and respond to a prompt. You might examine the author's rhetorical strategies in the passage or you might develop an argument that agrees or disagrees with the author's point of view. Some essay questions do not contain a reading passage, as in the following example:

Controversy is a fact of life in contemporary society. Think of a local, national, or international issue with which you are familiar that generates a great deal of controversy and debate. Then, using appropriate evidence, write an essay that carefully considers the opposing viewpoints on this issue and suggests a solution or compromise.

In modeling how to create a top-scoring essay response, let's examine another sample essay question:

British author C. S. Lewis once said that, "Friendship is unnecessary, like philosophy, like art. . . . It has no survival value; rather it is one of those things that give value to survival."

Think about his assertion. Then write an essay that defends, refutes, or qualifies Lewis's claim about the value of friendship. Use specific, appropriate evidence to develop your position.

Step One: Developing an Outline

If you spent the recommended 40 minutes writing your synthesis essay — and you should have! — you'll have a total of 80 minutes remaining for these final two essay questions. You can plan to spend 40 minutes on each one, although you may find that you're able to answer one more quickly than the other if you're particularly familiar with the material. Don't be concerned that you're not spending enough time on a given essay question if you know that you've written a good, thorough answer. You're being scored on content, not effort! You may answer the essay questions in either order, but you might be advised to save the easier of the two for last when your brain and hand are both wearing out.

Traditional essays generally don't demand as extensive an answer as the synthesis essay. You may plan to write a relatively straightforward five-paragraph essay in response to the standard essay questions. In this case, organize your outline by paragraph. Be sure to include your thesis statement in your first paragraph to make sure the AP Reader can understand your argument from the beginning. Then include one or two ideas or details in each of your supporting paragraphs. Write these main points in your outline so that you don't forget them when it comes time to write. Your final paragraph should contain a conclusion that wraps up your ideas and restates your thesis.

Step Two: Writing a Response

All the same rules apply when writing answers to the standard essay questions. Stick to your outline, stick to the point, and stick to the topic to produce the best and most concise response possible. The AP exam isn't a term paper, so you're not being scored on spelling and grammar. However, don't forget to include transition words to help guide the AP Reader through your argument and to follow the ideas you brainstormed in your outline.

Step Three: Revising Your Response

Remember that essay graders are not mind readers, so they will only grade what's on the page, not what you thought you were writing. At the same time, remember that essay graders do not deduct points for wrong information, so you don't need to spend time erasing errors. Just write a corrected sentence in the margin of your paper or, if you've skipped lines, on the line below the sentence with the mistake.

A Sample Response

How would you have responded to the essay question on C. S. Lewis's quote given earlier in the chapter? Review this sample response to see what one good answer looks like. Remember, there's no one right answer to a given essay question, although high-scoring responses will always be logical, well organized, and clearly written.

> Survival is the basic human motivation. People will go to incredible lengths to survive. The recent movie 127 Hours illustrates this basic instinct. A hiker, trapped by a boulder, makes the heart-wrenching choice to cut off his own arm in order to free himself and live to see another day. For most, just surviving is not good enough. People also want to live a life with meaning and filled with flourishing relationships

among family and friends. C.S. Lewis is correct in his assertion that friendship is not necessary for survival but gives value to the human existence.

Throughout history, men and women from all races, social classes, and various circumstances have found ways to survive in spite of overwhelming odds. In most cases, these people did not just survive but found a way to thrive in spite of their difficulties. How? Through friendships. In Mark Twain's classic American novel The Adventures of Huckleberry Finn, Huck Finn runs away from an abusive father. He goes as far as to fake his own death to escape and survive on his own. He seems happy to float down the river on a skiff and camp out on an island without anyone to accompany him. Even Huck doesn't seem to realize how much he needs a companion until he encounters Jim, the runaway slave. The two strike up an unlikely friendship (especially for the pre-Civil War South) and face their difficulties together, each relying on the other for support and camaraderie. Through every challenge, they stick together and find freedom.

Popular culture is also filled with tales of lone survivors. One thing most of these loners have in common is the connection to a loved one somewhere out there waiting for their safe return. Take the movie Castaway, for example. Tom Hanks's character is stranded on a deserted island after a plane crash. After he realizes that no one is going to rescue him, he sets out to survive. He makes a shelter. He lights a fire. He sharpens a stick for spear fishing. All the while, he continually opens the pocket watch his fiancé gave him during their last meeting. With his fiancé's picture included, the watch reminds him of what he has to live for. If he had no loved ones waiting for him, would he have fought so hard to survive? He spent years trying to get home. After building a raft to get off of the island and finally getting rescued by a freighter, he discovers his fiancé gave up on him and married someone else. Even though he loses the one that motivated him to survive, he seeks out other relationships to add value and meaning to his new life.

A person can't survive on friendships alone. However, a person cannot thrive without those relationships that provide value and meaning to life. Having friends is like wearing glasses. Sometimes a person doesn't even know that he has a vision problem until a friend brings life into focus.

Some More Advice

What have you learned about the free-response section of the AP English and Composition exam? Keep these ideas in mind as you prepare for the exam. When you become comfortable with these techniques, you will feel confident and prepared when you sit down to take the exam.

- Remember that the synthesis essay and the standard essay questions require different but similar approaches. You should be mentally prepared to address both of these essay types.

- Be sure to thoroughly read and evaluate all of the sources given with synthesis essay question. Make notes in your test booklet, and add any additional information or personal examples to further contextualize the provided sources.

- Make a clear and concise outline before you begin writing. This will help you organize your thoughts and speed up the actual writing process.

- Stay focused on the topic and answer the question that is asked! Addressing the question fully is the single most important way to earn points on this section.

- Handwriting is important and must legible! If the AP Reader can't read your writing, you'll get no points, even if your response is well conceived.

- Leave a few minutes at the end to quickly review and revise your answers. You don't need to check the spelling of every single word, but you do need to make sure that all of your ideas made it onto the page. Skipping lines while you write will leave room for you to add important words and ideas and make it easier for the scorer to read your handwriting.

Two Final Words: Don't Panic!

The free-response questions will ask you about concepts and situations that you may not have thought about before. However, remember that the essay questions seek to test your ability to synthesize information and write clearly and concisely on a variety of topics. There are no wrong answers, just faulty or incorrect approaches to writing the essays. Stay calm, read the essay questions and supporting material carefully, and put your thoughts in logical order with clear transitions. Following this process will help you get a great score, even if you've never heard of the authors or the concepts presented in the questions.

Approaching the Multiple-Choice Questions: The Passages

The multiple-choice section of the AP English Language and Composition exam will test your critical reading skills. The breadth and depth of the various kinds of knowledge you bring to the test — vocabulary, grammar, rhetorical strategies, even some expertise on certain topic — are measured only in your ability to apply them in your reading. The good news is that all of the answers to critical reading questions are found in the excerpt. Your job is to find those answers, by extracting meaning from complex, often dense, and sometimes archaic passages, and doing so under the pressure of time and without the aid of dictionaries or the Internet.

Most good readers (which you probably already are) apply critical-reading strategies intuitively. They deconstruct text without thinking much about what they are actually doing. It's no accident that strong readers read a lot, usually because they enjoy it, and the byproduct of that practice — besides the pleasure and knowledge they derive from it — is that they become very good at reading. Becoming an expert violinist, gymnast, or computer programmer requires thousands of hours of dedicated work. Even a video game whiz kid is the product of long hours of bleary-eyed, glued-to-the-screen practice. Keep this idea of useful practice in mind as you read a wide variety of materials. You'll find yourself becoming a better reader, and doubtless a better writer as well.

This book will help you do well on the AP English Language and Composition exam by helping you become a more accomplished reader — that is, by improving your ability to apply critical-reading strategies and by giving you focused reading practice. You will fill in some holes in your knowledge of nonfiction forms and rhetorical strategies, increase your vocabulary, and work on your ability to focus and be efficient in a timed assessment. Yes, there are some test-taking strategies included, even some tricks that will help you; familiarity with the types of questions on the exam will give you an advantage and a feeling of preparedness. But these "tricks" are really about becoming a better reader, someone who has developed the mental discipline to know what to do when faced with a challenging text.

TEST TIP

As you read a passage, try to grasp its basic idea or "gist." Read the entire passage before looking at any of the questions. If you understand the overall point, you will probably have a better feel for what each question is asking. Remind yourself that the questions are basically asking, "What is this author trying to say?"

What Is Nonfiction?

The multiple-choice section of the test measures your ability to read *nonfiction*. Thus, the AP English Language and Composition exam is not "literary" in the sense that its sister test, the AP English Literature and Composition exam, is. You will *not* be asked to analyze fiction, poetry, or drama on Section I of the exam. In general, nonfiction is "the literature of fact," as John McFee dubbed his nonfiction writing class at Princeton University. The main genre in this area is the essay, based on the autobiographical and self-reflective form established by the French writer Michel de Montaigne in 1580. The nonfiction passages on the exam will encompass many different genres and will address all sorts of topics, some familiar and some esoteric. However, all of them will be in some sense factual, presenting either documented historical facts or facts as the writer knows them or understands them. For example, passages may range from Barbara Tuchman's detailed description of the diplomatic maneuvers that led to World War I to Ernest Hemingway's relaxed account of writing short stories in a Paris café.

DID YOU KNOW?

The French Renaissance writer Michel de Montaigne (1533–1592) brought the essay to an early peak of perfection as a literary genre. His style combined the rigor of philosophy with the charm of personal anecdotes. His *Essais* (which translates as "attempts") had a huge influence on later writers such as Jean-Jacques Rousseau, Ralph Waldo Emerson, and Friedrich Nietzsche.

Most of what you will read on the AP English Language and Composition exam will be on some level persuasive — meant to make you think or feel a certain way, or at least make you understand how the author thinks or feels about a particular subject. You will encounter a wide range of expository modes: description, narration, definition, cause and effect, argument, process analysis, compare/contrast, and problem/solution. Many of the questions on the multiple-choice portion of the exam will ask you to analyze how the author tries to persuade the reader or how she or he organizes the material to achieve a certain effect. At least one passage will be research-based with notes, and you will be asked several questions about those notes.

What to Expect from the Passages

Don't expect to be familiar with the passages in the multiple-choice section of the AP English Language and Composition exam. You probably won't see the preamble to the United States Constitution or Martin Luther King Jr.'s "I Have a Dream" speech. And if a passage from Mark Twain is included, it is as likely to come from his book on Shakespeare as to come from *Life on the Mississippi*. The purpose of the exam is to test your ability to read and analyze unfamiliar texts. College Board looks for materials obscure enough not to be typically read or studied by high school students so that no one has an unfair advantage on the test. Variety is to be expected — from contemporary essays to historical accounts, from public orations to private diary entries, from scientific writing to impressionistic prose, and from all sorts of perspectives relating to gender, race, philosophy, politics, and environmental concerns.

There are also two important points to remember about the format of the passages. Most are excerpted material, meaning that there is text that comes before and after what you are reading. In addition, the passages are almost all anonymous, so you usually will not know the writer or the time period of the piece. (Here, your own wide reading may help you occasionally recognize the source of a passage.) Nevertheless, everything you need to know for the purpose of the exam is provided for you; it can be found in the content and language of the passage. If something of vital importance can't be gleaned from the passage, a footnote or brief introduction will provide it.

TEST TIP

In general, the passages included in the multiple-choice section of the AP English Language and Composition exam will not have introductory material such as a title, name of author, and details of historical context or significance. At most, a date of publication will situate the passage to some degree. This lack of information can be crucial: the context of a passage on war differs greatly if it was written by Julius Caesar rather than Abraham Lincoln. Read each passage carefully to try to determine the writer's viewpoint and historical context.

Finally, expect to be challenged and don't be surprised if you're occasionally bored. At least one of the excerpts will be a pre-1800 text, such as an eighteenth-century essay by Samuel Johnson. Such a passage will seem obscure even to an avid reader, and will certainly contain difficult and archaic vocabulary. As a twenty-first century student, you may wonder why you should be expected to know a word that was coined in Shakespeare's time and is rarely or never used today. The answer is that successful readers must have the ability to derive the meaning of a word from the context in which it is used, and the AP exam tests how well you can do this.

DIDYOUKNOW?

William Shakespeare (1564–1616) probably affected the course of the English language more than any other single writer. A modern reader of his plays and poems may be struck by the frequent appearance of "clichés," such as "tongue-tied," "a tower of strength," "slept not one wink," and "made a virtue of necessity." Of course, these were not clichés for Shakespeare, since he invented these phrases and hundreds more like them, all of which have become mainstays of English usage.

Ultimately, the exam is designed to measure your ability to read critically at the college level. To this end, the length of the test, as well as the archaic and esoteric nature of some of the passages, will challenge your ability to focus and concentrate. Most people can read about subjects they are interested in, even if the reading level is advanced. College-level reading and research will require you to read beyond your comfort zone and apply strategies to make sense of difficult material. Reading outside one's comfort zone is a mental discipline that requires practice and patience to attain.

TEST TIP

Do you get especially nervous when taking tests? Test anxiety is a common concern, particularly for high-stakes tests like the AP exams. If you find yourself getting nervous during the exam, put down your pencil, close your eyes, empty your mind, and take a few deep breaths. A short mental break may help you refocus and save you time in the long run.

Genres of Nonfiction

As noted above, nonfiction texts share the quality of being factual. Other than that, they may appear in dozens of forms or *genres*. To do well on the exam, it helps to be able to recognize quickly what genre of nonfiction each passage represents. The following is a list of major nonfiction genres, with some examples.

- **Essay:** a text written in the first person and describing or expressing strong opinions about some topic or life experience. Essays can be rigorous and analytical or relaxed and reflective. Many of the passages on the AP English Language and Composition exam are excerpts from essays. Here, in the opening of his essay "Degree," the Nobel laureate V. S. Naipaul examines the Indian attitude towards poverty:

"They tell the story of the Sikh who, returning to India after many years, sat down among his suitcases on the Bombay docks and wept. He had forgotten what Indian poverty was like. It is an Indian story, in its arrangement of figure and properties, its melodrama, its pathos. It is Indian above all in its attitude to poverty as something which, thought about from time to time in the midst of other preoccupations, releases the sweetest of emotions. This is poverty, our especial poverty, and how sad it is! Poverty not as an urge to anger or improving action, but poverty as an inexhaustible source of tears, an exercise of the purest sensibility."

- **Editorial:** a brief opinion piece on some current event or topical subject. Most editorials are written for newspapers, magazines, or websites, and they tend to date very quickly. Related to an editorial is the **op-ed article,** the name of which comes from "opposite the editorial page." It is usually written by someone unaffiliated with the editorial board. Here is the opening of an editorial for the April 1929 issue of *American Mercury* in which H. L Mencken mourns the passing of a senator*:*

"To be a fraud is safer and happier in Washington today than it has been since March 4, 1911. For James A. Reed, after eighteen years in the Senate, has hung up his sword and gone home to Missouri. His achievements, I suspect, are mainly writ in water. The cozeners and quick-salvers, thumbing their noses at his back, emerge from their dark retreats and prepare for an open season for gulls; there are deep, patriotic belches of relief in the very cloakrooms of the Senate itself. But let us not ask for too much. So were Grover Cleveland's achievements writ in water, and so, mainly, were Thomas Jefferson's. It is surely not unusual, under democracy, for a first rate man to fail."

TEST TIP

When you first receive your exam, glance through the multiple-choice section to see how many passages there are. Usually there will be 5 to 7 passages with a total of 50-55 questions on the test. Since you have 60 minutes to complete this section, you should spend about 8 to 12 minutes on each group of questions. Answer the easier questions first and return to the more difficult ones later. Make sure you fill in the bubbles on the answer sheet correctly!

- **Diary or Personal Journal:** a daily or frequent account of a person's life and reflections. In this excerpt from her diary written on July 15, 1944, 15-year-old Anne Frank expresses hope that the cruelty of the war is finally coming to an end:

"It's really a wonder that I haven't dropped all my ideals, because they seem so absurd and impossible to carry out. Yet I keep them, because in spite of everything I still believe that people are really good at heart. I simply can't build up my hopes on a foundation consisting of confusion, misery, and death. I see the world gradually being turned into a wilderness, I hear the ever approaching thunder, which will destroy us too, I can feel the sufferings of millions, and yet, if I look up into the heavens, I think that it will all come right, that this cruelty too will end, and that peace and tranquility will return again."

- **Letter:** a written communication to another person, often of an intimate nature. Once letters were exclusively written on paper and preserved manually, if at all. Today, letters include email and can be archived electronically. Here, in a letter from November 17, 1901, the Russian writer Anton Chekhov writes to his wife about the health of the great Russian novelist Leo Tolstoy (with a hint about Czarist censorship at the end):

"My sweet little spouse,

"The rumors reaching you about Tolstoy, his illness and even death, have no basis in fact. There are no particular changes in his health and have been none, and death is evidently a long way off. It is true he is weak and sickly-looking, but he hasn't a single symptom to cause alarm, nothing except old age. . . . Don't believe anything you hear. If, God forbid, anything happens, I will let you know by wire. I will call him "Grandpa," otherwise I daresay it won't reach you."

- **Biography:** the story of a person's life written by another person. Biography, which has been practiced for centuries, has become a particularly popular form of nonfiction. Here is an excerpt from Hayden Herrera's biography of the Mexican painter Frida Kahlo:

"It was not provincialism that made Frida borrow folk art modes. She was knowledgeable about art and she knew artists, critics, and art historians. When asked whom she admired, she mentioned Grunewald and Piero della Francesca, Bosch and Clouet, Blake and Klee. She loved the primitivism and fantasy of Gauguin and Rousseau, yet hers was distinct from theirs because it stemmed from Mexican popular tradition."

DIDYOU**KNOW?**

Frida Kahlo (1907–1954) was a Mexican painter known for her brutally honest depictions of herself in brightly colored and often surreal self-portraits. Kahlo had to overcome severe physical difficulties during her life. At age six, she contracted polio, and she suffered lifelong effects from a bus collision that damaged her spinal column.

- **Autobiography:** a person's life story written by the person her- or himself. An autobiography is usually a chronological presentation of the events in the writer's life with her or his thoughts about those events. Here, from Eleanor Roosevelt's autobiography, are her impressions upon meeting the 1960 Democratic nominee for president, John F. Kennedy:

"When he came to see me at Hyde Park I found him a brilliant man with a quick mind, anxious to learn, hospitable to new ideas, hardheaded in his approach. Here, I thought, with an upsurge of hope and confidence, is a man who wants to leave behind him a record not only of having helped his countrymen but of having helped humanity as well. He was not simply ambitious to be president; he wanted, I felt convinced, to be a truly great president. He neither desired nor expected his task to be easy. He saw clearly the position of the United States in the world today as well as the shortcomings at home and was both too honorable and too courageous to color these unpalatable facts or distort them."

- **Memoir:** a narrative that presents experiences and impressions from an author's life. Generally less formal than an autobiography, a memoir is based around a mood or attitude toward a particular section of the author's life. While an autobiography may have an assisting writer or a "ghostwriter," a memoir by definition relies entirely on the author's own words and impressions. Here, in an excerpt from his *Paris Album 1900–1914,* the French writer and filmmaker Jean Cocteau describes a distinctive countess:

"The evening was coming to an end. On the light-colored Savonnerie carpet, the music-stands and the listeners' chairs stood about untidily. All at once, among this musical wreckage, I saw the Comtesse de Noailles sitting surrounded by a group of ladies. She was devoting herself to extraordinary exercises. The nightingale practices before the singing season. He croaks, lows and squeaks and those who are not aware of his methods are amazed, as they stand at the foot of the night-dark tree. The Comtesse began in the same way."

- **Speech:** a public address usually presented to a large group of people. Here, in an excerpt from his "Iron Curtain" speech, delivered on March 5, 1946, in Fulton, Missouri, former British Prime Minister Winston Churchill lays out the parameters of what would be called "the Cold War":

"We understand the Russian need to be secure on her western frontiers by the removal of all possibility of German aggression. We welcome Russia to her rightful place among the leading nations of the world. We welcome her flag upon the seas. Above all, we welcome constant, frequent and growing contacts between the Russian people and our own people on both sides of the Atlantic. It is my duty however, for I am sure you would wish me to state the facts as I see them to you, to place before you certain facts about the present position in Europe. . . . From Stettin in the Baltic to Trieste in the Adriatic, an iron curtain has descended across the Continent. Behind that line lie all the capitals of the ancient states of Central and Eastern Europe. Warsaw, Berlin, Prague, Vienna, Budapest, Belgrade, Bucharest and Sofia, all these famous cities and the populations around them lie in what I must call the Soviet sphere, and all are subject in one form or another, not only to Soviet influence but to a very high and, in many cases, increasing measure of control from Moscow."

DIDYOUKNOW?

Winston Churchill's "iron curtain" speech, also known as the "Sinews of Peace" address, was not well received at first. In 1946, the public still generally thought of the Soviet Union as a close ally whose vital efforts helped defeat Nazi Germany. Many thought Churchill's speech was unnecessarily belligerent and warmongering. Subsequent Soviet repression of freedom movements in Hungary and Czechoslovakia, however, tended to bear out Churchill's concerns.

- **Criticism or Review:** an article that presents the writer's opinion about a work of art, such as a film, novel, play, or art exhibition. Here, in a review titled "An Ode to Toy" from June 17, 2010, Joe Morgenstern praises the computer-animated film *Toy Story 3:*

"When the strains of 'You've Got a Friend in Me' swell up in *Toy Story 3,* Randy Newman's now-classic song speaks for the toys, as always — for Woody, Buzz Lightyear, Mr. Potato Head and all the other treasured playthings who have basked in the love of their owner, Andy, and given the little boy their devotion in return. By now, though, the song can also speak for a studio that's become our friend. In an era of increasingly cheesy sequels churned out by entertainment conglomerates, Pixar has been the Fort Knox of honest feelings, and so it remains. Fifteen years after *Toy Story* burst upon the scene as the first full-length animated feature created completely on computers, the third film of the trilogy turns out to be gorgeously joyous and deeply felt."

- **Scientific Writing:** a book, article, or essay that presents an aspect of science in order to explain it or debate its legitimacy. Some science writing is geared toward other scientists, while some is aimed at a more general audience. Here, in an excerpt from *The Code Book,* Simon Singh explains the idea of an unbreakable code used to make bills that cannot be counterfeited:

"The story of quantum cryptography dates back to a curious idea developed in the late 1960s by Stephen Wiesner, then a graduate student at Columbia University. Sadly, it was Wiesner's misfortune to invent an idea so ahead of its time that nobody took it seriously. He still recalls the reaction of his seniors: 'I didn't get any support from my thesis advisor — he showed no interest in it at all. I showed it to several other people, and they all pulled a strange face, and went straight back to what they were already doing.' Wiesner was proposing the bizarre concept of quantum money, which had the great advantage of being impossible to counterfeit."

Representative Authors and Texts for AP English Language and Composition

In the course description, the College Board states that there is "no recommended or required reading list for an AP English Language and Composition course." However, the College Board does provide a list of authors that is "designed to illustrate the possibilities of nonfiction prose" and suggest "the range and quality of reading expected in the course."

The list below will give you a sense of the diversity of literature you will encounter on the test. When preparing for the exam, try to read a variety of texts. You might select a few authors from each major category — some old, some new. Read a variety of topics and notice the variations in approach. Read 4–5 works more carefully. Think about the authors' ideas, and also the rhetorical strategies and techniques they use to make their points to the reader. Study their various styles and use of language, syntax, and diction. Note what is most effective in their writing. These writers are listed here for a reason — they're known and respected for what they write and how they write it.

While many of the writers listed are known for more than what is shown as their representative works, this list shows works that are most characteristic of them or most suited to the exam format.

Pre-Twentieth Century

Writer	Representative Work(s)
Joseph Addison (1672–1719) English essayist, poet, playwright and politician	Founded *The Spectator* magazine with Richard Steele
Francis Bacon (1561–1626) English philosopher, statesman, scientist, lawyer, jurist and author	*The Advancement of Learning; Novum Organum*
James Boswell (1740–1795) Scottish lawyer, diarist, author	*The Life of Samuel Johnson*, a biography, and his journals
Thomas Carlyle (1795–1881) Scottish satirist, essayist, and historian	*Sartor Resartus; Signs of the Times*
Samuel Taylor Coleridge (1722–1834) English poet, literary critic and philosopher	*Biographia Literaria*
Charles Darwin (1809–1882) English naturalist	*On the Origin of Species*
Frederick Douglass (circa 1818–1895) American abolitionist, editor, orator, author, and statesman	*A Narrative of the Life of Frederick Douglass, an American Slave; My Bondage and My Freedom; Life and Times of Frederick Douglass*
Ralph Waldo Emerson (1803–1882) American philosopher, essayist, and poet	Various essays can be found at *http://www.rwe.org/*
Benjamin Franklin (1706–1790) one of the Founding Fathers of the United States, also a leading author and printer, satirist, political theorist, politician, and diplomat	*The Autobiography of Benjamin Franklin*
Margaret Fuller (1810–1850) American journalist, critic, and women's rights advocate	*Woman in the Nineteenth Century*
Edward Gibbon (1737–1794) English historian and member of Parliament	*The History of the Decline and Fall of the Roman Empire*
Thomas Hobbes (1588–1679) English political philosopher	*Leviathan*
Harriet Jacobs (Linda Brent) (1813–1897) American writer, abolitionist speaker and reformer	*Incidents in the Life of a Slave Girl*
Thomas Jefferson (1743–1826) third President of the United States, philosopher, and writer (among numerous other things)	primary author of the *Declaration of Independence; Declaration of the Causes and Necessity of Taking Up Arms*
Samuel Johnson (1709–1784) British author, poet, essayist, literary critic, biographer, and editor	*Dictionary of the English Language; Lives of the Most Eminent English Poets*
Charles Lamb (1775–1834) English essayist	*Specimens of English Dramatic Poets who Lived About the Time of Shakespeare; Essays of Elia*
John Locke (1632–1704) English philosopher	*An Essay Concerning Human Understanding*

(continued)

Pre-Twentieth Century *(continued)*

Writer	Representative Work(s)
Niccolò Machiavelli (1469–1527) Italian philosopher and writer, considered one of the main founders of modern political science	*The Prince*
John Stuart Mill (1806–1873) British philosopher	His collected works are easily accessed online: *http://www.gutenberg.org/browse/authors/m#a1705*
John Milton (1608–1674) English poet, author	*Areopagitica; Paradise Lost*
Michel de Montaigne (1533–1592) French writer, essayist	His collected essays (Montaigne is considered to be the father of the modern essay).
Thomas More (1478–1535) English lawyer, social philosopher, author, and statesman	*Utopia*
Thomas Paine (1737–1809) American author, pamphleteer, radical, intellectual, revolutionary, one of the founding fathers of the United States	*Common Sense; The American Crisis; The Rights of Man*
Francis Parkman (1823–1893) American historian	*The Oregon Trail: Sketches of Prairie and Rocky-Mountain Life; France and England in North America*
Walter Pater (1839–1894) English essayist, critic, and fiction writer	*The Renaissance*, especially *The Conclusion*
George Bernard Shaw (1856–1950) Irish playwright, critic, journalist; Nobel Prize in Literature	*The Intelligent Woman's Guide to Socialism and Capitalism; Treatise on Parents and Children; Pygmalian*
Richard Steele (1672–1729) Irish writer and politician, remembered as co-founder, with his friend Joseph Addison, of the magazine *The Spectator*	*The Tatler; The Spectator*
Jonathan Swift (1667–1745) Anglo-Irish satirist, essayist	*Gulliver's Travels; A Modest Proposal; A Tale of a Tub; Drapier's Letters*
Henry David Thoreau (1817–1862) American author, naturalist, critic	*Walden; Civil Disobedience*
Alexis de Tocqueville (1805–1859) French political thinker and historian	*Democracy in America; The Old Regime and the Revolution*
Oscar Wilde (1854–1900) Irish writer, poet, and playwright	*Intentions; De Profundis*
Mary Wollstonecraft (1759–1797) British writer, philosopher, and feminist	*A Vindication of the Rights of Woman*

(continued)

20th Century to the Present

Writer	Representative Work(s)
Edward Abbey (1927–1989) American author and essayist noted for his advocacy of environmental issues and criticism of public land policies	*The Monkey Wrench Gang; Desert Solitaire*
Diane Ackerman (1948–) American author, poet, and naturalist	*A Natural History of the Senses*
Paula Gunn Allen (1939–2008) Native American poet, literary critic, lesbian activist, and novelist	*The Sacred Hoop: Recovering the Feminine in American Indian Traditions*
Natalie Angier (1958–) American nonfiction writer and a science journalist for the *New York Times;* also a contributor to *Time* magazine	*Natural Obsessions*
Margaret Atwood (1939–) Canadian author, poet, critic, essayist, feminist and social campaigner	*Writing with Intent: Essays, Reviews, Personal Prose — 1983–2005; Second Words: Selected Critical Prose*
James Baldwin (1924–1987) American novelist, writer, playwright, poet, essayist and civil rights activist	*Notes of a Native Son; The Fire Next Time; No Name in the Street; The Devil Finds Work; The Evidence of Things Not Seen; The Price of the Ticket*
Dave Barry (1947–) Pulitzer Prize-winning American author and columnist; humorist	*The World According to Dave Barry; Dave Barry is NOT Making This Up*
Melba Patillo Beals (1941–) American journalist and member of the Little Rock Nine, a group of African-American students who were the first to integrate Central High in Little Rock, Arkansas	*Warriors Don't Cry; White is a State of Mind*
Simone de Beauvoir (1908–1986) French existentialist philosopher and writer	*The Ethics of Ambiguity; The Second Sex*
Lerone Bennett Jr. (1928–) American scholar, author and social historian	*When the Wind Blows; History of Us*
Wendell Berry (1934–) American writer, fiction, nonfiction, and poetry	Essay collections: *Citizenship Papers; The Way of Ignorance*
Susan Bordo (1947–) modern feminist philosopher and writer	*Unbearable Weight: Feminism, Western Culture, and the Body*
Jacob Bronowski (1908–1974) British mathematician and biologist	*The Ascent of Man; A Sense of the Future; Magic Science & Civilization; The Origins of Knowledge and Imagination*
William F. Buckley (1925–2008) American author, commentator, editor	Online @ *http://cumulus.hillsdale.edu/buckley/Standard/index.html*
Judith Butler (1956–) American feminist philosopher and writer	*Gender Trouble: Feminism and the Subversion of Identity*

(continued)

20th Century to the Present   (continued)

Writer	Representative Work(s)
Rachel Carson (1907–1964) American marine biologist and nature writer	*Silent Spring*
G. K. Chesterton (1874–1936) British journalist, novelist, essayist	*Eugenics and Other Evils*
Winston Churchill (1874–1965) British Prime Minister, historian, and writer	*The Second World War; A History of the English-Speaking Peoples*
Judith Ortiz Cofer (1952–) Puerto Rican author	*Sleeping with One Eye Open: Women Writers and the Art of Survival; The Myth of the Latin Woman*
Richard Dawkins (1941–) British ethologist, evolutionary biologist and popular science author	*The Selfish Gene*
Joan Didion (1934–) American novelist, essayist, memoir writer	*Slouching Towards Bethlehem; The Year of Magical Thinking*
Annie Dillard (1945–) Pulitzer Prize-winning American author and artist, best known for her narrative nonfiction	*Pilgrim at Tinker Creek*
Maureen Dowd (1952–) columnist for the *New York Times* and best-selling author	*Are Men Necessary?: When Sexes Collide;* also see current and archived columns in the *New York Times*
Elizabeth Drew (1935–) American political journalist and author	*Washington Journal: The Events of 1973–74; Portrait of an Election: The 1980 Presidential Campaign; On the Edge: The Clinton Presidency; Citizen McCain; George W. Bush's Washington*
W. E. B. Du Bois (1868–1963) American civil rights activist, historian, and author	*The Souls of Black Folk* and much more
Richard Ellmann (1918–1987) American literary critic and biographer	*Four Dubliners: Wilde, Yeats, Joyce, and Beckett*
Nora Ephron (1941–) American film director, producer, screenwriter, novelist, and journalist	Various screenplays: *Silkwood, When Harry Met Sally, Julie and Julia*
Timothy Ferris (1944–) American science writer	*The Science of Liberty; Coming of Age in the Milky Way*
M. F. K. Fisher (1908–1992) American writer	*Map of Another Town: A Memoir of Provence; To Begin Again: Stories and Memoirs*
Frances Fitzgerald (1940–) American journalist and author, known for her journalistic account of the Vietnam War	*America Revised; Cities on a Hill; Way Out There in the Blue: Reagan, Star Wars and the End of the Cold War; Rewriting American history,* a short article in *The Norton Reader;* and *Vietnam: Spirits of the Earth*
Tim Flannery (1956–) Australian palaeontologist and environmental activist	*The Weather Makers: The History & Future Impact of Climate Change*

(continued)

20th Century to the Present   (*continued*)

Writer	Representative Work(s)
Shelby Foote (1916–2005) American novelist and historian of the American Civil War	*The Civil War: A Narrative*
John Hope Franklin (1915–2009) United States historian	*Racial Equality in America; My Life and an Era: The Autobiography of Buck Colbert Franklin; Runaway Slaves: Rebels on the Plantation; Mirror to America: The Autobiography of John Hope Franklin*
Antonia Frasert (1932–) Anglo-Irish author	*The Weaker Vessel: Woman's Lot in Seventeenth-Century England; The Warrior Queens: Boadicea's Chariot; The Gunpowder Plot*
Thomas L. Friedman (1953–) American journalist, columnist and Pulitzer Prize-winning author	*The Lexus and the Olive Tree; The World Is Flat; Longitudes and Attitudes*
Paul Fussell (1924–) American cultural and literary historian, professor of literature	*The Great War and Modern Memory; Thank God for the Atom Bomb and Other Essays*
John Kenneth Galbraith (1908–2006) Canadian-American economist, writer	*A Life in Our Times*
Henry Louis Gates Jr. (1950–) American literary critic, educator, scholar, writer, editor	*Colored People; Tradition and the Black Atlantic: Critical Theory in the African Diaspora; Personal History: Family Matters*
Ellen Goodman (1941–) American journalist and Pulitzer Prize-winning syndicated columnist	*Making Sense; Value Judgments; Paper Trail*
Nadine Gordimer (1923–) South African writer, political activist and Nobel laureate	*The Conservationist; The Pickup; The Essential Gesture: Writing, Politics and Places*
Stephanie Elizondo Griest (1974–) Chicana author and activist from South Texas	*Around the Bloc: My Life in Moscow, Beijing, and Havana; 100 Places Every Woman Should Go*
David Halberstam (1934–2007) American Pulitzer Prize-winning journalist and author; known for his early work on the Vietnam War	*Summer of '49; The Next Century; The Fifties; October 1964*
Elizabeth Hardwick (1916–2007) American literary critic, novelist, and short-story writer.	*A View of My Own* (1962), *Seduction and Betrayal* (1974), *Bartleby in Manhattan* (1983), and *Sight-Readings* (1998).
Elva Trevino Hart Mexican-American writer	*Barefoot Heart: Stories of a Migrant Child* (memoir)
John Hersey (1914–1993) Pulitzer Prize-winning American writer and journalist	*Hiroshima*
Edward Hoagland (1932–) American author best known for nature and travel writing.	*Compass Points; Hoagland on Nature; Early in the Season*, plus numerous essays
Richard Holmes (1945–) British biographer	*Shelley: The Pursuit; Coleridge: Early Visions*

(*continued*)

20th Century to the Present   (continued)

Writer	Representative Work(s)
Bell Hooks (1952–) American author, feminist, and social activist	*Ain't I a Woman?: Black Women and Feminism; Yearning: Race, Gender, and Cultural Politics*
Zora Neale Hurston (1891–1960) American folklorist, anthropologist, and author	*Mules and Men; Their Eyes Were Watching God*
Evelyn Fox Keller (1936–) American author and physicist	*The Century of the Gene, Making Sense of Life: Explaining Biological Development with Models, Metaphors, and Machines*
Helen Keller (1880–1968) American author and lecturer	*The Story of My Life*
Martin Luther King Jr. (1929–1968) American clergyman and political leader	various speeches, letters, essays
Barbara Kingsolver (1955–) American novelist, author	*Animal, Vegetable, Miracle; Small Wonder: Essays, High Tide in Tucson*
Maxine Hong Kingston (1940–) Asian American author	*The Woman Warrior*
Paul Krugman (1953–) American columnist, author and Nobel Prize-winning economist	Op-ed columns for the *New York Times*; various books and articles
Alex Kuczynski (1967–) American author and reporter for the *New York Times*, columnist for the *New York Times Magazine*	*Beauty Junkies*
Lewis H. Lapham (1935–) American author, journalist	*Waiting for the Barbarians; Theater of War; Gag Rule; and Pretensions to Empire*
T. E. Lawrence (1888–1935) British army officer, known also as Lawrence of Arabia	*Seven Pillars of Wisdom; Revolt in the Desert*
Gerda Lerner (1920–) American historian and author	*Why History Matters; The Creation of Feminist Consciousness; Fireweed: A Political Autobiography*
Phillip Lopate (1943–) American author and media critic	*Waterfront: A Walk Around Manhattan; Against Joie de Vivre*
Barry Lopez (1945–) American environmental author and social critic	*Home Ground: Language for an American Landscape*
Norman Mailer (1923–2007) American writer, co-founder of "new journalism"	*The Executioner's Song; The Big Empty: Dialogues on Politics, Sex, God, Boxing, Morality, Myth, Poker and Bad Conscience in America*
Nancy Mairs (1943–) American author, writes about her experiences with multiple sclerosis	*Waist High in the World*
Peter Matthiessen (1927–) American writer and environmental activist	*In the Spirit of Crazy Horse, Travelin' Man, Shadow Country*

(continued)

20th Century to the Present   (continued)

Writer	Representative Work(s)
Mary McCarthy (1912–1989) American author and political activist	*Memories of a Catholic School Girl, Vietnam, Ideas and the Novel*
Frank McCourt (1930–2009) Irish-American writer	*Angela's Ashes*
Bill McKibben (1960–) American environmentalist and writer	*The Bill McKibben Reader: Pieces from an Active Life, Earth: Making a Life on a Tough New Planet*
John McPhee (1931–) American writer and pioneer of creative nonfiction	*Annuls of the Former World, Encounters with the Archdruid, Silk Parachute*
Margaret Mead (1901–1978) American anthropologist	*Sex and Temperament in Three Primitive Societies, Male and Female*
Jan Morris (1926–) Welsh historian and travel writer	*Locations, O Canada!, Contact! A Book of Glimpses*
John Muir (1838–1914) Scottish-born American naturalist, author, and early advocate of preservation of wilderness in the United States, co-founder of the Sierra Club	*The Story of My Boyhood and Youth*
Donald M. Murray (1923–2006) American journalist and teacher	*My Twice-Lived Life: A Memoir, The Lively Shadow: Living with the Death of a Child*
V. S. Naipaul (1932–) Trinidadian novelist and essayist, awarded the Nobel Prize in literature in 2001 for his life's work	*The Writer and the World: Essays*, or anything by this writer
Joyce Carol Oates (1938–) American novelist and essayist	*Where I've Been, And Where I'm Going: Essays, Reviews, and Prose*
Barack Obama (1961–) 44th President of the United States, president of *Harvard Law Review*	Keynote address at the Democratic National Convention in 2004
George Orwell (1903–1950) English author and journalist	*Politics and the English Language; 1984*
Cynthia Ozick (1928–) Jewish American writer	*Fame & Folly: Essays, Quarrel & Quandary, The Din in the Head: Essays*
Francine Prose (1947–) American writer	*Blue Angel; The Lives of the Muses: Nine Women & the Artists They Inspired*
David Quammen (1948–) award-winning science, nature and travel writer	*Monster of God: The Man-Eating Predator in the Jungles of History and the Mind*
Arnold Rampersad (1941–) biographer and literary critic, born in Trinidad	*Days of Grace: A Memoir, Jackie Robinson: A Biography*
Ishmael Reed (1938–) American poet, essayist, and novelist	*Barack Obama and the Jim Crow Media: The Return of the "Nigger Breakers," Mixing It Up: Taking on the Media Bullies and Other Reflections*

(continued)

20th Century to the Present (continued)

Writer	Representative Work(s)
David Remnick (1958–) American journalist and Pulitzer Prize-winning writer	*Lenin's Tomb: The Last Days of the Soviet Empire*
Mordecai Richler (1931–2001) Canadian author, screenwriter and essayist	*Oh Canada! Oh Quebec! Requiem for a Divided Country, Dispatches from the Sporting Life*
Sharman Apt Russell (1954–) American nature and science writer	*An Obsession with Butterflies: Our Long Love Affair with a Singular Insect, Anatomy of a Rose: Exploring the Secret Life of Flowers*
Carl Sagan (1934–1996) American astronomer, astrophysicist, and author	*Pale Blue Dot: A Vision of the Human Future in Space, Cosmos*
Edward Said (1935–2003) Palestinian-American literary theorist	*Out of Place*
George Santayana (1863–1952) Spanish-American philosopher and author	*The Sense of Beauty, The Life of Reason*
Arthur M. Schlesinger (1917–2007) Pulitzer Prize-winning American historian and social critic	*A Thousand Days: John F. Kennedy in the White House, The Disuniting of America: Reflections on a Multicultural Society, A Life in the 20th Century, Innocent Beginnings, 1917–1950*
David Sedaris (1956–) American humorist and writer	*Naked; Holidays on Ice; Me Talk Pretty One Day, Dress Your Family in Corduroy and Denim*
Richard Selzer (1928–) American surgeon and author	*The Exact Location of the Soul: New and Selected Essays; Raising the Dead: A Doctor's Encounter with His Own Mortality*
Leslie Marmon Silko (1948–) Native American author	*Yellow Woman and a Beauty of the Spirit: Essays on Native American Life Today*
Barbara Smith (1946–) American lecturer, author, and lesbian feminist	*Writings on Race, Gender and Freedom: The Truth That Never Hurts*
Red Smith (1905–1982) American sportswriter	*Views of Sport; Out of the Red*
Shelby Steele (1946–) American author and documentary film maker, specializing in the study of race relations	*The Content of Our Character*
Lincoln Steffens (1866–1936) American journalist, lecturer, and political philosopher, a famous muckraker	*The Shame of the Cities*
Ronald Takaki (1939–2009) American author	*Debating Diversity: Clashing Perspectives on Race and Ethnicity in America*
Lewis Thomas (1913–1993) American physician, researcher, and writer	*The Lives of a Cell: Notes of a Biology Watcher*

(continued)

20th Century to the Present   (continued)

Writer	Representative Work(s)
Barbara Tuchman (1912–1989) American historian and Pulitzer Prize-winning author	*The Guns of August*
Cynthia Tucker (1955–) American journalist and Pulitzer Prize-winning columnist	Her blog can be found at *http://blogs.ajc.com/cynthia-tucker/*
Laurel Thatcher Ulrich (1938–) Harvard University professor and women's historian	*Good Wives: Image and Reality in the Lives of Women in Northern New England, 1650–1750, A Midwife's Tale: The Life of Martha Ballard based on her diary, 1785–1812*
John Updike (1932–2009) American novelist and critic	*The Clarity of Things: What's American About American Art?, Due Considerations: Essays and Criticism, Still Looking: Essays on American Art*
Gore Vidal (1925–) American author and political activist	*Gore Vidal: Snapshots in History's Glare, Imperial America: Reflections on the United States of Amnesia*
Alice Walker (1944–) American author	*In Search of Our Mothers' Gardens: Womanist Prose, We Are the Ones We Have Been Waiting For*
Jonathan Weiner (1953–) American journalist, science writer	*Long For This World; The Next One Hundred Years: Shaping the Fate of Our Living Earth; The Beak of the Finch: A Story of Evolution in Our Time* (Pulitzer Prize)
Cornel West (1953–) African American philosopher, author, and civil rights activist	*The African-American Century: How Black Americans Have Shaped Our Century; Restoring Hope: Conversations on the Future of Black America; The War Against Parents: What We Can Do For America's Beleaguered Moms and Dads*
E. B. White (1899–1985) American writer	Essays of E.B. White
George Will (1941–) U.S. newspaper columnist, journalist, author, and baseball fan	Will has published numerous books, but search online for his editorials and columns in *Newsweek, The Washington Post*, and ABC News. He is syndicated across the nation.
Terry Tempest Williams (1955–) American author, naturalist, and environmental activist	*Mosaic: Finding Beauty in a Broken World*
Garry Wills (1934–) American historian and Pulitzer Prize-winning author	*Lincoln at Gettysburg: The Words That Remade America; Inventing America: Jefferson's Declaration of Independence*

(continued)

20th Century to the Present *(continued)*

Writer	Representative Work(s)
E. O. Wilson (1929–) American biologist, researcher, and Pulitzer Prize-winning author, specializing in the study of ants	*On Human Nature, The Ants, The Future of Life*
Edmund Wilson (1895–1972) American writer, literary and social critic	*The American Earthquake: A Documentary of the Twenties and Thirties, The Bit Between My Teeth: A Literary Chronicle of 1950–1965*
Tom Wolfe (1930–) American author and journalist, one of the founders of the New Journalism movement	*The Electric Kool-Aid Acid Test, The Right Stuff,* and 35th Jefferson Lecture in the Humanities titled "The Human Beast"
Virginia Woolf (1882–1941) English author	*A Room of One's Own, Women And Writing, Collected Essays*
Richard Wright (1908–1960) American author	*American Hunger, Black Boy*
Malcolm X (1925–1965) African-American Muslim minister, public speaker, and human-rights activist	*The Speeches of Malcolm X at Harvard, The Autobiography of Malcolm X*
Anzia Yezierska (circa 1880–1970) Polish-American novelist	*Red Ribbon on a White Horse; Bread Givers*

Approaching the Multiple-Choice Questions: Rhetorical Strategies

To do well on the multiple-choice section of the AP English Language and Composition exam, you must recognize the rhetorical strategy used in each passage. This includes the author's purpose in writing the passage, the author's assumptions about the reader or audience, and the means the author employs to accomplish his or her purpose. Seeing the rhetorical strategy will also help you focus on the author's main point, or the "big picture" the passage presents.

Author's Purpose

In general, authors of nonfiction write to persuade, inform or instruct, or entertain. Most of the passages you will read for the AP English Language and Composition exam will be written to persuade. However, many of them will combine one or more of these purposes. For example, a writer who employs satire or parody seeks to entertain the reader while also convincing him or her about something. In the following excerpt, a writer explains why American sports fans generally dislike soccer, and in the process expresses his own preference for basketball:

"Americans keep an eye on their watches. They like a tight schedule arranged with order and precision. It's satisfying to them that a basketball game can end with a "buzzer beater" at the last millisecond. On the other hand, a soccer game meanders to a close, with added time slapped on at the end. Foul shots in basketball always proceed from the foul line with military precision. Free kicks in soccer are allowed from the general area of a foul. And American fans view all that milling around in the center of the soccer field as a big waste of time. That's why there's a shot clock in basketball – to keep the game moving!"

Nonfiction passages feature the following modes of writing to accomplish a purpose.

- **Persuasive writing** attempts to convince the reader to agree with a point of view about a particular problem or controversy. The writer states a position or opinion and supports it with facts and examples. Persuasive writing may appeal to logic or emotion. Many of the passages on the AP English exam use this form of writing.

- **Narrative writing** tells a story or describes a situation in chronological order. Many nonfiction writers, such as Tom Wolfe and Joan Didion, employ all the resources of novelists to make their narrative writing more vivid. These include plot, characters, setting, and imagery.

DID YOU KNOW?

In his 1966 book *In Cold Blood,* American author Truman Capote (1924–1984) used all the techniques of fiction to write what he called a "nonfiction novel." The book detailed the events of a brutal murder case in Kansas. Since the success of Capote's book, many writers have used similar techniques to present historical events in vivid novelistic prose.

- **Descriptive writing** uses sensory language, rich detail, and figurative language to portray people, places, or things. Travel writers often employ descriptive writing to help a reader visualize a scene or appeal to all of a reader's senses.

- **Expository writing** seeks to inform, explain, instruct, clarify, or define. It generally features a main topic, supporting details and facts, strong organization, and logical transitions. Genres for expository writing include science and history books and articles, guidebooks, instruction manuals, textbooks, and lexicons.

TEST TIP

While reading a passage, ask yourself, "What is the author trying to accomplish with this piece?" If you determine the author's purpose is to persuade the reader, ask yourself, "What is the author's viewpoint on this topic? What is he or she trying to convince me to believe or accept?" Remember, it's completely irrelevant whether you agree with the author. The important thing is to understand the author's purpose and rhetorical strategy.

Organizational Patterns

Writers of nonfiction use various *organizational patterns* or *text structures* to shape their material. The pattern chosen helps the author accomplish his or her purpose. The AP English Language and Composition exam will ask you to identify these patterns and how they contribute to the author's overall plan. Some major organizational patterns include:

- **Cause/Effect.** The writer shows how actions or events and their results are related.

- **Compare/Contrast.** The writer shows how two or more people, things, or ideas are alike and how they are different. The writer may also use analogy and metaphor to make an imaginative comparison, as in describing a political candidate as if he or she is a marketable product like soap or beer.

- **Problem/Solution.** The writer describes a problem and proposes a solution.

- **Hypothesis/Support.** The writer presents a hypothesis or theory and provides details and examples to support it or refute it.

DIDYOU**KNOW?**

The theory of general relativity, developed by the German-born physicist Albert Einstein in a 1916 scientific paper, is now being proved essentially correct by highly accurate atomic clocks. Einstein theorized that gravity is basically acceleration. Thus, the stronger gravity is, the slower time runs. Atomic clocks placed at different altitudes show that height actually does affect the progression of time. A person in a penthouse ages faster (by billionths of a second) than a person in a basement.

- **Definition.** The writer defines something by carefully describing what characteristics it has and does not have.

- **Illustration.** The writer presents a topic and then gives examples to explain it further.

- **Chronological.** The writer presents facts or events in time order.

- **Directions.** The writer explains how something is done in sequential steps.

- **Classification.** The writer explains how concepts or terms are related.

Persuasive Writing Techniques

The multiple-choice section of the AP English Language and Composition exam will also require you to analyze the method of persuasive writing used in a passage. You should recognize the following three types of rhetorical strategies used in persuasive writing:

- **Appeal to reason.** The author employs logic to make an argument. In *inductive reasoning,* the author presents a specific case or example and then draws general conclusions from it. To be effective, the evidence presented should be clear and reliable and the conclusions drawn should apply to the specific case. Types of inductive arguments include:

  — *Part-to-whole,* where the whole is assumed to be like individual parts only larger.

    Example: Taking a practice test improved Kaylee's performance on the exam. Therefore, everyone in the class should take a practice test.

  — *Extrapolation,* where areas beyond the area of focus are assumed to be like the focused-on area.

    Example: In home entertainment, people have come to expect more choices about what TV programs to watch, what songs to listen to, and what games to play. Why not give them more choices with regard to their health care as well?

  — *Prediction,* where the future is assumed to be like the past.

    Example: Every time I go to the beach after a storm, the sand is full of seaweed. Since it stormed last night, I'll be stepping over lots of seaweed at the beach today.

In *deductive reasoning,* the author presents a generalization and then applies it to a specific case. To be convincing, the generalization should be based on reliable evidence.

  Example: Gene therapy is a promising new treatment option for many diseases. Tests indicate that someday gene therapy could be used to treat coronary artery disease.

Writers often employ a form of deductive reasoning called the *syllogism*, which has a major premise, a minor premise, and a conclusion.

Example:

Major premise: All the musicians in the school orchestra are A students.

Minor premise: Hubert plays the viola in the school orchestra.

Conclusion: Hubert is an A student.

DIDYOU**KNOW?**

The idea of the syllogism comes from the Greek philosopher Aristotle (384 BCE–322 BCE), who was a student of Plato and a teacher of Alexander the Great. Aristotle's writings on logic, ethics, and aesthetics are still studied closely today. It is thought that only about one-third of his original writings have survived.

- **Appeal to emotion.** The author uses an emotional argument designed to engage a reader's sympathies, values, and compassion. Emotional appeals often use sources such as personal interviews, anecdotes, testimony, and visual evidence to bolster an argument. For example, an argument in favor of a vegetarian diet might detail the treatment of cattle in slaughterhouses. An emotional appeal to fear may seek to make readers uneasy about their own safety, security, or health.

- **Appeal to morality.** The author tries to garner moral support for an argument by linking it to a value that is widely accepted. For example, an essay opposing increases in military spending might appeal to religious values of peace and brotherhood or political beliefs about imperialism or violence.

Three Persuasive Writing Strategies to Frame an Argument

You should recognize the three main types of strategies writers use to frame a persuasive argument.

- **Proposition of fact.** In this type of argument, the author seeks to convince the reader that a proposition is true or false. An argument of this kind might be "Is the violence in videogames and Hollywood movies responsible for violent acts in society?"

- **Questions of value.** In this type of argument, the author seeks to convince the reader that an action or activity was right or wrong, moral or immoral, ethical or unethical, or better or worse than another action or activity. For example: "Is it proper for a Supreme Court Justice to make speeches on national issues that might come before the Court someday?"

- **Questions of policy.** In this type of argument, the author tries to convince the reader than some action should be taken or some policy adopted. For example: "To improve public safety, should theatergoers be screened by metal detectors before they enter a theater?"

Logical Fallacies

Arguments that include common errors in reasoning or assumption are called logical fallacies. On the AP English Language and Composition exam, you may be required to identify instances in which authors use one or more of these.

- **Hasty generalization.** This argument is also called "jumping to conclusions." It bases its conclusion on too few samples to prove the point. Example: "Two people I know personally have never been vaccinated and neither has ever had a serious illness or physical condition. Therefore, vaccinations are largely unnecessary."

- **Faulty appeal to authority.** This argument attempts to justify a claim by misrepresenting the trustworthiness of a supposedly authoritative source, failing to acknowledge that experts disagree on the point, or appealing to a source who is not an expert. An example of the latter: Lebron James insists that children today spend too much time using social media on computers and cell phones.

DIDYOUKNOW?

The false appeal to authority is much like the bare assertion fallacy, or *ipse dixit* (Latin for "He himself said it"). This says, in effect, "It is so because I say it's so." In one of their famous debates for election as senator in 1858, Stephen Douglas attacked Abraham Lincoln in these words, "Mr. Lincoln has not character enough for integrity and truth, merely on his own *ipse dixit*, to arraign President Buchanan, President Pierce, and nine Judges of the Supreme Court, not one of whom would be complimented by being put on an equality with him."

- **Post hoc, ergo propter hoc.** (Latin for "after this, therefore because of this") This argument suggests that because one event precedes another, it also causes it. Example: Since digital books were introduced, no American writer has won the Nobel Prize for literature.

- **Ad Hominem.** (Latin for "against the man") This argument is an attack on a person's character instead of on the person's ideas or opinions. Example: "Having met the author and experienced his insufferable arrogance, I can safely dismiss his ideas about love and friendship."

- **Common Knowledge or Ad populum.** This argument is an appeal to the opinion of the masses, as if the agreement of large numbers of people makes it unnecessary to offer any more evidence for a contention. Example: With the highest ratings in its time slot, that detective show is obviously one of the best shows on television.

- **Bandwagon Appeal.** Similar to Ad Populum, this argument taps into people's desire to be like the group or to hold the trendy opinion. It argues that "everyone is doing this" or "the hip people believe this."

TEST TIP

Now that you've studied these logical fallacies, see how they're used in certain product advertisements and political campaign commercials. Make notes of which faulty appeal is used and why it is misleading. This will reinforce your ability to identify these appeals on the AP English Language and Composition exam.

- **Red Herring.** This argument avoids the key issue by introducing a separate issue as a diversion. Example: Some baseball hitters probably gained an advantage by using performance-enhancing steroids. Yet the season is so long and taxing on the players' bodies, it is no surprise that many would seek chemical assistance.

- **Straw Man.** This argument creates a "straw man" by exaggerating, overstating, or over-simplifying an opposing point of view. Example: My opponent would eliminate all government aid programs until children were left to starve and parents forced to take the most menial jobs just to survive.

- **Slippery Slope.** This argument is based on the idea that if a first step is taken, then a second and third step will follow inevitably, until a disaster occurs like a person sliding on a slippery incline until he or she falls to the bottom. Example: If our city council allows video cameras to be placed at intersections, soon they will install them in our neighborhoods. And next there will be a camera in front of each house and then inside each house. We can't allow this intrusion into our privacy to stand.

- **Appeal to Tradition.** This argument suggest that a course of action is proper or necessary simply because things have always been done that way. Example: The school year should begin on the first Tuesday after Labor Day, for that is when it always began when I was a child.

- **Glittering Generalities.** This argument uses "happy words" that sound important but actually have little or no real meaning. The words, such as *wonderful, fair,* and *decent,* are employed in general statements that can't be proved or disproved.

- **Begging the Question or Circular Reasoning.** This argument assumes as evidence the very conclusion it is trying to prove. Example: Useless courses like Home Economics should be dropped from the curriculum at our school. Think how much money is wasted on useless courses each year. Notice that the writer has not proved that the course is useless; it is just assumed to be so.

- **Either/Or.** Also called "false dichotomy," this argument deceptively reduces an argument to two oversimplified alternatives. Example: "We must immediately adopt green energy technologies completely, or else poison our planet with carbon-producing fuels."

- **Guilt by Association.** This argument relies on prejudice instead of careful thought. It seeks to impugn a person because of the actions or reputation of those with whom he or she associates. Example: His scientific work is suspect. Recently a colleague with whom he has been friendly for years was fired for plagiarizing an article in an academic journal.

TEST TIP

An argument that is slanted to pursue a specific agenda or philosophy is called propaganda. You may encounter an example of propaganda on the AP English exam. Look for extreme forms of logical fallacy and a willingness to distort the truth. Be prepared to note how the author uses biased language and "rigged" examples to reach a false conclusion.

Analyzing Organization and Development

Now that you have tools for analyzing a passage, you can use them to look for a pattern of organization and methods of development. A coherent piece of writing is a progression of ideas. Ask yourself: In this passage, what is the progression of thought from each sentence and idea to the next, from each paragraph to the next? Try to follow how each sentence, or even each clause or phrase, is related to and proceeds from the previous one. Try to follow as well the way in which one paragraph is related to and proceeds from the previous one. Sometimes, particularly in the older passages, our modern conception of paragraphing is lacking. If you are presented with an unusually long passage without conventional paragraph breaks, you might find it challenging to see shifts in ideas or tone to help you understand how the passage develops. Consider the following points about the organization of a passage:

- **If the passage is descriptive,** is it organized spatially or by order of importance? What is the overall effect?

- **If the passage is narrative,** is the chronological order of events interrupted by flashback, foreshadowing, or episodic events? Is the plot framed or circular?

- **If the passage is expository,** are any of the following devices or methods used: definition, cause and effect, inductive order, deductive order, comparison/contrast, division and classification, problem/solution, examples, analogy?

- **If persuasion is used**, what methods does the author use to bolster the argument? Does the author deal with opposing evidence? Where is the thesis — at the beginning or at the end? Does the author commit any logical fallacies?

- **Looking for transitions:** In addition, look for transition words and phrases to help you understand the progression of ideas in the passage. Transitions tell us how words, phrases, clauses, sentences, paragraphs — essentially ideas — are related to each other. For example, the use of the transition "for example" in this sentence shows how the idea that came before this phrase is related to the idea that comes next; you know that I'm about to use an example to illustrate the point I just made.

This strategy of looking for transition words is especially useful in the denser, pre-twentieth century passages. Even if the passage seems like complete gibberish to you, if the transition to the second paragraph begins with the word *however*, you actually know quite a bit about that passage — you know that the first part (however confusing) contrasts with the second part. In fact, frequently you will be asked, "How does the second paragraph develop from the first?" You need only to notice the word *however* to get that question correct. Now, if you actually understand a little of the gibberish in the second paragraph — even understand the main idea of the second paragraph — then you actually know more about the first paragraph than you originally thought. You may now be able to understand what was said in the context of its contrast to the second paragraph. The same rule applies to sentences, or even words, phrases, and clauses. Marking transitions in the text will help you understand the author's progression of thought.

Transition Words and Phrases

Words that show **cause and effect**:

therefore	because	thus

Word and phrases that can be used to **compare** two things:

likewise	also	while in	the same way
like	as	similarly	

Words that can be used to **contrast** two things:

but	still	although	on the other hand
though	while	however	yet
otherwise	despite	even though	

Words and phrases that can be used to show **time**:

while	first	meanwhile	soon	then
after	second	today	later	next
afterward	third	tomorrow	as soon as	
before	now	next week	about	
when	suddenly	during	until	
yesterday	finally			

Words and phrases that can be used to show **location**:

above	behind	by	near	throughout
across	below	down	off	to the right
against	beneath	in back of	onto	under
along	beside	in front of	on top of	
among	between	inside	outside	
around	beyond	into	over	

Words and phrases that can be used to **emphasize a point**:

again	truly	especially	for this reason
to repeat	in fact	to emphasize	

Words and phrases that can be used to **add information**:

again	another	for instance	for example
also	and	moreover	additionally
as well	besides	along with	other
next	finally	in addition	

Phrases that can be used to **clarify**:

that is	for instance	in other words

Words and phrases that can be used to **conclude or summarize**:

finally	as a result	to sum up	in conclusion
lastly	therefore	all in all	because

TEST TIP

Once you've filled in all your answers for the multiple-choice section of the AP English exam, go back and check your answers a final time. Make sure you've marked each answer clearly and accurately.

Methods of Development

As you read a passage, notice how the author develops his or her main point and supporting ideas. Does the author rely on a single method, or, more likely, does he or she combine a number of supporting elements to develop the passage? Look for these rhetorical elements and think about how they support the author's purpose.

- **Examples:** The author may include examples that are very specific and concrete or more speculative and hypothetical.

- **Anecdotes:** Anecdotes are short narratives, often personal, used to illustrate a point within a larger context of a passage. Ask yourself if the anecdote is relevant or if it appeals more to emotion than logic.

- **Narration:** The author may develop the passage as a story, usually ordered chronologically. All the elements of narrative fiction may be employed.

- **Description:** Descriptive pieces are supported by details and imagery, and — except in the most scientific, objective writing — meant to evoke an emotional response in the reader. Description is also often used to illustrate a point within a larger context of a piece where the dominant mode of exposition is not descriptive.

- **Figurative language:** Ideas are often supported through figurative language. In fact, an entire piece may be developed through an extended metaphor or an analogy. Again, these devices are often used in conjunction with other methods of development.

- **Logic or reasoning:** The author may use abstract reasoning to support the point. Some arguments are presented deductively — a general or universal idea is presented leading to a more specific point or application. Other arguments are presented inductively — specific points are provided leading to a general or universal conclusion. Look for examples of logical fallacies, like those described above. In general, you should focus on the big picture of how the argument is presented in terms of logic: inductive reasoning, deductive reasoning, and logical fallacy.

Time for a quiz
- Review strategies in Chapter 2
- Take Quiz 1 at the REA Study Center
  (www.rea.com/studycenter)

Approaching the Multiple-Choice Questions: Grammar, Usage, and Style

There are basically two types of questions on the multiple-choice portion of the AP English Language and Composition exam. One type is the overarching question that measures your understanding of the passage as a whole. This type of question asks you to consider how the author uses an overall rhetorical strategy and plan of organization to accomplish his or her purpose. The other kind of question asks you to focus on a very specific part of the passage, from a paragraph or a sentence to a particular phrase or word. These questions focus on points of grammar, usage, style, and tone. The good news is that even if you don't completely understand the passage as a whole, you can still figure out the answers to many of the focused questions. At the same time, by figuring out the focused questions you often will gain a better understanding of the passage as a whole.

One caution — some students refuse to believe that meaning is derived from a complex interplay of content, structure, and language, preferring to think that this complexity is some kind of figment of their English teacher's imagination and not the writer's careful creation. These students often have great difficulty with the AP English Language and Composition exam. Remember, good writing is purposeful writing, and the best writing often feels effortless because it has been crafted to achieve an effect. As you work through the multiple-choice section of the exam, approach every word, detail, image, figure of speech, allusion, syntactic construction — basically every part of the passage — as a choice made by the author, not as a happenstance. In addition, assume that these elements do not exist in isolation but rather are interrelated: they combine to help the writer achieve a specific purpose. Thus, diction and syntax affect style, and style affects tone.

Grammar and Usage

The multiple-choice section of the AP English Language and Composition exam is not a grammar test, and you will not be asked to identify types of sentences or parts of speech. However, you will see questions that are related to grammar. You must be able to understand how one word relates to another word in a sentence, or how a word relates to an entire sentence. You must be able to identify the antecedent of a word or phrase. You should be able to tell what word is modified by another word. You should be familiar with parallel sentence construction, and grammatical terms such as "period," which refers to a long, grammatically complex sentence. In other words, you must be alert to how issues of grammar and usage can affect style and content.

Later in this book, you will review the rules of grammar and usage more generally for help in writing compositions. Here, you'll look at the areas of grammar and usage that are most helpful in answering the multiple-choice questions.

Antecedents and Pronoun Reference

An *antecedent* is a noun, clause, or phrase to which a pronoun or other part of speech refers. Good writers make sure that every pronoun clearly refers to a specific word or phrase. Unclear pronoun reference can lead to ambiguity or even confusion — a problem that we will look at more closely in the section on composition. Here is an example sentence that employs pronouns and antecedents.

When Jasmine discovered that **her** bicycle was not in the garage, **she** immediately wondered if **her** friend Doreen had borrowed **it**.

The pronouns *her* and *she* refer to Jasmine, while the pronoun *it* refers to the bicycle. To clarify the antecedents, you might ask yourself, "Whose bicycle is it?" The answer is "Jasmine's," so the pronoun *her* refers to *Jasmine*. You might also ask yourself, "What had Doreen perhaps borrowed?" The answer is Jasmine's bicycle, so the pronoun *it* refers to *bicycle*.

TEST TIP

When a question on the AP English Language exam asks you to find an antecedent, the answer will probably not be simple. Be prepared to look beyond the immediate sentence. Use the strategy of asking questions such as Who? What? When? Where? and Why?

Asking questions like this works easily with simple sentences. However, on the AP English exam, you will see much more complex sentences and paragraphs. The antecedent to a pronoun may be hard to decipher — in fact, it may occur two or three sentences earlier than the pronoun that refers to it. Read the following two passages and look for the antecedents of the pronouns in bold type.

> First, it is important to note that men and women regard conversation quite differently. For women **it** is a passion, a sport, an activity even more important to life than eating because **it** doesn't involve weight gain.
>
> —Merrill Markoe, *What the Dogs Have Taught Me*

> The contrast would be too painful, the shock too great, but for the intervention of the Fool, whose well-timed levity comes in to break the continuity of feeling when it can no longer be borne, and to bring into play again the fibres of the heart just as **they** are growing rigid from over-strained excitement. The imagination is glad to take refuge in the half-comic, half-serious comments of the Fool, just as the mind under the extreme anguish of a surgical operation vents itself in sallies of wit. The character was also a grotesque ornament of the barbarous times, in which alone the tragic ground-work of the story could be laid. In another point of view **it** is indispensable, inasmuch as while it is a diversion to the too great intensity of our disgust, it carries the pathos to the highest pitch of which it is capable, by showing the pitiable weakness of the old king's conduct and its irretrievable consequences in the most familiar point of view.
>
> —William Hazlitt, *Characters of Shakespeare's Plays*

In the first passage, the first pronoun *it* refers to the noun *conversation,* while the second pronoun *it* refers to the noun *activity.* (The activity, of course, is making conversation.) As you can see, the second passage is much more complex, as it is written in the ornate prose style of the early nineteenth century. It's fairly easy to identify the antecedent of the pronoun *they:* it refers to the noun *fibres.* To find the antecedent of the pronoun *it,* you might ask yourself, "What is indispensable and why?" Here the pronoun *it* refers to the noun *character* — Hazlitt is saying that the character of the Fool, with its comic relief, is indispensable to Shakespeare's play *King Lear*. However, the pronoun *its* refers to the nearby noun *conduct,* and not to the word *character*.

A similar type of question might ask what a certain word refers to. For example,

The word "character" is used as another name for which of the following?

(A) levity

(B) imagination

(C) comments

(D) the Fool

(E) sallies of wit

As you've seen, the word *character* refers to "the Fool," a character in the play *King Lear*. Several questions on the AP English exam will ask you to identify similar connections between words or phrases.

Clauses, Phrases, and Modifiers

The AP English Language and Composition exam will ask you to identify clauses and phrases that are used as modifiers. A *clause* is a group of words that contains a subject and a verb. An *independent clause* can stand alone as a complete sentence. A *dependent clause* (or subordinate clause) may begin with a subordinating conjunction, such as *since, when, because, after,* or *while*. A prepositional phrase is a group of words that begins with a preposition that links to an object. Common prepositions include *at, on, in, above, beyond, beneath,* and similar words that express a position or state.

A *clausal modifier* acts like an adjective or adverb in the structure of a sentence. Clauses can appear at the beginning, middle, or end of a sentence, as in the following examples.

Adjective clause:

Everyone recognized the actress *who emerged from the limousine at the premier.*

The gift, *which had been purchased months before,* was wrapped and gathering dust in the corner.

Adverb clause:

> *Once the game went into overtime,* the crowd rose to its feet and maintained a continuous roar.

> The fans realized, *once the winning touchdown was scored,* that they had witnessed a classic.

A *phrasal modifier* can also function as an adjective or an adverb in a sentence.

Prepositional phrase as adjective:

> The singer *in the sequined dress* performed a program of wonderful jazz songs.

> Hailstones began falling, threatening the windshield *of his new sports car.*

Prepositional phrase as adverb:

> *Throughout our neighborhood,* people helped each other recover from the storm.

> We finally found our dog Charlie sitting disconsolately *between two unfamiliar houses.*

An *appositive* is a noun or noun phrase that renames another noun nearby. It may come at the beginning or end of a sentence or be "embedded" in the middle.

> *An accomplished chef,* Ricardo prepared delicious meals for the visitors.

> Austin learned a great deal about the rigors of Olympic training from Natalya, *a former gymnast.*

> I played with Lollipop, *our neighbors' spritely little pug,* for a few minutes each evening.

Another phrasal modifier is a *verbal phrase,* which is made up of a verbal (a verb that also functions as another part of speech) and all of its modifiers and objects. A verbal phrase can be a participial phrase, a gerund phrase, or an infinitive phrase, and it can function in a sentence as various parts of speech.

> *Washing her car in the driveway,* Betsy noticed a scratch on the hood. (The phrase in italics is a participial phrase that functions as an adjective modifying *Betsy.*)

> *Washing her car* is the last thing Betsy has to do today. (The phrase in italics is a gerund phrase that functions as a noun and the subject of the sentence.)

> Betsy likes *to wash her car on sunny summer afternoons.* (The phrase in italics is an infinitive phrase that functions as a direct object in the sentence.)

An infinitive phrase can also function as the subject of a sentence.

To mount an exhibition of his paintings and drawings was a longstanding dream.

A less common phrasal modifier is the *absolute phrase,* which is a word group that modifies an entire sentence and consists of a noun plus at least one other word. An absolute phrase may appear at various places in a sentence.

His jacket red amidst the white snowfall, the hunter could be seen from miles away.

The hunter could be seen from miles away, *his red jacket glowing amidst the white snowfall.*

The hunter, *red jacket almost glowing in the snow,* could be seen from miles away.

Now look at a passage that will test your knowledge of clauses and phrases.

"We hold these truths to be self evident: that all men are created equal; that they are endowed by their creator with certain inalienable rights; that among these rights are life, liberty, and the pursuit of happiness; that to secure these rights, governments are instituted among men, deriving their just powers from the consent of the governed; that whenever any form of government becomes destructive of these ends, it is the right of the people to alter or to abolish it, and to institute new government, laying its foundation on such principles, and organizing its powers in such form, as to them shall seem most likely to effect their safety and happiness."

This sentence contains 112 words! So, where do you begin? First, look for the main clause. "We hold these truths to be self-evident." The rest of the sentence following the colon is a series of subordinate or dependent clauses that lists the "truths" that Jefferson says are "self-evident." Jefferson organizes the clauses for you, using parallel structure; but he clearly separates the clauses from each other with semi-colons as well. Of course, some of the subordinate clauses contain other complicating phrases, but you can look at these subordinate clauses as separate units now, separate units that all exist in service to illustrating the self-evident truths. Will the AP English exam ask you to identify the phrases and clauses in the technical way just described? No, but it might ask you a question such as this one: How do the clauses beginning with "that" function in the sentence? And now you know; they illustrate the "truths" about people and their natural rights that Jefferson considers "self-evident." You also might see a question such as this one:

The series of dependent clauses beginning with "that" do all of the following EXCEPT

(A) They create a parallelism that adds coherence to the sentence.

(B) They present a list of items exemplifying the "truths."

(C) They assert the concepts Jefferson says that declaration will assume.

(D) They incorporate abstract nouns and adjectives to help illustrate the truths.

(E) They employ a series of metaphors to illustrate the "truths."

Of course, (E) is the bad choice, or rather the good choice because you are seeking the answer choice that doesn't belong. Notice that the grammar skills you employed to analyze the sentence in order to understand it were exactly the skills you needed to answer the question.

DIDYOUKNOW?

A committee of the Continental Congress that included John Adams, Benjamin Franklin, and others chose the young Virginian Thomas Jefferson to write the Declaration of Independence because of his "happy talent for composition" (Adams' phrase). Amid a tense atmosphere, Jefferson secluded himself on June 11 and began drafting the document. He wrote several versions before he was satisfied. The committee made a few changes to his final draft and submitted it to the full Congress on June 28. The document was approved and then released to the public on July 4, 1776.

Sentence Types and Parallel Structure

In your study of grammar, you doubtless have learned the main types of sentences. This knowledge will come in handy on the AP English Language and Composition exam, for you will be asked about parallel structure, compound subjects and predicates, and subordinate clauses. The main sentence types are:

- **Simple sentence.** An independence clause containing a subject and a verb.

- **Compound sentence.** A sentence formed by joining two independent clauses using a coordinating conjunction, a semicolon, or a conjunctive adverb.

- **Complex sentence.** A sentence made up of an independent clause and one or more dependent clauses joined by subordinating conjunctions.

- **Compound-Complex Sentence.** A sentence formed from two or more independent clauses and one or more dependent clauses joined by one of a variety of conjunctions or punctuation marks.

A *coordinating conjunction (and, but, or, nor, for, yet, so)* joins two simple sentences or independent clauses. If the clauses are closely related, they may also be joined with a semicolon.

> I wore a heavy sweater to class, *yet* I still felt chilly all morning.

> I wore a heavy sweater to class; I still felt chilly all morning.

A simple sentence may have a compound subject or a compound predicate.

Compound subject:

> The *necessity* to act quickly and the *ability* to do so led us to our decision.

Compound predicate:

> Genius *scorns* the well-trod path and *seeks* the unmarked trail that leads to discovery.

You may also see questions about parallel structure or syntax, as in the passage from the Declaration of Independence above. Authors use parallel structure to present their ideas clearly and in sequence, so that the reader can follow the argument more easily.

> The particular man aims to be somebody; to set up for himself; to truck and higgle for a private good; and, in particulars, to ride that he may ride; to dress that he may be dressed; to eat that he may eat; and to govern, that he may be seen.
>
> —*Ralph Waldo Emerson*

The AP exam might ask you to identify the parallel elements in the Emerson sentence, or to choose an edit that would improve the parallel structure. In addition, you might be asked a question like the following:

Which word is grammatically and thematically parallel to the word *tone* in the following sentence?

> You do not assume indeed the solemnity of the pulpit, or the tone of stage-declamation: neither are you at liberty to gabble on at a venture, without emphasis or discretion, or to resort to vulgar dialect or clownish pronunciation.
>
> —*William Hazlitt*

(A) pulpit

(B) stage-declamation

(C) solemnity

(D) venture

(E) liberty

The correct answer is (C) solemnity.

Another type of sentence is the *periodic sentence,* which may appear as an answer choice on the AP exam. It is a long sentence that begins with dependent clauses and withholds the main point until the end. Here is an example translated from an ancient Greek writer:

> For when the greatest of all wars broke out and a multitude of dangers presented themselves at one and the same time, when our enemies regarded themselves as irresistible because of their numbers and our allies thought themselves endowed with a courage that could not be excelled, we outdid them both in a way appropriate to each.
>
> —Isocrates, *Panegyricus*

Syntax

Syntax is defined as the "arrangement of words in meaningful patterns." Sentences, which are syntactical units composed by words, do not have meaning until they are put together. When we examine an author's use of syntax, we are examining devices that the author may have manipulated to create an emotional or intellectual effect. Sentence length and structure — repetition, rhythm, parallelism — all contribute to help the audience better understand the author's message. The items below are common techniques for manipulating syntax:

- **Sentence Length and Type:** Are the sentences simple, compound, complex, or compound-complex? Are they short or long? Shorter sentences imply a less formal style; for example, J.D. Salinger uses short sentences in the novel *The Catcher in the Rye* to express the rapid thought processes of a disillusioned teenager. Longer sentences imply a more formal style; for example, Vladimir Nabokov uses long sentences packed with imagery to express his impressions of the past in his autobiography *Speak, Memory*. A series of shorter sentences tend to quicken the pace of the writing, while longer sentences slow it down.

As always, consider how sentence length and type work with the other elements of style to achieve the writer's purpose.

Notice the different impacts of a passage written as a long sentence and then as a series of short, staccato sentences:

> It is easier to just avoid the topic of our future energy crisis instead of facing the same difficult questions with no really satisfying answers and with also the same political posturing from both sides of the question, repeated over and over again.

> Our future energy crisis? It's easier to just avoid the topic. Instead of facing the same hard questions with no really satisfying answers. And there's also the same political posturing from both sides. Over and over again.

- **Sentence Variety:** Most writing is a combination of both long and short sentences as well as sentence types. Where does the author use sentence variety to create meaning? Are short sentences or fragments used for special emphasis? Are long sentences or run-ons used for a specific effect? Look (and listen) for the diversion from the pattern as a point of special meaning and emphasis. Notice how Emerson uses short sentences to introduce and conclude a thought:

  > There are degrees in idealism. We learn first to play with it academically, as the magnet was once a toy. Then we see in the heyday of youth and poetry that it may be true, that it is true in gleams and fragments. Then, its countenance waxes stern and grand, and we see that it must be true. It now shows itself ethical and practical.

- **Specialized Sentence Structures:** What specialized sentence structure does the author use? Sometimes this terminology makes it onto the exam, so it is helpful to you as a critical reader to be aware of these structures and their effects. Knowing these six sentence structures is beneficial: *balanced, periodic, cumulative, inverted, imperative,* and *antithesis.*

  — *Balanced Sentence:* In a balanced sentence, two coordinate but contrasting structures are placed next to each other like the weights on a balanced scale. Thus, a balanced sentence creates a contrasted thought:

  > "Many are called but few are chosen" (Matthew 22:14)

  > "I come to bury Caesar, not to praise him" (Shakespeare, *Julius Caesar*)

When you read a balanced sentence out loud, you tend to pause between the balanced parts. That pause is marked by some kind of fulcrum — usually a coordinating conjunction or a mark of punctuation.

— *Periodic Sentence:* As we've seen, a periodic sentence builds to a climactic statement in its final main clause or phrase. Herman Melville used the structure when he wrote this comment about Benjamin Franklin:

> "Printer, postmaster, almanac maker, essayist chemist, orator, tinker, statesman, humorist, philosopher, parlor man, political economist, professor of housewifery, ambassador, projector, maxim-monger, herb-doctor, wit: Jack of all trades, master of each and mastered by none — the type and genius of the land, Franklin was everything but a poet."

— *Cumulative Sentence:* A cumulative sentence reverses the order of the periodic sentence. Instead of withholding the main idea until the last clause, the writer states it immediately and then expands on it with examples, details, and/or clarifications. Here is an example from Annie Dillard:

> "Her moving wings ignited like tissue paper, enlarging the circle of light in the clearing and creating out of the darkness the sudden blue sleeves of my sweater, the green leaves of jewel-weed by my side, the ragged red trunk of a pine."

— *Inversion:* In an inversion sentence the typical subject-verb order is reversed. Consider the sentence, "Gone are the days when everyone had read the same books, seen the same movies, and dined at the same restaurants." The typical word order would be, "The days when everyone had . . . are gone." Because inversion is infrequently used in prose, it calls attention to the part of the sentence that is out of typical order, and thus creates a special emphasis.

— *Imperative:* The imperative sentence is when the subject is the understood "you," telling or even commanding the audience to do something. There is no hedging or qualifying in the imperative, so the form is very strong and assertive: "Seek simplicity, and distrust it" (Alfred North Whitehead).

— *Antithesis:* An antithesis balances two opposite or contrasting words, phrases, or clauses:

> "Ask not what your country can do for you; ask what you can do for your country." (John F. Kennedy)

This quote is also an example of a balanced sentence.

TEST TIP

When you find an example of unusual syntax in a passage on the AP exam, such as inversion or antithesis, mark it and write a brief note. Although it might not be the focus of a question, understanding its purpose will help you understand the passage.

- **Repetition.** Bad writing is repetitive; good writing effectively uses repetition to create meaning. Anyone who has ever heard or read Martin Luther King, Jr.'s famous 1963 speech at the Lincoln Memorial remembers the "I have a dream" refrain. As you read a passage that employs repetition, consider the words or phrases that are repeated. Are certain sentence structures also repeated? You will notice these repetitive words, phrases and sentences when you read; think about how these stylistic choices affect the meaning. Here, from *Julius Caesar*, is Antony's funeral oration, in which Shakespeare uses repetition for an ironical effect:

> The noble Brutus
>
> Hath told you Caesar was ambitious:
>
> If it were so, it was a grievous fault,
>
> And grievously hath Caesar answer'd it.
>
> Here, under leave of Brutus and the rest —
>
> For Brutus is an honourable man;
>
> So are they all, all honourable men —
>
> Come I to speak in Caesar's funeral.
>
> He was my friend, faithful and just to me:
>
> But Brutus says he was ambitious;
>
> And Brutus is an honourable man.
>
> He hath brought many captives home to Rome
>
> Whose ransoms did the general coffers fill:
>
> Did this in Caesar seem ambitious?
>
> When that the poor have cried, Caesar hath wept:
>
> Ambition should be made of sterner stuff:
>
> Yet Brutus says he was ambitious;

And Brutus is an honourable man.

You all did see that on the Lupercal

I thrice presented him a kingly crown,

Which he did thrice refuse: was this ambition?

Yet Brutus says he was ambitious;

And, sure, he is an honourable man.

DIDYOU**KNOW?**

Martin Luther King, Jr.'s "I Have a Dream" speech was delivered from the steps of the Lincoln Memorial to a huge crowd gathered there on August 28, 1963. The speech called for racial equality and an end to discrimination in America, and is regarded as one of the greatest speeches in history. King used all the resources of rhetoric, including the language and cadences of the church, to deliver his message. At the end, King summed up his message with some partly improvised lines on the idea of "I have a dream."

- **Rhythm:** Does the language have rhythm? Rhythm is not only a characteristic of poetry, but good prose is often rhythmic as well. Rhythm is created in a number of ways. Parallel syntax is the repetition of word order or form either within a single sentence or in several sentences that develop the same central idea. Once again, consider this famous line from The Declaration of Independence:

"We hold these truths to be self evident: that all men are created equal; that they are endowed by their creator with certain inalienable rights; that among these rights are life, liberty, and the pursuit of happiness; that to secure these rights, governments are instituted among men, deriving their just powers from the consent of the governed …"

This is a long, complicated sentence (even in this abridged form), but the parallel syntax and repetition of the relative clauses not only creates the grammatical coherence necessary for comprehension, but it also produces an equal emphasis on each clause as well as a rhythmic lyricism that distinguishes Thomas Jefferson's masterpiece. Rhythm can also be created by the repetition of words or sentences of similar length, especially short ones. Again, you may have been criticized for using this technique in your own writing, but good writers use these elements to make their writing "sing." Listen for patterns in syntax as you read, but also pay attention to breaks in the pattern. They are just as significant.

- **Sentence Beginnings and Endings:** Do any sentences begin or end with a significant word or phrase? Do any sentences have the main idea "hidden" in the middle, in an interrupter, so as to create surprise or suspense?

- **Allusion and Quotation:** Allusions to Shakespeare or Greek philosophers? Latin words and/or phrases? A little French? A verse from a famous poem? These stylistic choices combined with elevated diction are usually characteristics of formal writing meant to appeal to an educated audience. Sometimes, however, such allusions are delivered with a verbal wink at the reader. Look for humor and incongruity — the audience probably still needs to be educated to understand it, but the style may not be formal. Is the language purposefully inflated to create irony, parody, or humor? Here is an example that uses a quote from T. S. Eliot's *The Waste Land*:

  > "'April is the cruelest month,' said the poet, and boy, don't I believe him. With taxes due on the fifteenth of April, every American feels the pinch of impending penury as the deadline approaches."

DIDYOUKNOW?

T. S. Eliot (1888—1965) used allusion frequently in his poem *The Waste Land*. For example, the opening passage of the poem — "April is the cruelest month, breeding/lilacs out of the dead land, mixing/memory and desire" — parodies a passage about April in the General Prologue of Geoffrey Chaucer's *Canterbury Tales*.

Punctuation and Capitalization

Any questions about punctuation on the AP English Language and Composition exam will probably concern an author's use of punctuation marks to control the flow of an argument, to create parallel structure, or to set off an appositive. Nevertheless, you should pay close attention to punctuation marks as you read; this will help you decipher difficult passages and figure out the author's main point. In the passage from the Declaration of Independence that you read before, the colon after the main clause introduces clarifying material in the form of a list of subordinate clauses. You can usually replace a colon with the phrase "in other words" or "for example":

"We hold these truths to be self-evident" *for example,* "that all men are created equal," etc.

The semicolons in the passage are used to create a strong separation between each subordinate clause. Semicolons connect independent clauses that are closely related in meaning. When faced with very dense and difficult text, such as some of the passages on the AP exam, allow the punctuation to help you hear what you are reading in your mind. The author placed the punctuation marks to adjust the pace and flow of his or her writing. If you practice reading difficult text out loud with the pace and expression that the punctuation implies, you will improve your reading comprehension.

TEST **TIP**

Remember that passages from the eighteenth or nineteenth centuries may include unusual punctuation and capitalization. For example, eighteenth century writers such as Samuel Johnson and Jonathan Swift capitalized many more nouns than we do today. Writers also used commas with almost every subordinate clause or separate phrase. According to Naomi S. Baron, "The punctuation that emerged in the eighteenth and nineteenth centuries was consistent in just two respects: it was prolific and often chaotic."

You may be asked about capitalization, as in the question, "Why is the second use of the word "Reason" capitalized in this sentence?"

> He cared not at all for reason, that niggling, small-bore tool of hobbyist philosophers, but he reverenced with all his soul that true Reason that had manifested itself in the unfettered minds of thinkers for thousands of years.

The answer is: "The author wants to emphasize the enduring nature of a certain approach to the idea of reason."

Remember, any questions on the AP English exam about punctuation and capitalization will generally focus on how the author uses them to clarify meaning or make a special point.

Diction

Diction refers to word choice. A writer creates the tone and meaning of a work through the careful choice of words and style of language used. A writer may use archaic, or old-fashioned, words such as *thee* and *thou*; dialect or regional speech patterns; words with similar meanings that have positive or negative connotations (such as the words *high-spirited* or *disruptive* to describe a mischievous child); colloquialisms (such as "It's possible that the whole thing would *blow up in our faces*"); and jargon and technical language (such as "If the physician takes the vitals and the BP is too high, she must get the patient to a clinic stat!").

Certainly it is important for you to be able to understand the vocabulary used in the passages on the AP English Language and Composition exam. However, you must also be aware of the difficult or obscure terms that appear in the test questions themselves. Are you familiar with the word *pedantic*? Do you recognize when something is *churlish* or *inimitable*? If not, you may have trouble answering the multiple-choice questions on the test. A list of key terms is included in this book for you to study. Think of this list as a good start, nothing more. The best way to get a good score on the AP English exam is to expand your vocabulary — that is, to read, read, read. Keep notes on new words that you encounter. Write down the entire sentence or paragraph in which each one appears. Skim through a dictionary on occasion. And try to work some of your new acquisitions into your own conversation or writing.

For practice, read the following passage and then answer the question that follows.

> This realm, in which [Karl] Jaspers is at home and to which he has opened the ways for us, does not lie in the beyond and is not utopian; it is not of yesterday nor of tomorrow; it is of the present and of this world. Reason has created it and freedom reigns in it. It is not something to locate and organize; it reaches into all the countries of the globe and into all their pasts. And although it is worldly, it is invisible. It is the realm of *humanitas*, which everyone can come to out of his own origins. Those who enter it recognize one another, for then they are "like sparks, brightening to a more luminous glow, dwindling to invisibility, alternating and in constant motion. The sparks see one another, and each flames more brightly because it sees others" and can hope to be seen by them.
>
> —Hannah Arendt, *Men in Dark Times*

The speaker's tone in this passage is primarily one of

(A) cautious ambivalence

(B) lyrical tribute

(C) satirical bombast

(D) poignant remorse

(E) acerbic cynicism

First, you should examine the answers one by one and see how they compare to your analysis of the passage. "Cautious ambivalence" means a careful middle feeling between two extremes or two opposed feelings simultaneously. This does not suit the passage, for the writer seems sure of her thoughts and feelings. "Lyrical tribute" means a poetic and intensely emotional praising of someone or something. That certainly seems to fit this passage, so you should consider this possibly the correct choice. "Satirical bombast" means inflated and pretentious writing used to make fun of something. Although the language in this passage is elevated in places, it certainly does not seem bombastic, and it is not satirical in intent. "Poignant remorse" means a sadly mixed feeling of regret, which does not fit the positive tone of this passage. And "acerbic cynicism," which means acidly or bitingly negative, is not reflected in this ringing endorsement of Jasper's "realm." The best answer is (B) lyrical tribute. Arendt in this passage is praising the writer and theologian Karl Jaspers for working in a realm of the spirit where freedom reigns and where others, no matter their origins, can interact with one another.

DIDYOUKNOW?

Hannah Arendt (1906–1975) was a German American writer and philosopher and one of the most influential political writers of the twentieth century. Much of her work analyzes the nature of political power and the roots of totalitarianism. In her book *Eichmann in Jerusalem* describing the trial of the Nazi Adolf Eichmann, she coined the phrase "the banality of evil" to describe the thoughtless way that ordinary people obey orders that lead to evil acts.

Point of View, Style, and Tone

On the multiple-choice section of the AP English exam, most of the questions will analyze the overall effect of the passage and how the author achieves that effect. This involves questions of point of view, style, and tone.

Point of view, of course, can refer to first-person, third-person, or omniscient. However, the point of view you will be looking at is the author's attitude to his or her material and the main point that the author is trying to convey. Point of view, when not stated directly, is presented through an author's style and tone.

Style is the author's characteristic manner of expression. It may feature short, staccato sentences or long, flowing sentences with lots of imagery. In other words, style is the way that the author uses language to present his or her point of view. In this way, one of the essential attributes of style is the repetition of patterns. The other component of style is deviation from the customary patterns. Ernest Hemingway, for example, deviates from his usual short sentences and few descriptive words when he describes nature. In those passages, you will find long, complex sentences and lyrical descriptions of nature, such as a river, to show the peace that people obtain when they escape the jarring, destructive effects of civilization and are comforted by the healing beauty of nature.

Expectation (the pattern) and surprise (the deviation from the pattern) are the component parts of style. A discussion of style is also a discussion of the well-chosen word or phrase. A discussion of the well-chosen word or phrase depends on your ability to be discriminating about language and to recognize good writing. For example, colloquial word choice is not standard formal usage and employs idiomatic or slang expressions; this kind of word usage develops a casual tone. Scientific, Latinate (words with Latin roots or origins), or scholarly language is formal and employs rigidly standard rules of usage. Concrete words form vivid images in the reader's mind, while abstract language is more appropriate for a discussion of philosophy. Allusive style uses many references to history, literature, or other shared cultural knowledge to provoke or enlighten the reader. Appeals to the senses make the writing more concrete and vivid. Rhythmic prose can mimic a process or inject a playful tone into the passage.

Authors employ other poetic devices in their writing to emphasize important ideas. When an author makes the choice to use similes or metaphors, or any of the other common poetic or rhetorical devices, usually, it is because the author wants to draw attention to that particular characteristic and perhaps suggest a more complex relationship to the implied or stated theme.

If the author suddenly varies sentence structure or the length of a sentence, you should take note. Short sentences or fragments usually signal important ideas — introductions or summations. If, in the midst of a variety of sentence structures and lengths, the author inserts two or three short, simple sentences in a row you should note this change as being significant. To emphasize a crucial detail or idea, an author may use a special sentence pattern, such as a balanced sentence or an inverted construction.

An author can choose from a variety of specialized sentence patterns or structures to create emphatic sentences. Most sentences in the English language are loose sentences or cumulative sentences; that is, the main idea appears at the beginning of the sentence (subject first, then predicate, then additional clauses or modifiers) and much of the predicate part of the sentence can be cut off without serious damage to the main idea. Any time an author wishes to call attention to an important idea, he or she can use a different sentence structure. These different structures are called "emphatic" because they emphasize the ideas contained therein.

Your most important task in analyzing style is to understand its relationship to the purpose or main idea of a passage. You will be asked to characterize the author's style in each passage. Like tone, an author's style is formed from rhetorical elements working together; style is always a reflection of the author's purpose and intended audience, as well as the specific occasion for the writing. When you think about style, consider the following:

- **Formal or Informal:** As you read, try to quickly assess whether the writing is more formal or informal. While there are many degrees of these two categories, making this initial judgment will help you read the passage with more understanding and answer the multiple-choice questions more easily. Just remember that archaic language in the passage, which makes it difficult for you to read, does not necessarily mean that the writing is especially formal. Pay attention to all the elements of style discussed in this section.

- **Diction:** How would you characterize the author's choice of words? Is it colloquial, idiomatic, scientific, Latinate, concrete, abstract, scholarly, or allusive? Does the language include slang, jargon, or dialect? Is the word choice inflated or understated? Consider incongruity as well. Is an informal idiom or slang word used in an otherwise formal passage? What effect is the author trying to create with this contrast?

- **Figurative Language:** Which literary devices — personification, metaphor, simile, allusion, hyperbole — does the author use? Remember, figurative language has denotation or literal meaning, and connotation or the ability to evoke nuanced feeling. Passages with figurative language tend to be more formal and/or lyrical; however, passages that include slang would suggest an informal, colloquial style.

- **Imagery:** Does the author use imagery? If the author uses imagery, to what senses does the author appeal? How does the use of imagery reinforce the author's main point? Is the imagery pleasant or distasteful, beautiful or frightening? Are there incongruous images, like a dagger lying on a checkerboard, or a beautiful flower growing through the cracks in a sidewalk on a rough urban street? Does a particular sense dominate the description? Why?

- **Verbal Sound Effects:** Which literary devices of sound — alliteration, assonance, consonance, rhyme — does the author use? While you probably won't be asked specific questions using these terms on the test, it is important to know how these elements influence style. Both alliterative words and rhyming words create connections to each other and tend to make an impression in the reader's mind. Consider the Ben Franklin maxim,

> "One today is worth two tomorrows."

The connection in meaning between "today," "two," and "tomorrow" are emphasized by the alliterated *t* sound. Look at another Franklin maxim:

> "If you would know the value of money, go and try to borrow some; he that goes a-borrowing goes a sorrowing."

Here of course the rhyming words become even more connected in meaning by their connection in sound. In addition, the repetition of sounds of words in close proximity, both initial sounds as well as sounds within words, contribute to the feeling of a passage. Soft words repeating soft sounds *(l, m, n, s, f* sounds) can create a calming effect while harsher sounds *(t, k, p* sounds) might create an exciting or discordant effect.

Look at these lines from Washington Irving's short story "Rip Van Winkle." Rip is the fictional character who falls asleep in the Catskill Mountains for twenty years, and this is the line Irving uses to bring us in to the section of the story that will begin Rip's long slumber:

> "From an opening between the trees he could overlook all the lower country for many a mile of rich woodlands. He saw at a distance the lordly Hudson, far, far below him, moving on its silent but majestic course, with the reflection of a purple cloud, or the sail of a lagging bark, here and there sleeping on its glassy bosom, and at last losing itself in the blue highlands."

Notice how Irving combines the repetition of the soft sounds here in the initial and internal syllables of the words in this sentence with the imagery to create this sleepy fantasy.

Tone is the writer's attitude toward the subject and the audience, and it encompasses diction, point of view, style, syntax — every possible resource of writing. The tone might be described as lyrical or playful or elegiac. The tone of a passage can be obvious, but it can also be subtle and misleading. For example, satire is often included on the multiple-choice section of the AP English Language and Composition exam. Satire uses humor and irony to criticize people or social institutions. It is related to, but not quite the same as, sarcasm. In satire, the writer takes on a role, and so may be hiding his or her true feelings about the subject. A satirical passage criticizing the excessive claims or rhetoric of a public figure might present a mocking version of a tribute to the person.

Instead of genuinely espousing the person's greatness, the writer is actually disparaging his or her lack of proportion or self-awareness. Successful satire can be quite subtle, and an inexperienced reader might miss its true tone. If you sense that a passage is satirical, ask yourself whether the writer is being serious or is teasing and mocking the subject. Look for examples of hyperbole or bombastic language that go over the top in their praise.

TEST TIP

When you confront the five answer choices describing the tone of a passage, see if you can eliminate one or two of them immediately because they obviously don't fit the passage. For example, the tone of a tough-minded political tract is probably not going to fit the description *lyrical* or *innocent*.

Finally, remember that almost every group of multiple-choice questions on the AP English exam will include a question about the tone of the passage. Here you will meet with descriptive words such as *reverent, condescending, terse, judicious, effusive,* and many more. A list of terms that might be used to describe the tone of a passage is included here. You should learn these words and their meanings. Yet the list contains only some of the possibilities. It's up to you to find and learn the meaning of as many descriptive terms as you can before taking the AP exam. Doing so will certainly increase your chances of making a good score.

Terms to Describe Tone, Style, and Attitude

acerbic	bombastic	conciliatory	diffident
accusatory	callous	condescending	disapproving
admiring	candid	contemplative	disdainful
ambivalent	capricious	confident	disgusted
angry	choleric	contemptuous	disillusioned
appreciative	churlish	contentious	dismissive
apprehensive	clinical	cynical	dramatic
bantering	colloquial	defensive	earnest
benevolent	compassionate	detached	ecstatic
biting	complimentary	determined	effusive
bitter	concerned	didactic	elegiac

enthusiastic	ironic	pedantic	self-deprecating
facetious	irreverent	petty	self-effacing
factual	jovial	petulant	sentimental
fanciful	judgmental	pretentious	sincere
fervent	judicious	prudent	smug
flippant	learned	reassuring	solemn
harsh	lugubrious	reckless	somber
hopeful	malicious	reconciled	strident
hortatory	mocking	remorseful	superficial
idiosyncratic	mock-serious	respectful	sympathetic
impartial	moralistic	restrained	taunting
incisive	mournful	reverent	terse
indignant	neutral	sanguine	threatening
inflammatory	nostalgic	sarcastic	turgid
informal	objective	sardonic	urbane
informative	obsequious	satiric	urgent
insipid	optimistic	scholarly	worshipful
insolent	patronizing	scornful	zealous

Approaching the Multiple-Choice Questions: Documenting Sources

For the multiple-choice questions on the AP English Language and Composition exam, you will need to be familiar with the various styles and uses of documentation. Although it's not necessary to memorize all the documentation styles, it is important to have certain skills, such as the ability to analyze footnotes. In order to answer the documentation questions, your close reading of materials and familiarity with the nature of academic discourse with documentation will help you on the AP English Language test. Although there are different rules or guidelines, these documentation styles have similar elements: selection of headings, punctuation and abbreviations, citation of references, and many other elements that are a part of a publication or manuscript.

Documentation Styles

1. MLA – Modern Language Association: used in English and foreign language and literature courses, as well as in other disciplines in the humanities. MLA recommends the use of a parenthetical system of documentation. Citations are in parentheses within the text to point to sources in an alphabetized list of works cited that appears at the end of the essay.

2. Turabian/Chicago: used by different groups of scholars in the humanities, literature, history, and the arts, and scholars in the physical, natural, and social sciences. *The Chicago Manual of Style* presents two basic documentation systems: (1) notes and bibliography and (2) author-date.

3. APA – American Psychological Association: used by psychologists, anthropologists, and business managers for scientific writing.

4. CSE – Council of Science Editors: used by students in the Biological Sciences.

On the AP English Language test there are multiple-choice questions that address the footnoted nonfiction passages. Generally, a footnote is indicated in the text with a superscript number. Multiple footnotes in a text are numbered in order. Each footnote is placed at the bottom of the page where the number appears. The footnote may be preceded by the same superscript number as in the text or by a full-size number followed by a period. Alternatively, citations may appear at the end of a text as numbered endnotes.

DID YOU KNOW?

The Chicago Manual of Style is a guide to style for American English that has been continuously published since 1906 by the University of Chicago Press. It has grown from its first edition of 203 pages to a comprehensive reference work that included more than 1,000 pages in its sixteenth edition. More than any other guide, it is responsible for a uniform standard of citation style for research publications.

In MLA style, only one sentence is used in a footnote or endnote:

[5]David K.C. Cooper, <u>Open Heart: The Radical Surgeons Who Revolutionized Medicine</u> (New York: Kaplan Publishing: 2010) 156.

A bibliography entry contains three sentences (author, book title, publishing information):

Cooper, David K.C. <u>Open Heart: The Radical Surgeons Who Revolutionized Medicine.</u> New York: Kaplan Publishing, 2010.

TEST TIP

Remember that the basic purpose of a footnote is to inform the reader about the source for a quotation or statistic included in a nonfiction text. Questions about the purpose of a footnote may include answers that sound plausible, but do not explain why the footnote was actually necessary.

When you read an essay or nonfiction passage with documentation, especially with footnotes, you should think about the questions that follow:

- What type of publication is it?

Print:

— book

— encyclopedia

— journal article

— magazine article

— newspaper article

— anthology

— government publication

Nonprint:

— online journal or magazine article

— online encyclopedia

— web-based images, videos or documents

— podcast

— online database

— TV or radio program

— film

— interview

— lecture

— speech

DIDYOUKNOW?

The term *podcast* is a neologism combining the word "broadcast" and the word "pod" from the iPod. This form of media, which can include both audio and video, is used to present academic lectures, slide shows, and video clips, and is used increasingly by universities and businesses.

- What is the author's full name?

- Is there more than one author?

- What is the full title (including subtitle)?

- Who is the editor/s or translator/s (if there is one)?

- What is the edition (if the book is a second or later edition)?

- What is the number of the volume and the total number of volumes (if the book is a multivolume work) in the series?

- What is the series name (if the book is part of a series)?

- What is the city of publication?

- Who is the publisher?

- What is the year of publication?

- When was the webpage last updated and what date was it viewed?

Questions About Documentation

For questions about annotated material, you need to be able to identify the information the notes reveal about the passage and the reason they are included. You might not recognize the format in the selection (APA, MLA, Chicago style, CSE), but knowing the exact style is not important. Questions about documentation usually appear in the following format:

The purpose of footnote _____ is to inform the reader _____.

The number _____ in the footnote most probably indicates _____.

Taken as a whole, the footnotes suggest that _____.

In line _____ of the footnote, the word _____ refers to _____.

According to footnote _____, which of the following is the source for the quotation: _____?

The footnotes imply all of the following about the passage EXCEPT _____.

Which of the following is an accurate reading of footnote _____?

TEST TIP

If you are asked which of the answer choices "is an accurate reading" of a footnote, read the answers carefully to see that the information matches that in the footnote. The wrong answers will probably include elements from the footnote that are presented or interpreted incorrectly.

Time for a quiz
- Review strategies in Chapter 2
- Take Quiz 2 at the REA Study Center
  (www.rea.com/studycenter)

Approaching the Multiple-Choice Questions: Analyzing a Passage

In this chapter we will analyze a sample passage from the multiple-choice section of the AP English exam and present a strategy or thought process for answering each question. The passage presented here is typical of those on the AP exam; it is anonymous, formal and ornate in its prose style, and mostly self-explanatory. This analysis will demonstrate how a logical approach to the multiple-choice questions can result in finding the right answers.

Sample Passage with Multiple-Choice Questions

Questions 1–10. Read the following passage carefully before you choose your answers. *This passage is taken from a nineteenth-century essay.*

Nothing is more clear than that every plot, worth the name, must be elaborated to its *dénouement* before anything be attempted with the pen. It is only with the *dénouement* constantly in view that we can give a plot its indispensable air of consequence, or causation, by making the incidents, and especially
(5) the tone at all points, tend to the development of the intention.

DIDYOU**K**NOW?

In dramatic structure, the *dénouement* includes events between the falling action and the actual final scene of the story or play. The word comes from an Old French word meaning "to untie." The *dénouement* is when the complexities of a plot are untied or unraveled for the reader or audience.

There is a radical error, I think, in the usual mode of constructing a story. Either history affords a thesis — or one is suggested by an incident of the day — or, at best, the author sets himself to work in the combination of striking events to form merely the basis of his narrative-designing, generally, to fill in (10) with description, dialogue, or autorial comment, whatever crevices of fact, or action, may, from page to page, render themselves apparent.

I prefer commencing with the consideration of an *effect*. Keeping originality always in view — for he is false to himself who ventures to dispense with so obvious and so easily attainable a source of interest — I say to myself, in the (15) first place, "Of the innumerable effects, or impressions, of which the heart, the intellect, or (more generally) the soul is susceptible, what one shall I, on the present occasion, select?" Having chosen a novel, first, and secondly a vivid effect, I consider whether it can be best wrought by incident or tone — whether by ordinary incidents and peculiar tone, or the converse, or by peculiarity both (20) of incident and tone — afterward looking about me (or rather within) for such combinations of event, or tone, as shall best aid me in the construction of the effect.

I have often thought how interesting a magazine paper might be written by any author who would — that is to say, who could — detail, step by step, (25) the processes by which any one of his compositions attained its ultimate point of completion. Why such a paper has never been given to the world, I am much at a loss to say — but, perhaps, the autorial vanity has had more to do with the omission than any one other cause. Most writers — poets in especial — prefer having it understood that they compose by a species of fine (30) frenzy — an ecstatic intuition — and would positively shudder at letting the public take a peep behind the scenes, at the elaborate and vacillating crudities of thought — at the true purposes seized only at the last moment — at the innumerable glimpses of idea that arrived not at the maturity of full view — at the fully-matured fancies discarded in despair as unmanageable — at the (35) cautious selections and rejections — at the painful erasures and interpolations — in a word, at the wheels and pinions — the tackle for scene-shifting — the step-ladders and demon-traps — the cock's feathers, the red paint and the

TEST TIP

When confronted with archaic or ornate prose, try to determine word meanings from near-by context clues and the broader context of the passage. When you encounter unfamiliar words that you can't decipher, circle them or jot them down in the margin. You might find clues to their meanings further on in the text.

black patches, which, in ninety-nine cases out of the hundred, constitute the properties of the literary *histrio.*

(40) I am aware, on the other hand, that the case is by no means common, in which an author is at all in condition to retrace the steps by which his conclusions have been attained. In general, suggestions, having arisen pell-mell, are pursued and forgotten in a similar manner.

For my own part, I have neither sympathy with the repugnance alluded to, (45) nor, at any time, the least difficulty in recalling to mind the progressive steps of any of my compositions, and, since the interest of an analysis or reconstruction, such as I have considered a *desideratum,* is quite independent of any real or fancied interest in the thing analyzed, it will not be regarded as a breach of decorum on my part to show the *modus operandi* by which some one of my (50) own works was put together.

1. The author of the passage can best be described as a person who

   (A) is eager to learn from various authors their different modes of composing a narrative

   (B) is reluctant to reveal his secrets of composition to the public

   (C) believes that there are many equally valid ways to compose a successful narrative

   (D) is comfortable with describing his own method of composing a narrative

   (E) aspires to be a writer but has yet to discover a successful mode of composition

2. In line 2 of the passage, the French term *dénouement* refers to the

   (A) reading public

   (B) most respected literary critics of the day

   (C) main theme of the literary work

   (D) plot of the composition

   (E) culmination or ending of the narrative

DIDYOU**KNOW?**

The word *pell-mell* means "in frantic disorderly haste." The American writer Washington Irving wrote, "I went to work pell-mell, blotted several sheets of paper with choice floating thoughts" — a quote which demonstrates the method that the author of the passage is criticizing.

3. What is the "radical error" that the author refers to in the first sentence of the second paragraph?

   (A) not basing the story on an incident of the day

   (B) not letting the plot unfold as the writing proceeds

   (C) not beginning with the idea of a final effect

   (D) not being open to various means of composing a story

   (E) not filling in sufficiently the "crevices of fact"

4. According to the author, no detailed description of the process of composition has hitherto been published primarily due to

   (A) "autorial vanity" (line 27)

   (B) "ecstatic intuition" (line 30)

   (C) "vacillating crudities of thought" (lines 31–32)

   (D) "cautious selections and rejections" (line 35)

   (E) "painful erasures and interpolations" (line 35)

5. Which of the following words is grammatically and thematically parallel to "novel" (line 17)?

   (A) "first" (line 17)

   (B) "vivid" (line 17)

   (C) "effect" (line 18)

   (D) "peculiar" (line 19)

   (E) "converse" (line 19)

6. In context, the phrase "history affords a thesis" (line 7) is best interpreted as having which of the following meanings?

   (A) History can be reduced to a unifying idea.

   (B) History is like a complicated plot.

   (C) History seems to validate a theory.

   (D) History proves to be based on a false idea.

   (E) History provides a theme for a story.

7. Read the section below from lines 36–39.

   . . . in a word, at the wheels and pinions — the tackle for scene-shifting — the step-ladders and demon-traps — the cock's feathers, the red paint and the black patches, which, in ninety-nine cases out of the hundred, constitute the properties of the literary *histrio*.

   The meaning of this section is reinforced by which earlier phrase?

   (A) "its ultimate point of completion" (lines 25–26)

   (B) "poets in especial" (lines 28–29)

   (C) "would positively shudder" (line 30)

   (D) "take a peep behind the scenes" (line 31)

   (E) "at the innumerable glimpses of idea" (lines 32–33)

8. In the sentence beginning "Most writers" (lines 28–39), the author employs which of the following rhetorical devices?

   I.   parallel syntax

   II. personification

   III. elevated diction

   (A) I only

   (B) III only

   (C) I and III only

   (D) II and III only

   (E) I, II, and III

9. "The repugnance alluded to" (line 44) refers to

   (A) other writers' refusal to reveal their methods of composition

   (B) the public's disapproval of contemporary fiction

   (C) novelists' disparagement of poets

   (D) other writers' difficulties with composition

   (E) other writers' skepticism about the author's methods of composition

10. The author's tone in the passage as a whole is best described as

(A) harsh and strident

(B) authoritative and self-assured

(C) superficial and frivolous

(D) cautious and conciliatory

(E) informal and self-deprecating

Analyzing the Passage and Answering the Questions

First, you should read the passage through twice. On the first reading, you will notice the elaborate language and the difficult syntax. The passage was probably written before the twentieth century. Read carefully and try to get a general feeling for the author's purpose and main point. The passage is obviously written by an experienced author, and concerns the best method of composing a story. As you read the passage a second time, mark distinctive features such as the italicized words *dénouement, effect, histrio, desideratum,* and *modus operandi,* and the long sentence with parallel elements of syntax in lines 28–39. Ask yourself what the author is trying to say and who the audience for the essay might be.

TEST TIP

If you change your answer to a multiple-choice question, be sure to erase your original answer completely. Otherwise, the machine that grades this section may count your answer wrong because of double marking.

Now you're ready to begin answering the multiple-choice questions. Remember that on the actual AP exam, if one of the questions seems too difficult, you can move on to the next question and come back to the other one later.

1. This question asks how the author of the passage can best be described. The author mostly criticizes other writers, so (A) is not correct. The author is not at all reluctant to reveal his secrets of composition, saying, "it will not be regarded as a breach of decorum on my part to show the *modus operandi* (mode of operation) by which some one of my own works was put together. Thus, (B) is incorrect.

The author criticizes "the usual mode of constructing a story," and seems to think his own approach is superior. Therefore, (C) would seem to be incorrect. In his detailed thoughts about the process of composition, the author reveals himself as a seasoned writer, so (E) is not correct. As we've seen, the author is ready to share with the reader his own methods of composition, so (D) is the correct answer.

2. This question asks about that tricky italicized word that you marked, *dénouement.* Instead of analyzing the answers, first try to figure out the meaning of the word from the context clues in the paragraph. The author says that every plot "must be elaborated to its *dénouement*" before the actual writing begins. He also says that only by keeping the *dénouement* in view can a writer give a plot "its indispensable air of consequence, or causation." This sounds like he is talking about how the story ends or how the plot is resolved. Now scan the answer choices. Answer choice (E) is "the culmination or ending of the narrative." This fits your guess about the meaning in context of the word *dénouement*. Answer choice (E) is correct.

TEST TIP

If you have a hard time understanding a question, try circling or underlining key words or phrases from the question stem and restating them in your own words. Focus on the overall meaning of the question.

3. First, you should reread the full sentence where the quoted phrase appears. Then read the sentences that follow it. The author elaborates on another writer's faulty (in the author's view) method of composition. The first sentence of the next paragraph is the most important clue: "I prefer commencing with the consideration of an *effect*." This is the author's preferred way of constructing a story, so a "radical error" to him would be a method that did not start this way. Thus, "not beginning with the idea of a final effect" is to him a "radical error" in the usual way of constructing a story. Answer choice (C) is correct.

4. As you read this question, notice the word *hitherto,* which means "up to this time." The question asks why the author believes that no detailed description of the writing process has been published yet. Go back to paragraph 4, where the author discusses how interesting such a descriptive article ("magazine paper") would be. Notice the following sentence: "Why such a paper has never been given to the world, I am much at a loss to say — but, perhaps, *the autorial vanity has had more to do with the omission than any one other cause.*" You can see that

the author believes that "autorial vanity" (the self-regard of other authors) is the main cause of this "omission." Now you can check the other answers, just in case. Choice (B), "ecstatic intuition," describes how other authors want the public to view their methods of composition, not the reason for their reluctance to share them. The other answer choices all come from the author's list of the shoddy ways (in his view) that other writers develop their ideas. Thus, your original notion is confirmed; answer choice (A) is correct.

5. This is another tricky question. A word that is grammatically parallel to another word serves the same purpose in the sentence, while a thematically parallel word reinforces the theme in the same way. Go to line 17 and reread the first part of the sentence where the word "novel" appears: "Having chosen a novel, first, and secondly a vivid effect." Here, the author's syntax can be a bit difficult for a twenty-first century reader. The word "novel" here does not refer to the literary form, but instead is an adjective meaning "unusual." Earlier in the paragraph, the author spoke of "keeping originality always in view," and if something is original it is novel. Now you can see that the author is actually saying (in modern terms) "Having first chosen a novel effect, and secondly having chosen a vivid effect." Thus the words "novel" and "vivid" both modify the noun *effect* and are parallel grammatically — and also thematically, since they explain the sort of effect the author is seeking. Answer choice (B), "vivid," is correct.

6. To understand the context of the phrase this question is asking about, reread the entire paragraph where it appears. Notice that the author is talking about what he sees as the errors in composition that other authors make. This includes how they get ideas for their stories: "Either history affords a thesis — or one is suggested by an incident of the day." You can tell that "history" here is being referred to as a source for narrative or thematic ideas, as for an historical novel. To "afford a thesis" means to provide a theme or idea. Thus, choices (A), (C), and (D) would seem to be incorrect because they indicate that the phrase is making a comment on history itself. Answer choice (B) seems plausible because it compares history to a plot, but that is not the exact idea of the phrase in context. Answer choice (E) is correct.

7. The key to answering this question correctly is making sure you understand the quoted section of text. Read the section again carefully. The images are somewhat obscure, but you can probably get the basic idea: "wheels and pinions" refers to simple gears, and "the tackle for scene-shifting" is the machinery used to raise and lower scenery in a theater; "step-ladders" are found backstage, as are "cock's feathers" for costumes and red paint for painting scenery. Even the word *histrio* refers to histrionics or theatrical

performance. The author is describing a writer's mind or "workshop" as if it were the backstage area of a theater where the scenery and costumes and other properties are created and moved around. With this in mind, you should look for the phrase that refers to the theater; this type of phrase would "reinforce" the idea of the text section. Sure enough, the only answer phrase that is related to the theater is "take a peep behind the scenes." Answer choice (D) is correct.

8. To begin, reread the sentence from lines 28–39. It is the longest, most complex sentence in the passage, and we've already looked at it for other questions. Check to see if each kind of rhetorical device listed is found in this sentence. First, look for parallel syntax. Notice that several phrases begin with the word *at:* "at the elaborate and vacillating crudities of thought — at the true purposes seized only at the last moment — at the innumerable glimpses of idea that arrived not at the maturity of full view — at the fully-matured fancies discarded in despair as unmanageable — at the cautious selections and rejections — at the painful erasures and interpolations." This is a perfect example of parallel syntax. Next, look for personification, which is treating an animal, object, or idea as if it had human qualities. The passage is talking about writers and their methods of composition, but it doesn't personify those methods or anything else. Finally, look for instances of elevated diction, or fancy word choices. This author certainly uses lots of fancy words and phrases, from "vacillating crudities" to "erasures and interpolations" to "the literary *histrio.*" So I and III are found in this sentence, but not II. Look for the answer that includes I and III only. Answer choice (C) is correct.

9. To answer this question, you must understand the meaning of the phrase "the repugnance alluded to." Rereading the complete sentence, you can see that the author does not have sympathy with this "repugnance," so it is something he disagrees with or disapproves of. The word "repugnance" means "strong dislike or distaste for something." Remember that the author does not agree with other authors who decline to share their working methods with the public. So "the repugnance alluded to" (*alluded* means "referred to") is the refusal of other writers to share or reveal their ways of composing a story. It has nothing to do with the public's disapproval (B), novelists' disparagement of poets (C), or other writers' difficulties with composition (D) or skepticism about the author's way of working. Thus, answer choice (A) is correct.

10. At this point, after having analyzed this passage thoroughly, you probably have a pretty good grasp of the author's tone. Let's look at each answer choice in turn. While the author's criticism of other writers is harsh, his style seems too balanced

and controlled to be labeled "strident," which means "loud, vociferous, and discordant." His tone is certainly authoritative, as he apparently is a published author of wide experience, and he is so self-assured that he feels free to criticize other professional writers. He does not strike the reader as being superficial and frivolous, as his reasoning is subtle and logical. He is anything but cautious and conciliatory (the latter word means "appeasing by being friendly or agreeable"). He is also far from informal, and nowhere close to being self-deprecating. He is not shy about exhibiting his knowledge, opinions, and methods. After this analysis, you can see that answer choice (B) is correct.

Not all the passages on the AP English Language and Composition exam will be this difficult to analyze. For example, many passages will come from twentieth century writers whose style is much easier for modern readers to understand. However, this example has demonstrated the thought processes required to answer the multiple-choice questions correctly. As you can see, the best study method is to read as much and as widely as possible and to keep adding to your vocabulary — until you feel like a human dictionary!

DIDYOU**KNOW?**

The passage in this chapter is from an essay by the American writer Edgar Allan Poe (1809–1849). The essay, called "The Philosophy of Composition," appeared in 1846 and is one of the most influential descriptions of the composition process ever written. In it, Poe describes in great detail how he planned and wrote his poem "The Raven."

Time for a quiz
- Review strategies in Chapter 2
- Take Quiz 3 at the REA Study Center
  (www.rea.com/studycenter)

Take Mini-Test 1
on Chapters 3–7
Go to the REA Study Center
(www.rea.com/studycenter)

Approaching the Essay Questions: Writing an Essay

The free-response or essay section of the AP English Language and Composition exam is composed of three prompts, which you are given a total of 135 minutes to complete (a recommended 15 minutes for reading the sources for the synthesis prompt and 120 minutes for writing your essays). Currently there are three types of free-response questions on the AP exam with some subset variations within these categories. These include the Synthesis Essay, the Rhetorical Analysis or Style Analysis Essay, and the Persuasive Essay.

Just like reading, writing is a skill that needs to be developed and practiced. Ideally, your English classes have provided a continuous cycle of writing, editing, revising, and feedback, and your other content area courses have emphasized writing as well. There is no substitute for this kind of instruction and practice in your development as a writer. However, the time constraints on the AP English exam add an extra level of difficulty because the exam asks you to address complex prompts without the benefit of the full writing process most good writers rely on. So, while you may be a fine writer — and truly advanced for your grade — this kind of on-demand, timed writing will probably be challenging and a bit stressful for you. It certainly is a skill that needs to be practiced before the exam.

The AP English Language and Composition exam assumes that you are fluent in Standard English syntax and grammar and that you are able to organize your thoughts in coherent, well-expressed expository prose. Most students will be familiar with the standard thesis and support essay with its introduction, body paragraphs, and conclusion. Beyond an ability to use this basic form, however, students need to be aware of the different stylistic effects created by different syntactic and lexical choices. That is to say, when you choose a particular word or construct a very short or very complex sentence, you need to be in control of your choices, realizing how these choices affect your reader and the overall impact of your essay. This awareness is useful in both the analysis and creation of expository prose.

DIDYOUKNOW?

Do you want to continue your development as a writer? The Iowa Writers' Workshop is a creative writing program that began at the University of Iowa in 1936. The program requires students to take classes in literature and participate in workshop courses, which meet weekly. At these workshops, students read their work aloud and submit to criticism by a roundtable made up of the instructor and their fellow students. Alumni of this prestigious program have won seventeen Pulitzer Prizes.

Essays on the AP English exam are scored on a scale of 0 to 9 points, with the point count and standards being tailored to suit each essay question. Two trained Readers will score each paper. If the scores of the two Readers differ by more than one point, a third Reader will be consulted. Many hours are spent training Readers so that they can score different kinds of responses to the essays with great consistency. Though the essays are read quickly, they are always read accurately and thoroughly!

The Readers understand that these are first-draft essays, so they are not expecting perfection. Content counts much more than grammar, word choice, or spelling; however, seldom does an essay with even as few as three or four significant errors receive the top score. It is wise, therefore, to proofread and correct your writing before going on to the next prompt. Rearranging or rewording some of your sentences is acceptable, but make sure your changes are clearly marked and that your paper is legible. You must address the given task carefully: do not deviate from the topic or dwell too long on one point. You should attend to subtle nuances of language in your essay. A mediocre paper is one that fails to identify and to analyze subtleties of meaning. Better-quality papers recognize and respond to the emotional shadings of the topic. See the scoring rubric below:

Scoring Rubic for Essay Questions

Scores of 9–8: These are superior essays. They feature a clear statement of position, thoughtful support, convincing examples, and stylistic maturity (varied sentence structure, nuanced diction, strong organization). Although there may be a few minor grammar or spelling errors, the author demonstrates a superior control of language in writing the essay.

Scores of 7–6: These are proficient essays. They have a clear thesis that is supported by specific and convincing proof, but they are less nuanced, sophisticated, and/or original than the 8/9 essays. The author's writing is less seasoned and assured and thus displays occasional lapses of diction, tone, syntax, or organization. Although there may be errors of grammar and spelling,

(continued)

Scoring Rubic for Essay Questions *(continued)*

the author demonstrates a solid control of language. Well-written papers with "6" content may earn a 7, and "7" content essays with weaker writing may earn a 6.

Score of 5: These are mediocre, but adequate, essays. The thesis may not be quite clear, the argument not as well developed, and/or the organization may not be especially effective. The writing generally conveys the author's ideas, but the style is less sophisticated and there are some grammatical and spelling errors. **A score of 5 is considered the lowest passing score an AP Reader can give an essay.**

Score of 4: These essays are judged as not adequate. Though 4 essays generally follow a standard multi-paragraph thesis and support format, the paragraphs tend to be short (three or four sentences) indicating a lack of adequate development. Essays will receive a score no higher than 4 if they do *any one* of the following:

(A)   oversimplify or over-generalize the issues;

(B)   present a misreading or a partial misreading of the presented text;

(C)   revert to simpler tasks such as paraphrasing rather than arguing a point or analyzing a problem or a text;

(D)   write only in general terms, ignoring fine distinctions;

(E)   fail to discuss the issue thoroughly and satisfactorily;

(F)   misstate or mismanage the evidence;

(G)   fail to include sufficient details;

(H)   fail to establish the importance to the writer;

(I)   treat only one aspect of a two-sided issue;

(J)   cite examples but fail to consider the consequences;

(K)   cite stylistic techniques but fail to explain their effect or impact on the author's purpose;

(L)   characterize the passage without analyzing the language;

(M)   display awkward or inconsistent control of syntax, diction, and/or mechanics. Though the prose in these essays generally conveys the writers' ideas, the syntax may be awkward, repetitive, and/or overly simplistic; the diction may be immature or inappropriate; and basic spelling and punctuation rules are at times lacking.

(continued)

Scoring Rubic for Essay Questions *(continued)*

Scores of 3–2: These are weak essays. They lack clear organization and adequate support for the thesis, the writing style is simplistic, and there are frequent grammar and spelling errors.

Scores of 1: These are poor essays. Although they may mention the question, they lack clarity, have little or no evidence, and contain consistent grammar and spelling errors. They are badly written, unacceptably brief, or disastrously off topic.

The Writing Process

The purpose of the essay or free-response section of the AP English exam is to test your ability to "move effectively through the stages of the writing process," from reading a prompt carefully and using sources to drafting, revising, editing, and reviewing an effective, sophisticated essay. In this section, you will review the writing process and see how the steps can be adapted to your needs for the essay portion of the AP English exam.

Thinking About Your Own Method of Composition

To write successful essays, you should focus not only on the finished product, but on the process necessary to achieve a polished, clear, coherent piece of writing. Your approach to this process has two aspects. First, you must develop through repeated practice your own repertory of routines, strategies, and skills for composing, revising, and editing many different kinds of text. Second, you should also develop a keen awareness about your own individual method of composition — including both strengths and weaknesses — which will be most beneficial when you get stuck in the planning stages or in the middle of creating a piece of writing. No doubt your writing teacher has used established research, theory, and practice to help you overcome any problems you might have with the writing process. At this point, you should think of yourself as a capable, experienced writer.

As you examine the writing process, remember that it is not — and should not be — a formulaic series of rigidly defined steps. Instead, the steps should be seen as overlapping and continuously repeating; new ideas may occur at the revising or editing stage, for example, and lead you to rewrite — and greatly improve — a paragraph. Thus, even the most experienced writer often has to rethink an approach or "go back to the drawing board" under certain circumstances. With this in mind, you should consider alternate strategies for each step of the writing process, and try to identify habits and methods that work best for you in different writing situations.

The following sections will review the steps of the writing process that are appropriate for your work on the free-response section of the AP English exam: prewriting, drafting, revising, editing, and reviewing. On exam day there won't be time to complete each step of the writing process as you would for a term paper. You must basically perform the stages in rapid succession, with lots of overlapping. However, you should work on these steps in your practice essays. This will help you improve your method of composition and give you confidence in the skills needed for the pressurized situation of the essay test.

Prewriting

Prewriting: Clarifying the Task

You should not begin writing until you are certain about what the prompt or assignment requires. Therefore you need to read the writing prompt carefully, and note the key words or phrases that describe the writing task, such as *compare, contrast, explain, describe, offer a solution, present a rebuttal,* etc. Points to think about include:

- **Purpose**. What is the reason for writing, or what is to be accomplished at the end?

- **Preparation**. What actions should be taken before beginning, such as reading a passage or consulting a source?

- **Components**. What are the required elements in the assignment (outlines to follow, questions to answer, conclusions to draw)?

- **Evaluation**. What criteria will the Readers use to determine if you have satisfied the prompt or completed the assignment successfully?

It may help to clarify your task if you paraphrase the prompt for yourself. Also, refer back to the prompt as often as needed during the writing process.

TEST TIP

One of the worst mistakes you can make on an essay question for the AP English exam is to fail to do what the prompt requires. Make sure you know exactly what the prompt is asking and shape your response accordingly.

Prewriting: Thinking and Planning

Once the task has been clarified, you can think about possible approaches to take or topics to address. On a timed prompt, as in the AP English exam, the writer must decide on an approach fairly rapidly. For a larger assignment like a term paper, you might do additional reading on several related topics while pondering the best course to take in planning and writing the paper.

Again, although the writing process is presented here as a series of orderly steps, it is not generally so tidy in execution. The steps are iterative — they influence each other and recur constantly. You should remember that the original ideas or approach that you settle on may have to be revised after the drafting process has begun. Or, once the editing has begun, you may notice that more information is needed or an argument needs to be bolstered with better examples. Be aware that the process may double back on itself before the polished finish product is achieved.

Prewriting: Determining the Purpose

To focus your purpose for writing, you should write a *thesis statement* that lays out the overall point of view or argument that you want to make about the topic. A thesis statement written in the planning stage may have to be revised during drafting. Nevertheless, it will serve as a guide for developing the essay or paper. Typically, a thesis statement appears at the end of the introductory paragraph. Remember that a good thesis statement, while subject to disagreement from those with other viewpoints, is supportable with evidence from supplied text, sources (as in the synthesis essay), or your own knowledge, experience, or past reading.

Before beginning to draft an essay, or any piece of writing, the student writer might complete these statements:

My purpose in writing this is to . . .
My main points are . . .
And my conclusion is that . . .

Prewriting: Thinking About the Audience

Remember to direct your writing to a specific audience — in this case, to the AP Readers who will evaluate your writing. Imagine that you are presenting your information or making your argument to the Reader face-to-face. You might even imagine the

Reader asking questions such as "What is your main point? How can you prove that? What sources support that? What conclusions can be drawn from this?"

To satisfy the expectations of the AP Readers, keep the following points in mind as you plan and draft your response:

- The Reader will judge whether the response completely addresses the prompt.

- The Reader will evaluate your ability to articulate, sustain, and support an argument.

- The Reader will examine your use of appropriate examples from the reading passage, the provided sources, or your own reading or personal experience.

- The Reader will evaluate the writing on its logic, structure, fluency, coherence, and use of the conventions of Standard English.

On the synthesis essay, the Reader may also look at your ability to quote from and cite source material correctly.

Prewriting: Strategies for Generating Content

You will find it much easier to draft an essay when you have a plan or outline to follow. The following strategies can be used to generate ideas before drafting. Remember, should you choose to employ one of these strategies, it must be done quickly to meet the time restrictions for the AP exam.

- **Brainstorming.** List ideas at random that could be of use in the essay. Don't worry about the syntax or proper grammar at this point. Any potentially relevant idea should be jotted down.

DIDYOUKNOW?

The term "brainstorming" was popularized by an advertising executive named Alex F. Osborn in his 1953 book *Applied Imagination*. For the past decade Osborn had worked on ways to solve problems creatively. He noticed that group-thinking sessions, by encouraging employees to offer more imaginative ideas, often led to better solutions. Today, brainstorming is often used by individuals to generate ideas.

- **Making an outline.** Make a cursory outline of ideas, which will serve to organize the material into main ideas and supporting details.

- **Using a graphic organizer.** You can use one of a variety of graphic organizers to generate ideas. For example, an essay with a compare/contrast structure could be organized around a T-chart or Venn diagram that lists how two things are alike and different. If you're a visual thinker, you could use a spider cluster to connect supporting details to a main topic or idea. A flow chart could be used to show a logical or chronological flow of ideas from start to finish.

Drafting

Drafting: Main Idea or Argument

The next stage of the writing process after prewriting is drafting or actually writing the essay. Having settled on what the task is, who the audience is, and what ideas you want to present, you should draft an opening sentence and paragraph that includes the *thesis statement or main argument* The opening paragraph should articulate your main argument or point to be made and briefly describe what the essay is about.

Remember that the opening of an essay must clearly announce the topic or the main point, as in the following:

"This passage from George Orwell's essay "Politics and the English Language" demonstrates the author's pessimistic view that "the slovenliness of our language makes it easier for us to have foolish thoughts." Orwell's point is well taken and certainly is applicable to today's media-driven society. In fact, regarding the use of English in a political context, things have become much worse since Orwell's time, as a glance at our recent political discourse clearly shows."

If the prompt calls for you to take one side of an argument, this point of view should be included in the opening. For example,

"While social media such as email, text messaging, Twitter, and other forms seems to bring people together, its actual effect is to separate people by lessening the impulse and opportunity for them to interact face to face."

Drafting: Thinking About the Audience

As in the Prewriting stage, you should think about your target audience (i.e., the AP Reader) during the Drafting stage. Try to estimate how much the audience knows about the topic and fill in the gaps. Also try to anticipate questions, objections, or alternate viewpoints that the audience might have, and answer these in the course of the essay. Your essay should exhaust such possible questions as:

- Why is this so?

- What is significant or important about this idea or example?

- What does this point have to do with the main argument?

- What about this claim, which contradicts your main argument?

TEST TIP

As you draft your essay, mentally test each idea as if you had a skeptical person looking over your shoulder. Ask yourself if the idea is written clearly, if it follows logically from an earlier point, and if it needs to be defended against some obvious objection or opposing viewpoint. You may want to address important objections towards the end of the essay.

Drafting: Creating Paragraphs

Think of the first sentence of each paragraph as a sub-topic sentence or main idea. The sentences that follow it should then support the idea with examples, definitions, quotes, explanations, and other details. When the paragraphs of an essay are composed properly, the reader often can read only the first sentences of each paragraph to get a good idea of what the essay is about.

You should also vary the length of your paragraphs. An occasional short paragraph can be used effectively for emphasis. The writer should double-check a long paragraph to see that it does not include more than one main idea, which can be confusing to the audience or disturb the flow of the argument. An effective essay should also feature a variety of sentence lengths and types of sentences.

Since there is no set number of paragraphs necessary for a successful AP exam essay, you should let your response develop organically from your argument, sources, and examples. Don't use the simple five-paragraph formula. It is too restrictive and artificial; it forces you to think in terms of the formula instead of a well-developed argument. Your essay may have three body paragraphs or six — whatever is needed to develop your ideas thoroughly.

Drafting: Logical Transitions

A successful piece of writing flows because one idea seems to lead seamlessly to the next. Be mindful of showing the connections between ideas so that the argument doesn't "jump around" or seem disconnected. Some important reminders about logical transitions include:

- **Use repetition for emphasis.** Repeating key words and phrases signals that they are important.

- **Use consistent word choice to prevent confusion.** The reader should not be thinking, "Does this term mean the same thing as that one?"

- **Announce each sub-topic and then discuss it.** Don't bring up an idea and leave it hanging.

- **Use words that show the stages of your presentation or argument.** They may be numerical words, such as *first, second,* and *third.* They may also be words like *at first, initially, then, next, finally,* and *in conclusion.*

- **Use words that connect ideas.** Words such as *because, therefore, however, in addition to, despite,* and *consequently* show strong connections between sentences and paragraphs and help the reader follow the main ideas or argument.

Drafting: A Strong Conclusion

A successful essay should culminate in a strong conclusion that wraps up the argument in a logical way. A good conclusion may also:

- Present a solution to a problem

- Call for a particular action

- List consequences

- Briefly expand on the main idea

There is no need for you to rehash, word for word, the thesis statement or main idea of the essay in the conclusion. Likewise, major new ideas or supporting claims should not be introduced and left hanging in the last paragraph. Instead, you should briefly review the main point or the main argument that the essay presents. Occasionally, you may find that you've phrased the main idea more clearly in the conclusion than in the introduction. In such a case, you might decide that the new version should be moved to the beginning of the essay. A writer should compare his or her introduction and conclusion to assure that they don't contradict each other and that they are not identical in wording.

Other points to consider about a successful conclusion include:

- Avoid citing additional text in the conclusion.

- Strive for a conclusion that wraps up the argument effectively, that gives the essay a "finished" feel.

- Avoid clichéd ending phrases such as "in conclusion" or "to sum up." Try to make a smooth, clever transition to your essay's ending.

Revising

Revising: What to Consider

The revising stage is when you should "re-view" the entire essay to see if you've actually written what was planned or intended. In the classroom, you can find out what needs to be revised by reading the draft aloud to the class and asking for questions or comments. When working alone on the AP essays, however, you must revise by looking at your work as an outside critic would, asking yourself questions such as "Does this need to be cut? Does this statement need more support? Do the paragraphs or main point need to be reordered? Does something need to be restated more clearly?"

DIDYOU**KNOW?**

Samuel Langhorne Clemens, better known as Mark Twain (1835–1910), knew the value of revising. In one of his notebooks, he wrote: "The time to begin writing an article is when you have finished it to your satisfaction. By that time you begin to clearly and logically perceive what it is that you really want to say."

Remember, with the time constraints of the AP essay test section, you probably will perform some (and perhaps most) of your revising and editing tasks as you draft. Things to consider during revision include:

- Audience

- Structure

- Content

- Logic

- Coherence

- Voice

- Style

- Tone

Revising: Think of Your Audience

At the revising stage, as at the other stages of writing, you should consider who will be reading the essay and how much they know about the topic. Try to imagine a Reader who is coming to the essay with limited knowledge of the subject matter. In that case, does something need to be defined or explained? Are the explanations already in the essay clear enough? Are there sufficient supporting details? Is the main point stated clearly and concisely? Thinking about the audience first will make the revision process much easier.

TEST TIP

Obviously, the Readers of the AP essays will be examining many responses to the same set of prompts. A clever introduction or transition, a neat turn of a phrase, a closely reasoned paragraph that includes a humorous aside—these kinds of elements will make your essay stand out and help you get a better score on the overall exam.

Revising: Structure

In revising your essay, you should consider whether the structure includes a strong introduction, a clear sequence of main points and supporting details, and a strong conclusion without appearing to be formulaic or rigid. Could a reader easily fill in an outline of the main points in the essay or paper? Do the topic sentences of the paragraphs serve as a sort of skeleton of the essay? Are there sections or sentences that would be more effective if moved to another location?

Revising: Content and Flow

At the revising stage, you should also examine the content and flow of the essay. Ideas should be presented clearly and accurately, in language that is consistent without being too repetitive. For example, if the subject has been referred to consistently as "the Civil War," it may be confusing to the reader if it is suddenly called "the War Between the States" or "the Great Rebellion." Look for synonyms and restatements that might cause problems with clarity.

Also look for logical connections of ideas. When ideas are presented in a logical order with connector words that emphasize how they are related, the essay flows for the reader. You should also look for unnecessary details that might be interesting in themselves but do not belong in the essay and are best eliminated.

Revising: Voice, Style, and Tone

The revising stage is also the time to consider how the writing sounds to the audience. A formal essay should be written in Standard English that is accurate and expressive without being ornate or florid. Problems with voice can often be detected by reading the essay silently to yourself. If you can't imagine reading your words to a typical audience, then there might be a problem with overwriting. The most effective writing style for the AP essay test is formal without being pompous or pretentious.

Also check your essay for a consistent voice and tone. Revise any passages that are too casual or full of jargon. Avoid slang words or colloquial language. While wit is desirable, sarcasm or cheap jokes are never appropriate.

Revising: Active Voice vs. Passive Voice

Active voice is when the emphasis is on a subject doing something, instead of something being done to it. Using the active voice tends to make your writing sound more forceful and assured. For example,

Passive Voice: The idea was thought by experts to be too controversial at the beginning.

Active Voice: At the beginning, experts considered the idea too controversial.

While both versions say the same thing, the sentence with the active voice places the emphasis on the subject (experts) doing something. Sometimes you may use the passive voice on purpose — as here, if the desired emphasis is on the idea itself. However, in general, it is best to use active voice as much as possible.

Revising: Conciseness and Sentence Variety

Try to revise your work for conciseness by cutting out unnecessary words and phrases. Redundant phrases include words that can be eliminated without changing the meaning, such as *advance planning, commute back and forth,* and *end result.*

Often writers who are working quickly will include too many prepositional phrases and infinitives. By eliminating as many of these as possible, you can be more concise.

> Too many prepositions: As of now, they are not in a position to make a decision due to the fact that there is a majority of the board members who are not in possession of the evidence.

> More concise: They cannot make a decision because a majority of the board members do not have the evidence.

Another way to make writing more lively and interesting is to vary the length of sentences and paragraphs. You might also insert an occasional question or exclamation for variety.

Editing

Editing: Spelling, Grammar, and Punctuation

The editing stage of the writing process is when the writer polishes the work and corrects mistakes. This is also called *proofreading*. You must perform this step quickly due to the time constraints of the exam. On the AP essay test, an error in grammar or usage is not considered a disaster. Nevertheless, misspelled words, grammatical errors such as subject-verb disagreement or inconsistent verb tense, or punctuation errors such as misplaced commas not only make the final product look sloppy, they can also confuse the intended meaning. By editing to correct mistakes, you demonstrate your commitment to the quality of your work.

Editing: Word Choice

The editing stage provides an opportunity for you to check that you've used strong, accurate words, particularly nouns and verbs. You should also try to avoid sexist language by using gender-neutral terms.

The wise *person* can *get* a large return on his money.

Wise *investors* can *earn* a large return on their money.

DIDYOU**KNOW?**

The French novelist Gustave Flaubert (1821–1880) was a fanatical believer in finding the right word (or *"le mot juste,"* as he called it in French). Flaubert would spend hours testing one word after another until he found the one that had precisely the meaning and sound that he sought. His devotion to his craft led him to refer to "the agonies of art."

You should also replace slang, technical jargon, and padded phrases.

To be successful, the young composer had to *work his tail off* every day.

To be successful, the young composer had to *work extremely hard* every day.

By the age of two months, the child *at the developmental median* will smile *upon visual contact* with his or her *female parent's* face.

At two months, the *average* child will smile *at the sight* of his or her *mother's* face.

TEST **TIP**

You should avoid using idioms, slang, and jargon in your essays. They do not belong in formal writing. If you notice an instance of one of these as you check your work, cross it out and replace it with a more straightforward or formal phrase.

Editing: Attribution of Sources

During the editing stage, you should check that the quotations in the essay are accurate, enclosed in quotation marks, and correctly attributed. In an essay based on a nonfiction passage, you should include only brief quotations (inside quotation marks), since the Reader is already familiar with the passage. In a more elaborate term paper, you would include the source in parentheses at the end of the paragraph or in a list at the end of the paper, depending on the style required.

Reviewing

Reviewing: Final Check for Errors

Ordinarily, the final stage of the writing process would be sharing or publishing your work. However, for the AP English essay exam your final step is to skim your essay in search of any final changes that need to be made. Check once more for errors in spelling or punctuation, and add any words or phrases that were left out. (These can be added with editing marks, such as a caret below the line and the written phrase above the line where it belongs.) Don't worry about cross-outs or last-second additions. You will not be scored on neatness — just make sure that your corrections are legible. The AP Readers understand that each of your essays is basically a first draft, not a polished final copy. Of course, it may happen that you are still writing when time is called. While it is best to end with a reasoned conclusion, you may have to finish with a quick sentence or two of summation. Don't fret too much — the introduction and body of your essay are most important, and you can still make a decent score without a carefully composed ending.

Time for a quiz
- Review strategies in Chapter 2
- Take Quiz 4 at the REA Study Center
  (www.rea.com/studycenter)

Approaching the Essay Questions: Grammar, Punctuation, and Spelling

While your score on the essay section of the AP English Language and Composition exam will be based almost entirely on your ability to organize your thoughts and write fluently, it is still helpful to review the basics of Standard English for formal writing. This chapter looks at sentence structures, clear pronoun references, correct capitalization and punctuation, spelling tips, and other aspects of writing formal English.

Parts of Speech

- **Noun:** a word that names a person, place, thing, or idea. Proper nouns naming a particular person or place are capitalized, while common nouns are not.

    Common nouns: farmer, borough, basketball, democracy

    Proper nouns: Barack Obama, Norway, Golden Gate Bridge

- **Pronoun***:* A word *(he, it, they, somebody)* used in place of a noun that identifies people, places, things, or ideas without renaming them. The noun that a pronoun replaces is its antecedent; a pronoun placed too far from its antecedent in a sentence may be vague in its reference.

- **Verb:** a word that expresses action (action verbs) or state of being (linking or helping verbs).

    Action verb: The girl *threw* the ball.

    Linking verb: Dolores *was* late for class.

    Helping verb: Juan *is* buying lunch for us today.

- **Adjective:** a word that modifies a noun or pronoun and answers such questions as What kind? Which one? How many?

    Examples: *heavy* rain, the *orange* sunset, *nine* players

- **Adverb:** a word that modifies a verb, adjective, or another adverb and answers such questions as How? When? Where? How often? To what extent?

    Examples: Our lawyer argued *effectively* that the case should be dismissed.

    His fingers turned *almost* blue in the frosty air.

DIDYOUKNOW?

There are more than 100 prepositions in the English language, which give it the flexibility and accuracy it has in describing relationships of one thing to another. Three of the most frequently used words in English are the prepositions *in, of,* and *to.*

- **Preposition:** a word that expresses a relationship between a noun or pronoun and another word in a sentence. The noun or pronoun that usually follows a preposition is called its object. The preposition, its object, and modifiers form a prepositional phrase.

    Examples: *from* the store, *in* the dirt, *throughout* the play

- **Conjunction:** a word that connects words or groups of words. Conjunctions include coordinating conjunctions *(and, but, so, yet, for, nor, or),* correlative conjunctions *(either/or, not only/ but also, neither/nor),* and subordinating conjunctions *(after, although, as, as if, because, before, even if, even though, how, if, inasmuch, lest, now that, since, unless, until, where, wherever, while).*

- **Gerund:** a present participle that always functions as a noun.

    Example: *Swimming* is my favorite sport.

- **Infinitive:** a phrase made up of the word "to" and the base form of a verb (to love, to decide). It can function as an adjective, adverb, or noun.

- **Interjection:** a word or phrase that generally expresses strong emotion, such as surprise or delight.

  Example: *Incredible!* Scientists have located the wrecked ship at the bottom of the sea.

- **Participle:** a verb form that usually ends in *-ed* or *-ing* and can function as an adjective but with certain characteristics of a verb.

  Examples: *canned* peas, *battering* winds

Sentence Parts

- **Subject:** A noun or pronoun that is partnered with an action verb or being verb. The subject may also be understood as (you), as in the sentence "Take me home, please."

- **Predicate:** A verb that expresses the subject's action or state of being. The subject and predicate do not always appear next to each other or in the normal order.

  Examples: The *worker* on the tower *yelled* for assistance.

  The *worker has* often *yelled* for assistance from the tower.

  Has the *worker yelled* for assistance from the tower?

- **Direct Object:** A noun or pronoun that follows a verb and answers the question Whom? or What?

- **Indirect Object:** A noun or pronoun that follows a verb and answers the question To whom? or For What?

- **Phrase:** A group of related words that does not have a subject and predicate pair and does not express a complete thought, such as a prepositional phrase or a verbal phrase.

- **Clause:** A group of related words that contains a subject and predicate. An *independent clause* expresses a complete thought, while a *dependent clause* does not.

  Independent clause: Hatteberg hit a double.

  Dependent clause: if Hatteberg hits a double

- **Conjunctions for Compounding Sentence Elements:** The coordinating conjunctions *and, but, or,* and *nor* join subjects, predicates, adjectives, adverbs, prepositional phrases, and dependent clauses within a sentence in a process called *compounding*. Subordinating conjunctions connect a dependent clause to an independent clause.

Sentence Structures

- A **declarative sentence** makes a statement and ends with a period.

  Example: My vegetable garden extends from the garage wall to the back fence.

- An **interrogative sentence** asks a question and ends with a question mark.

  Example: Who sold the tickets to today's game?

- An **exclamatory sentence** expresses strong emotion and often ends with an exclamation point.

  Example: What a wonderful movie that was!

- An **imperative sentence** gives an order or makes a request.

  Examples: Hand me the tape measure. Please hold still while I measure your waist.

- A **simple sentence** is an independent clause and expresses a complete thought.

  Example: Taking photographs is my favorite hobby.

- A **compound sentence** contains two or more independent clauses connected by a coordinating conjunction or a semicolon.

  Example: Taking photographs is my favorite hobby, but I also enjoy painting.

- A **complex sentence** contains an independent clause and one or more subordinate clauses.

  Example: While taking photographs is my favorite hobby, I also enjoy painting.

- A **compound-complex sentence** contain two or more independent clauses and one or more subordinate clauses.

  Example: Taking photographs is my favorite hobby, but I also enjoy painting because the blank canvas is such a challenge to me.

TEST TIP

Your use of syntax is an important part of your performance on the AP essay exam. Try to use a variety of sentence types in your responses. You might even include a rhetorical question.

Effective Sentence Structure and Preferred Usage

Proper sentence structure and usage of grammatical elements makes writing much easier to read and understand. Here are some points to remember.

- **Parallel structure** means that sentence elements that are alike in function should also be alike in construction. This adds to the clarity, economy, and force of a piece of writing.

   Not parallel: **Dancing** and **ability to sing** are two requirements for the lead role in this play.

   Parallel: **Dancing** and **singing** are two requirements for the lead role in this play.

   Not parallel: She likes **to dance** but not **singing**.

   Parallel: She likes **to dance** but not **to sing**.

   Not parallel: The director wondered **who the new actress was** and **about her experience in the theater.**

   Parallel: The director wondered **who the new actress was** and **what experience she'd had** in the theater.

   Not parallel: The director emphasized **collective effort, mutual support,** and **being responsible as a group** for the success of the production.

   Parallel: The director emphasized **collective effort, mutual support,** and **group responsibility** for the success of the production.

   Not parallel: The angry shopper wanted **to exchange** the item, **to obtain** a refund, or **a conversation** with the store manager.

   Parallel: The angry shopper wanted **to exchange** the item, **to obtain** a refund, or **to speak** to the store manager.

- **Avoid run-on sentences and comma splices.** A run-on sentence is when two independent clauses are joined together without a coordinating conjunction. A comma splice is when two independent clauses are joined with only a comma.

Sample Run-on Sentence:

The article advocates a world government this would actually make individuals everywhere less free.

Correcting a Run-on Sentence:

Add a period.

The article advocates a world government. This would actually make individuals everywhere less free.

Add a comma and a coordinating conjunction.

The article advocates a world government, *but* this would actually make individuals everywhere less free.

Add a subordinating conjunction to turn an independent clause into a dependent clause.

While the article advocates a world government, this would actually make individuals everywhere less free.

Add a semicolon if the two sentence halves have a strong logical connection.

The article advocates a world government; this would actually make individuals everywhere less free.

Sample Comma Splice Sentence:

Some students think it is difficult to write well, it just requires regular practice.

Correcting a Comma Splice:

Change the comma to a period.

Some students think it is difficult to write well. It just requires regular practice.

Add a coordinating conjunction.

Some students think it is difficult to write well, but it just requires regular practice.

Add a subordinating conjunction to turn an independent clause into a dependent clause.

Although some students think it is difficult to write well, it just requires regular practice.

Add a semicolon if the two sentence halves have a strong logical connection.

Some students think it is difficult to write well; it just requires regular practice.

DID YOU KNOW?

An exception to the comma splice rule is the usual punctuation of Julius Caesar's famous declaration: "I came, I saw, I conquered."

- **Clear pronoun reference** means that each pronoun in a sentence refers clearly and unmistakably to one particular noun. If necessary, the writer should rephrase the sentence to make the meaning clear.

Unclear: While storing the goblet in the antique cabinet, Kazuo broke it.

Clear: While storing the goblet in the antique cabinet, Kazuo broke the goblet.

Unclear: If the customers don't buy all the scarves, pack them away under the counter.

Clear: If any of the scarves are unsold, pack them away under the counter.

Unclear: The boss told Ernesto that he would be getting a raise.

Clear: The boss congratulated Ernesto on the raise he would be getting.

Unclear: While the city coffers were full, they made poor use of it.

Clear: While the city government had a lot of money, the council members made poor use of it.

Unclear: I arrived late to the play, which was foolish.

Clear: In arriving late to the play, I felt foolish.
Or
I arrived late to the play, which was in any case a foolish piece of work.

TEST TIP

In questions of pronoun reference, don't assume that the reader understands what you mean. It's better to repeat words and clarify the reference than to leave the reader confused: "When the salt shaker fell into the mixing bowl, the salt shaker broke."

- **Appropriate verb tense** means that the writer indicates whether the action occurred in the past, present, or future and stays consistent with the appropriate verb tense.

  Inconsistent: Elizabeth Bishop **is** celebrated for her ability to see original details in a setting, and she **used** this skill to add color to her poems.

  Consistent: Elizabeth Bishop **is** celebrated for her ability to see original details in a setting, and she **uses** this skill to add color to her poems.

  Inconsistent: Last year, our class **completed** a project in which we **would have to interview** older relatives about past events in American history.

  Consistent: Last year, our class **completed** a project in which we **had to interview** older relatives about past events in American history.

  Inconsistent: If the weather **would** cooperate, we **can** start the game on time.

  Consistent: If the weather **would** cooperate, we **could** start the game on time.

- **Subject/verb agreement** means that a subject and verb must agree in number; that is, both must be either singular or plural.

  Singular: **Caden has passed** every test this semester.
  There **is** another **test** today.

  Plural: **Caden and Laura have passed** every test this semester.
  There **are** more **tests** this week.

- **Pronoun agreement** means that a pronoun agrees in person, number, and gender with its antecedent.

  Incorrect person agreement: If a **person** hopes to succeed, **you** have to work hard.

  Correct: If a **person** hopes to succeed, **he or she** has to work hard.
  If **you** hope to succeed, **you** have to work hard.

  Incorrect number agreement: If **somebody** hopes to succeed, **they** have to work hard.

  Correct: If **somebody** hopes to succeed, **he or she** has to work hard.
  If **people** hope to succeed, **they** have to work hard.

Incorrect gender agreement: If a **person** hopes to succeed, **he** has to work hard.

Correct: If a **person** hopes to succeed, **he or she** has to work hard.

             If **people** hope to succeed, **they** have to work hard.

DIDYOUKNOW?

A gender-neutral pronoun does not assign a gender to the person under discussion. English is one of the languages that does not have a gender-neutral third person pronoun. In the past writers almost always used *he* to refer to a generic individual. However, in the interest of equality between the sexes, writers generally use *he or she* to refer to a generic person, or try to avoid such constructions altogether.

- **Idioms** are phrases that mean something different than the meanings of the individual words would indicate. In general, writers should use idioms sparingly, if at all, in formal writing.

  Examples:

  The supervisor **turned a blind eye** to the employees' disgruntled behavior. (pretended not to see)

  Of the dozens of job applicants, few looked **down at heel.** (shabby and untidy)

  Coaches advised the rookie quarterback to **bear down** and try to make progress every day. (focus and concentrate)

Capitalization

A successful piece of writing avoids errors in *capitalization.* Words that should be capitalized include:

- the first word in a sentence:

  Archery provides a great test of control and accuracy.

- the first word of a direct quote:

  Ford Madox Ford's greatest novel begins, "This is the saddest story I have ever heard."

- proper nouns:

  National Football League, White House, Wimbledon

- proper adjectives:

  Swedish ambassador, Merino wool

- titles:

  Mrs. Rodriguez, Dr. Bass, Senator Hollings, Lieutenant Riggins

- peoples and nationalities:

  Egyptians, Kurds, Chickasaws, Canadians

- the major words in titles of books, plays, poems, etc.:

  The Old Man and the Sea, The Two Gentlemen of Verona, "Stopping by Woods on a Snowy Evening"

- names of organizations, schools, government agencies:

  the United Nations, Notre Dame University, Department of Energy

- heavenly bodies:

  Saturn, Milky Way, Halley's Comet

- nations, states, cities:

  Poland, Montana, Eau Claire

TEST TIP

Resist the urge to capitalize too many words in your essay. For example, the word *league* in "National Hockey League" should be capitalized, but in "league policy" it is not. In the same way, words like *captain, professor,* and *supervisor* are not capitalized unless they are part of a title with a person's last name.

Punctuation

Try to read this paragraph.

take some more tea the march hare said to alice very earnestly ive had nothing yet alice replied in an offended tone so i cant take more you mean you cant take less said the hatter its very easy to take more than nothing lewis carroll

Now try again.

> "Take some more tea," the March Hare said to Alice, very earnestly.
>
> "I've had nothing yet," Alice replied in an offended tone, "so I can't take more."
>
> "You mean you can't take less," said the Hatter. "It's very easy to take more than nothing."
>
> —*Lewis Carroll*

This example illustrates how *punctuation* helps the reader understand what the writer is trying to say. The most important role of punctuation is clarification. In speech, words are accompanied by gesture, voice, tone, and rhythm that help convey a desired meaning. In writing, punctuation alone must do the same job.

There are many rules about how to use the various punctuation marks. The rules are sometimes difficult to understand because they are described with so much grammatical terminology. Therefore, this discussion of punctuation will avoid as much terminology as possible. If you still find the rules confusing, and your method of punctuation is somewhat random, try to remember that most punctuation takes the place of pauses in speech. As you write your essays for the AP English Language and Composition exam, listen for the natural pauses in your sentences. This will help you place your commas, periods, and dashes in a way that helps the Reader understand your meaning.

End Punctuation

There are three ways to end a sentence:

1. a period
2. a question mark
3. an exclamation point

The Period

Periods end all sentences that are not questions or exclamations. In speech, the end of a sentence is indicated with a full pause. The period is the written counterpart of this pause.

> Go get me my paper. I'm anxious to see the news.
> Into each life some rain must fall. Last night some fell into mine.

When a question is intended as a suggestion and the listener is not expected to answer or when a question is asked indirectly as part of a sentence, a period is also used.

> Mimi wondered if the parade would ever end.
> Will you please send the flowers you advertised.

Periods also follow most abbreviations and contractions.

Wed.	Dr.	Jr.	Sr.
etc.	Jan.	Mr.	Mr.
Esq.	cont.	a.m.	U.S.

Periods (or parentheses) are also used after a letter or number in a series.

a. apples	1. president
b. oranges	2. vice president
c. pears	3. secretary

Errors to Avoid

Be sure to omit the period after a quotation mark preceded by a period. Only one stop is necessary to end a sentence.

> She said, "Hold my hand." (no period after the final quotation mark)
> "Don't go into the park until later."
> "It's not my fault," he said. "She would have taken the car anyway."

For certain abbreviations, particularly those of organizations or agencies, no period is used. Check in a dictionary if in doubt.

AFL-CIO	NAACP	GM
FBI	NATO	IBM
TV	UN	SEC

The Question Mark

Use a question mark to end a direct question even if it is not in the form of a question. In writing, the question mark denotes the rising tone of voice used to indicate a question in speech. If you read the following two sentences aloud, you will see the difference in tone between a statement and a question composed of the same words.

> Mary is here.
> Mary is here?

Here are some more examples of correct use of the question mark. Pay special attention to the way it is used with other punctuation.

Where will we go next?

Would you like coffee or tea?

"Are you staying here," he asked, "or will you be coming with us?"

"Will they ever give us our freedom?" the prisoner asked.

"To be or not to be?" was the question asked by Hamlet.

Who asked, "When?"

Question marks indicate a full stop and lend a different emphasis to a sentence than do commas. Compare these pairs of sentences.

Was the sonata by Beethoven? or Brahms? or Chopin?

Was the sonata by Beethoven, or Brahms, or Chopin?

Did they walk to the park? climb the small hill? take the bus to town? or go skating out back?

Did they walk to town, climb the small hill, take the bus to town, or go skating out back?

The Exclamation Point

An exclamation point ends an emphatic statement. It should be used only to express strong emotions, such as surprise, disbelief, or admiration. If it is used too often for mild expressions of emotion, it loses its effectiveness.

Let go of me!

Help! Fire!

It was a wonderful day!

Who shouted "Fire!" (*Notice no question mark is necessary*)

Fantastic!

"Unbelievable!" she gasped. (*Notice no comma is necessary*)

Where else can I go! (*The use of the exclamation point shows that this is a strong statement even though it is worded like a question.*)

Interjections

An interjection is a word or group of words used as an exclamation to express emotion. It need not be followed by an exclamation point. Often an interjection is followed by a comma if it is not very intense.

Oh dear, I forgot my keys again.

Ouch! I didn't realize that the stove was hot.

Oh, excuse me. I didn't realize that you were next on line.

Punctuating for Pauses

There are five ways to indicate a pause shorter than a period.

1. dash

2. colon

3. parentheses

4. semicolon

5. comma

The Dash

Use the dash (—) to indicate a sudden or unexpected break in the normal flow of the sentence. It can also be used in place of parentheses or of commas if the meaning is clarified. Usually the dash gives special emphasis to the material it sets off.

Could you — I hate to ask! — help me with these boxes?

When we left town — a day never to be forgotten — they had a record snowfall.

She said — we all heard it — "The safe is not locked."

These are the three ladies — Mrs. Jackson, Miss Harris, and Ms. Forrest — you hoped to meet last week.

The sight of the Andromeda Galaxy — especially when seen for the first time — is astounding.

That day was the longest in her life — or so it seemed to her.

DID YOU KNOW?

The American poet Emily Dickinson (1830–1886) used dashes prolifically in her poems. In fact, most modern editions of her poetry change the punctuation because her use of so many dashes is considered eccentric and difficult for readers to negotiate. Here is a stanza from one of her poems, with the original capitalization and use of dashes:

The Brain—is wider than the Sky—
for—put them side by side—
The one the other will contain
With ease—and You—beside

A dash is often used to summarize a series of ideas that have already been expressed.

> Carbohydrates, fats, and proteins — these are the basic kinds of food we need.
>
> Jones, who first suggested we go; Marshall, who made all the arrangements; and Kline, who finally took us there — hese were the three men I admired most for their courage.
>
> James, Howard, Marianne, Angela, Catherine — all were displeased with the decision of the teacher.

The dash is also used to note the author of a quotation that is set off in the text.

> Nothing is good or bad but thinking makes it so.
>
> *—William Shakespeare*

> Because I could not stop for Death,
> He kindly stopped for me;
>
> *—Emily Dickinson*

The Colon

The colon (:) is the sign of a pause about midway in length between the semicolon and the period. It can often be replaced by a comma and sometimes by a period. Although used less frequently now than it was 75 years ago, the colon is still useful, for it signals to the reader that more information is forthcoming on the topic. The colon can also create a slight dramatic tension. It is used to introduce a word, a phrase, or a complete statement (clause) that emphasizes, illustrates, or exemplifies what has already been stated.

> He had only one desire in life: to play baseball.
>
> The weather that day was the most unusual I'd ever seen: It snowed and rained while the sun was still shining.
>
> In his speech, the president surprised us by his final point: the conventional grading system would be replaced next year.

Notice that the word following the colon can start with either a capital or a small letter. Use a capital letter if the word following the colon begins another complete sentence. When the words following a colon are part of the sentence that precedes the colon, use a lowercase letter.

> Jean thought of only two things the last half hour of the hike home: a bath and a bed.
>
> The thought continued to perplex him: Where will I go next?

When introducing a series that illustrates or emphasizes what has already been stated, use a colon.

> Only a few of the graduates were able to be there: Jamison, Mearns, and Linkley.
>
> In the basement, he kept some equipment for his experiments: the test tubes, some chemical agents, three sunlamps, and the drill.

Long quotations set off from the rest of the text by indentation rather than quotation marks are generally introduced with a colon.

The first line of Lincoln's Gettysburg address is familiar to most Americans:

> Four score and seven years ago our fathers brought forth on this continent a new nation, conceived in liberty and dedicated to the proposition that all men are created equal.

It is also customary to end a business letter salutation with a colon.

> Dear Senator Jordan:
>
> Dear Sir or Madam:

TEST TIP

The best way to avoid making punctuation errors in your essays is to rely on what you know. If you rarely use colons or semicolons in your writing, don't try using them in your responses. It's better to employ basic sentence structures that are used correctly than to fail at trying to include more elaborate sentence structures and punctuation.

In informal letters, use a comma.

> Dear Chi-Leng,
>
> Dear Father,

Finally, a colon is used between numbers when writing the time, between the volume and number or volume and page number of a journal, and between the chapter and verse in the Bible.

4:30 P.M.

The Nation, 34:8

Genesis 5:18

Parentheses

To set off material that is only loosely connected to the central meaning of the sentence, use parentheses [( )].

Most men (at least, most that I know) like wine, women, and song but have too much work and not enough time for such enjoyments.

On Tuesday evenings and Thursday afternoons (the times I don't have classes), the television programs are not too exciting.

Watch out for other punctuation when you use parentheses. Punctuation that refers to the material enclosed in the parentheses occurs inside the marks. Punctuation belonging to the rest of the sentence comes outside the parentheses.

I thought I knew the poem by heart (boy, was I wrong!).

For a long time (too long as far as I'm concerned), women were thought to be inferior to men.

We must always strive to tell the truth. (Are we even sure we know what truth is?)

When I first saw a rose (don't you think it's the most beautiful flower?), I thought it must be man-made.

The Semicolon

Semicolons (;) are sometimes called mild periods. They indicate a pause midway in length between the comma and the colon. Writing that contains many semicolons is usually in a dignified, formal style. To use them correctly, it is necessary to be able to recognize main clauses—complete ideas. When two main clauses occur in a single sentence without a connecting word *(and, but, or, nor, for),* the appropriate mark of punctuation is the semicolon.

It is not a good idea for you to leave the country right now; you should actually try to stay as long as you possibly can.

Music lightens life; literature deepens it.

In the past, boy babies were often dressed in blue; girls, in pink. (*"were often dressed" is understood in the second part of the sentence.*)

Notice how the use of the comma, period, and semicolon gives a sentence a slightly different emphasis.

Music lightens life; literature deepens it.

Just as music lightens life, literature deepens it.

Music lightens life. Literature deepens it.

A semicolon lends a certain balance to writing, particularly in long, involved sentences or paragraphs, that would otherwise be difficult to achieve. Nonetheless, you should be careful not to overuse it. A comma can just as well join parts of an ordinary sentence with two main ideas. A semicolon is more appropriate if there is a striking contrast in the two ideas expressed.

Ask not what your country can do for you; ask what you can do for your country.

It started out as an ordinary day; it ended being the most extraordinary of her life.

Our power to apprehend truth is limited; to seek it, limitless.

If any one of the following words or phrases is used to join together compound sentences, it is often preceded by a semicolon.

then	however	thus	furthermore
hence	indeed	consequently	also
that is	nevertheless	anyhow	in addition
in fact	on the other hand	likewise	moreover
still	meanwhile	instead	besides
otherwise	in other words	henceforth	for example
therefore	at the same time	even now	

Here are some examples of a semicolon used to join the independent clauses of a compound sentence.

For a long time, people thought that women were inferior to men; *even now* it is not an easy attitude to overcome.

Being clever and cynical, he succeeded in becoming president of the company; *meanwhile*, his wife left him.

Cigarette smoking has never interested me; *furthermore*, I couldn't care less if anyone else smokes or not.

Some say Bach was the greatest composer of all time; *yet* he still managed to have an ordinary life in other ways: he and his wife had twenty children.

We left wishing we could have stayed much longer; *in other words*, they showed us a good time.

When a series of complicated items is listed or if there is internal punctuation in a series, a semicolon is sometimes used to make the meaning clearer.

You can use your new car for many things: to drive to town or to the country; to impress your friends and neighbors; to protect yourself from rain on a trip away from home; and to borrow against should you need money right away.

The scores from yesterday's games came in late last night: Pirates-6, Zoomers-3; Caterpillars-12, Steelys-8; Crashers-9, Links-8; and Greens-15, Uptowns-4.

In October a bag of potatoes cost 69¢; in December, 99¢; in February, $1.09; and in April, $1.39. I wonder if this inflation will ever stop.

The semicolon is placed outside quotation marks or parentheses, unless it is a part of the material enclosed in those marks.

I used to call him "my lord and master"; it made him laugh every time.

The weather was cold for that time of year (I was shivering wherever I went); nevertheless, we set out to hike to the top of that mountain.

The Comma

Of all the marks of punctuation, the comma (,) has the most uses. Before you tackle the main principles that guide its usage, be sure that you have an elementary understanding of sentence structure. There are actually only a few rules and conventions to follow when using commas; the rest is common sense. *The worst abuse of commas comes from those who overuse them or who place them illogically.* If you are ever in doubt as to whether or not to use a comma, do not use it.

In a Series

When more than one adjective (an adjective series) describes a noun, use a comma to separate and emphasize each adjective.

the long, dark passageway

another confusing, sleepless night

an elaborate, complex plan

the haunting, melodic sound

the old, gray, crumpled hat

In these instances, the comma takes the place of "and." To test if a comma is needed, try inserting "and" between the adjectives in question. If it is logical, you should use a comma. The following are examples of adjectives that describe an adjective-noun combination that has come to be thought of almost as one word. In such cases, the adjective in front of the adjective-noun combination needs no comma.

a stately *oak tree*	my worst *report card*
an exceptional *wine glass*	a borrowed *record player*
a successful *garage sale*	a porcelain *dinner plate*

A comma is also used to separate words, phrases, and whole ideas (clauses); it still takes the place of "and" when used this way.

an apple, a pear, a fig, and a banana

a lovely lady, an indecent dress, and many admirers

She lowered the shade, closed the curtain, turned off the light, and went to bed.

John, Frank, and my Uncle Harry all thought it was a questionable theory.

One question about the use of commas in a series is whether or not one should be used before the final item. Usually "and" or "or" precedes the final item, and many writers do not include the comma before the final "and" or "or." However, it is advisable to use the comma, because often its omission can be confusing. For example, look at these cases:

No: Would you like to shop at Saks, Lord and Taylor and Macy's?

No: He got on his horse, tracked a rabbit and a deer and rode on to Canton.

No: We planned the trip with Mary and Harold, Susan, Dick and Joan, Gregory and Jean and Charles. *(Is it Gregory and Jean or Jean and Charles or Gregory and Jean and Charles?)*

With a Long Introductory Phrase

Usually if a phrase of more than five or six words precedes the subject at the beginning of a sentence, a comma is used to set it off.

After last night's fiasco at the disco, she couldn't bear the thought of looking at him again.

Whenever I try to talk about politics, my husband leaves the room.

It is not necessary to use a comma with a short introductory phrase.

In January she will go to Switzerland.

After I rest I'll feel better.

At Grandma's we had a big dinner.

During the day no one is home.

If an introductory phrase includes a verb form that is being used as another part of speech (a "verbal"), it must be followed by a comma. Try to make sense of the following sentences without commas.

No: When eating Mary never looked up from her plate.
Yes: When eating, Mary never looked up from her plate.

No: Because of her desire to follow her faith in James wavered.
Yes: Because of her desire to follow, her faith in James wavered.

No: Having decided to leave Mary James wrote her a letter.
Yes: Having decided to leave Mary, James wrote her a letter.

Above all, common sense is the best guideline when trying to decide whether or not to use a comma after an introductory phrase. Does the comma make the meaning clearer? If it does, use it; if not, there is no reason to insert it.

To Separate Sentences with Two Main Ideas (Compound Sentences)

To understand this use of the comma, you need to have studied sentence structure and be able to recognize compound sentences. When a sentence contains more than two subjects and verbs (clauses) and the two clauses are joined by a connecting word *(and, but, or, yet, for, nor)*, use a comma before the connecting word to show that another clause is coming.

I thought I knew the poem by heart, but he showed me three lines I had forgotten.

Are we really interested in helping the children, or are we more concerned with protecting our good names?

Jim knows you are disappointed, and he has known it for a long time.

If the two parts of the sentence are short and closely related, it is not necessary to use a comma.

He threw the ball and the dog ran after it.

Jane played the piano and Charles danced.

Errors to Avoid

Be careful not to confuse a compound sentence with a sentence that has a compound verb and a single subject. If the subject is the same for both verbs, there is no need for a comma.

No: Charles sent some flowers, and wrote a long letter explaining why he had not been able to come.

No: Last Thursday we went to the concert with Julia, and afterward dined at an old Italian restaurant.

No: For the third time, the teacher explained that the literacy level of high school students was much lower than it had been in previous years, and, this time, wrote the statistics on the board for everyone to see.

To Set Off Interrupting Material

There are so many different kinds of interruptions that can occur in a sentence that a list of them all would be quite lengthy. In general, words and phrases that stop the flow of the sentence or are unnecessary for the main idea are set off by commas.

Abbreviations after names

Did you invite John Paul, Jr., and his sister?

Martha Harris, Ph.D., will be the speaker tonight.

Interjections: An exclamation added without grammatical connection.

Oh, I'm so glad to see you.

I tried so hard, alas, to do it.

Hey, let me out of here.

No, I will not let you out.

Direct address

Roy, won't you open the door for the dog?

I can't understand, Mother, what you are trying to say.

May I ask, Mr. President, why you called us together?

Hey, lady, watch out for the car!

Tag questions: A question that repeats the helping verb and is in the negative.

I'm really hungry, aren't you?

Jerry looks like his father, doesn't he?

You'll come early, won't you?

We are expected at nine, aren't we?

Mr. Jones can chair the meeting, can't he?

Geographical names and addresses

The concert will be held in Chicago, Illinois, on August 12.

They visited Tours, France, last summer.

The letter was addressed to Ms. Marion Heartwell, 1881 Pine Lane, Palo Alto, California 95824. *(No comma is used before a zip code.)*

Transitional words and phrases

On the other hand, I hope he gets better.

In addition, the phone rang six times this afternoon.

To tell the truth, I don't know what to believe.

Parenthetical words and phrases

You will become, I believe, a great statesman.

We know, of course, that this is the only thing to do.

In fact, I planted corn last summer.

The Mannes affair was, to put it mildly, a surprise.

Bathing suits, generally speaking, are getting smaller.

Unusual word order

The dress, new and crisp, hung in the closet.
(Normal word order: The new, crisp dress hung in the closet.)

Intently, she stared out the window.
(Normal word order: She stared intently out the window.)

Nonrestrictive Elements: Not essential to the meaning

Parts of a sentence that modify other parts are sometimes essential to the meaning of the sentence and sometimes not. When a modifying word or group of words is not vital to the meaning of the sentence, it is set off by commas. Since it does not restrict the meaning of the words it modifies, it is called "nonrestrictive." Modifiers that are essential to the meaning of the sentence are called "restrictive" and are not set off by commas. Compare the following pairs of sentences:

The girl *who wrote the story* is my sister. (essential)

My sister, *the girl who wrote the story*, has always been drawn to adventure. (nonessential)

John Milton's poem *Paradise Lost* is a masterpiece of powerful blank verse. (essential — Milton wrote other poems)

Dante's great work, *The Divine Comedy*, marked the beginning of the Renaissance and the end of the Dark Ages. (nonessential — Dante wrote only one great work)

My parakeet Simian has an extensive vocabulary. (essential — because there are no commas, the writer must have more than one parakeet)

My parakeet, Simian, has an extensive vocabulary. (nonessential — the writer must have only one parakeet, whose name is Simian)

The people who arrived late were not seated. (essential)

George, who arrived late, was not seated. (nonessential)

She always listened to her sister Jean. (essential — she has more than one sister)

She always listened to her husband, Jack. (nonessential — obviously, she has only one husband)

To Set Off Direct Quotations

Most direct quotes or quoted materials are set off from the rest of the sentence by commas.

"Please read your part more loudly," the director insisted.

"I won't know what to do," said Michael, "if you leave me now."

Be careful not to set off indirect quotations or quotes that are used as subjects or complements.

"To be or not to be" is the famous beginning of a soliloquy in Shakespeare's *Hamlet.* (subject)

Back then my favorite song was *"A Summer Place."* (complement)

She said she would never come back. (indirect quote)

"Place two tablespoons of chocolate in this pan" were her first words to her apprentice in the kitchen. (subject)

To Set Off Contrasting Elements

Her intelligence, *not her beauty*, got her the job.

Your plan will take you further from, *rather than closer to*, your destination.

In Dates

She will arrive on April 6, 1992.

He left on 5 December 1990.

In January 1987 he handed in his resignation.

In January 1987, he handed in his resignation.

Spelling

At first glance, one would expect *blew* and *sew* to rhyme. Instead, *sew* rhymes with *so*. If words were spelled the way they sound, one would expect *so* to rhyme with *do* instead of *dough* and would never expect *do* to rhyme with *blew. And what about plough and tough?* Confusing, isn't it?

Words are not always spelled phonetically, and it sometimes seems that the spellings of words in English is totally illogical. Nevertheless, it's important to spell properly in formal writing. Poor spelling is usually a sign of haste or carelessness, and it is often taken as a sign of ignorance or illiteracy. Learning to spell correctly is indeed more difficult for some people than for others. Like any other skill, however, it can be mastered with time and patience. There are many helpful practices to improve spelling: using the dictionary, keeping a list of difficult or irregular words, familiarizing oneself with word origin, and studying the word list and the rules in this chapter.

If you have absolutely no idea how to spell a word, it might seem like you cannot look it up in a dictionary. Yet even with the most difficult words, you probably will have a general idea of how it is spelled. Even if you know only the first few letters of the word, you should be able to find it in a dictionary or glossary.

Example: Check the spelling of the word *miscellaneous.*

You probably know that *misc-* are the first four letters of the word and might even know a few more letters by sounding the word out. Although phonetics is not a reliable source for spelling, it can be helpful when using the dictionary. In this particular problem, it most likely is the ending *-aneous* that gives you difficulty. Since in the English language there are few words beginning with the letters *misc-*, you should have little trouble finding *miscellaneous* in the dictionary.

Example: Check the spelling of *occasionally.*

Here, you are probably concerned with the number of *c*'s and *s*'s. If you look up the word with the beginning *oca-*, there is no listing. The next logical choice is to check the word with two *c*'s, which will be found a few entries later. You can even skim the page when a general idea of the spelling is known.

As you can see, checking spelling is a matter of trial and error. Use the dictionary when you are not sure of a word's spelling — and sometimes even when you feel certain. Also, make sure that you have found the correct word, not a homonym or a word with a similar form, by checking the word's definition.

Word Analysis

A basic knowledge of the English language, especially familiarity with its numerous prefixes, can help build vocabulary and also strengthen spelling skills. For example, if you know that *inter-* means *between* and that *intra-* means *within,* you're not likely to spell *intramural* as *intermural.* (The former means within the limits of a city, a college, etc.)

The following table lists some common Latin and Greek prefixes, which form part of the foundation of the English language.

Prefix	Meaning	English Example
ab-, a-, abs-	away, from	abstain
ad-	to, toward	adjacent
ante-	before	antecedent
anti-	against	antidote
bi-	two	bisect
cata-, cat-, cath-	down	cataclysm
circum-	around	circumlocution
contra-	against	contrary
de-	down, from	decline
di-	twice	diatonic
dis-, di-	apart, away	dissolve
epi-, ep-, eph-	upon, among	epidemic
ex-, e-	out of, from	extricate
hyper-	beyond, over	hyperactive
hypo-	under, down, less	hypodermic
in-	in, into	instill

(continued)

(continued)

Prefix	Meaning	English Example
inter-	among, between	intercede
intra-	within	intramural
meta-, met-	beyond, along with	metaphysics
mono-	one	monolith
non-	no, not	nonsense
ob-	against	obstruct
para-, par-	beside	parallel
per-	through	permeate
pre-	before	prehistoric
pro-	before	project
super-	above	superior
tele-, tel-	far	television
trans-	across	transpose
ultra-	beyond	ultraviolet

Spelling Lists

There are some words that consistently give writers trouble. The list below contains about 100 words that are commonly misspelled. In studying this list, readers will find that certain words are more troublesome than others. These in particular should be reviewed.

Commonly Misspelled Words		
accommodate	February	professor
achievement	height	prominent
acquire	immediately	pursue
among	interest	quiet
apparent	its, it's	receive
arguing	led	procedure
argument	lose	profession
athletics	losing	receiving
belief	marriage	recommend
believe	mere	referring

(continued)

(continued)

Commonly Misspelled Words		
beneficial	necessary	remember
benefited	occasion	repetition
bureau	occurred	rhythm
business	occurrence	sense
category	occurring	separate
comparative	opinion	separation
conscious	opportunity	similar
controversial	parallel	studying
define	particular	succeed
definitely	performance	succession
definition	personal	surprise
describe	personnel	technique
description	possession	than
despair	possible	their, they're, there
disastrous	practical	then
effect	precede	thorough
embarrass	prejudice	to, too, two
environment	prepare	tomorrow
exaggerate	prevalent	transferred
existence	principal	unnecessary
existent	principle	villain
experience	privilege	write
explanation	probably	writing
fascinate	proceed	

As a handy reference, it is a good idea to set aside an area in a notebook to list problem words. Add to it any new words that are pose spelling problems for you.

Spelling Rules

Prefixes

Prefixes (such as *dis-*, *mis-*, *in-*, *un-*, and *re-*) are added to words without doubling or dropping letters.

dis + appear = disappear	dis + service = disservice
dis + solved = dissolved	dis + satisfied = dissatisfied
mis + information = misinformation	mis + spelled = misspelled
mis + understand = misunderstand	in + capable = incapable
in + definite = indefinite	in + numerable = innumerable
un + usual = unusual	un + seen = unseen
un + named = unnamed	re + elect = reelect
re + search = research	

Suffixes

When forming adverbs from adjectives ending in *al,* the ending becomes *ally.*

normal	normally	real	really
occasional	occasionally	legal	legally
royal	royally		

Words ending in *n* keep the *n* when adding *ness.*

openness	stubbornness	suddenness	brazenness

All words ending in *ful* have only one *l.*

cupful	cheerful
forgetful	doleful
mouthful	graceful
helpful	meaningful
spoonful	handful

Add *ment* without changing the root word's spelling.

adjust + ment = adjustment	develop + ment = development
amaze + ment = amazement	

Silent *e*

When a suffix beginning with a vowel is added, a word ending in a silent *e* generally drops the *e.*

admire + able = admirable	allure + ing = alluring

believe + able = believable	come + ing = coming
dare + ing = daring	deplore + able = deplorable
desire + ous = desirous	explore + ation = exploration
fame + ous = famous	imagine + able = imaginable
move + able = movable	note + able = notable

However, the word retains the *e* when a suffix beginning with a consonant is added.

arrange + ment = arrangement	glee + ful = gleeful
like + ness = likeness	spite + ful = spiteful
time + less = timeless	

With *judgment, acknowledgment,* and other words formed by adding *ment* to a word with a *dge* ending, the final *e* is usually dropped, although it is equally correct to retain it.

When adding *ous* or *able* to a word ending in *ge* or *ce,* keep the final *e* when adding the suffix. The *e* is retained to keep the soft sound of the *c* or *g.*

courageous	manageable	outrageous
changeable	advantageous	traceable

IE + EI

In words with *ie* or *ei* in which the sound is e, (long *ee*), use *i* before *e* except after *c.*

Examples: *i* before *e:*

believe	pier	shield	wield
chief	priest	siege	yield
niece	reprieve		

Examples: Except after *c:*

ceiling	conceit	conceive	deceive	perceive	receive

The following words are some exceptions to the rule and must be committed to memory.

either	conscience	weird	reign
leisure	height	freight	weigh
neither	forfeit		
seize	neighbor		

Except before *ing,* a final *y* usually changes to *i.*

rely + ance = reliance	study + ing = studying
modify + er = modifier	modify + ing = modifying
amplify + ed = amplified	amplify + ing = amplifying

When preceded by a vowel, a final *y* does not change to *i.*

annoying, annoyed

destroying, destroyed, destroyer

journeyman, journeyed, journeyer

Doubling the Final Consonant

In one-syllable words that end in a single consonant preceded by a single vowel, double the final consonant before adding a suffix that begins with a vowel.

drop + ing = drop(p)ing	clap + ed = clap(p)ed
man + ish = man(n)ish	snap + ed = snap(p)ed
quit + ing = quit(t)ing	

However, when a suffix begins with a consonant, do not double the final consonant before adding the suffix.

man + hood = manhood	glad + ly = gladly
bad + ly = badly	fat + ness = fatness
sin + ful = sinful	

This is also the case in multisyllabic words that are accented on the final syllable and have endings as described above.

admit + ed = admitted   begin + ing = beginning

commit + ed = committed

      BUT

commit + ment = commitment

However, in words with this type of ending, in which the final syllable is not accented, the final consonant is not doubled.

happen + ing = happening   profit + able = profitable

comfort + ed = comforted   refer + ence = reference

confer + ence = conference

Only three words end in *ceed* in English. They are *exceed, proceed,* and *succeed.* All other "seed-sounding" words (except *supersede)* end in *cede.*

intercede	recede
concede	accede
secede	precede

Remember that certain letter combinations, such as *ough,* are pronounced differently in different words: *plough, rough, through.*

Approaching the Essay Questions: Rhetorical Modes

In Chapter 4, we looked at the rhetorical strategies used by authors of nonfiction to help you analyze passages and answer multiple-choice questions. In this chapter we will briefly review rhetorical modes with an eye towards using them effectively in your own essays for the AP English Language and Composition exam. On the style-analysis essay, you will be using rhetorical tools to analyze an author's writing methods in a passage. On the persuasive and synthesis essays, you will be using these tools to present logical, structured arguments about topics that are provided. It helps to be familiar with these rhetorical modes and methods so that each time you are faced with a prompt you can choose the approach that best helps you accomplish the required writing task.

Deciding on Your Writing Purpose

The modes of writing you will use on your responses include *expository*, *persuasive*, *descriptive*, and *narrative*. You might use a combination of all of these on one essay. Before you choose your writing mode, you must decide on your purpose for writing:

- **To inform or instruct** — The essay seeks to explain, describe, or define something. This type of essay should be tightly organized, with a series of main points and supporting details.

- **To persuade** — The essay seeks to convince the reader to believe something or agree with a certain point of view. This type of essay is logically organized to present an argument step by step.

- **To entertain** — The essay seeks to evoke laughter, sadness, suspense, nostalgia, or other emotions. Generally this type of essay has a looser, more improvisatory structure.

When you read a writing prompt, think about what it is asking you to do. For example, a prompt might ask you to *explain* how an author uses irony in a passage to criticize social conditions. Another prompt might instruct you to *support or refute* an argument, or to *take a position* on a viewpoint expressed in a passage. As you've seen, the AP essay prompts generally direct you to inform, explain, or persuade in your writing. Nevertheless, you should also try to entertain, at least to a certain extent; using humor or pathos can be effective ways to stir your reader's emotions and make your writing more interesting.

TEST TIP

It might be helpful to underline the words in the prompt that describe your writing task. Then you can refer back to the prompt as you write to make sure you are following the instructions.

Choosing an Organizational Pattern

The pattern you choose to organize your essay should help you accomplish the task in the prompt. Certain organizational patterns are better suited to certain purposes for writing. Look at each pattern below, along with an example of a thesis statement that introduces the pattern.

- **Cause/Effect:** Presents the relationship between an action and its result.

  "The poor writing skills of many American students today are mainly due to the widespread use of social media and the bad writing habits it engenders."

- **Compare/Contrast:** Explores how two or more people, things, or ideas are similar or different.

  "Today's movies, with their technical sophistication and more realistic characters and settings, are far superior to the Hollywood assembly-line films of the 1930s and 1940s."

- **Problem/Solution:** Describes how a problem can be solved or remedied.

  "To address the energy crisis in our country, new cars, trucks, and SUVs should be converted to run on natural gas, which is cheap, abundant, and relatively clean."

DIDYOU**KNOW?**

Perhaps the most famous "problem/solution" essay in the English language is "A Modest Proposal" by Jonathan Swift (1667–1745). Its subtitle is "For Preventing the Children of Poor People in Ireland from Being a Burden to Their Parents or Country, and for Making Them Beneficial to the Public." Swift's "modest proposal" is that these children should become food for the populace. Of course, Swift's purpose is satire: to show the callousness of a society that failed to care for its children.

- **Hypothesis/Support:** Examines a hypothesis or theory by providing details and examples to support it or refute it.

  "Maslow's theory of motivation, or 'hierarchy of needs,' can be verified by thinking about common examples we all see in everyday life."

- **Definition:** Defines something by listing the characteristics it has and does not have.

  "Is our system of government today a true democracy? To answer that question one must examine our society's success in drawing ordinary citizens into the process."

- **Illustration:** Provides a topic and gives examples to explain it or elaborate on it.

  "The days of 'one size fits all' marketing practices are over, as is obvious from developments such as targeted marketing and boutique shops for every taste."

Using Rhetoric to Persuade

Rhetoric is defined as "speaking or writing effectively." It includes all the tools and methods a writer uses to appeal to an audience, including figurative language, style, and tone. In your essays for the AP English exam, you must use rhetoric to write fluently and persuasively.

In Aristotle's classical rhetoric, there are three ways of persuading readers or listeners:

- **Logos or logic** — This is the use of logic or reason to persuade. Use facts, statistics, and hard evidence to make this kind of argument. (The word "logic" is derived from the Greek word *logos,* which means "word.")

- *Ethos* **or ethics** — This is an ethical appeal that emphasizes your own credibility and standing. Use balanced language, fairness to both sides of a question, and the judgments of experts to make this kind of argument. (Our word "ethics" is derived from the Greek *ethos.)*

- *Pathos* **or emotion** — This is the use of an emotional appeal to persuade. Use examples and language designed to evoke pity, astonishment, or outrage in the reader. *(Pathos* in Greek means "suffering" and "experience." It is the basis for our word "pathetic.")

Also, remember the three principal strategies for framing a persuasive argument:

- **Present a proposition of fact.** Convince the reader that a proposition is true or false.

- **Present a question of value.** Convince the reader that an action is right or wrong, moral or immoral, ethical or unethical, acceptable or unacceptable.

- **Present a question of policy.** Convince the reader that a policy should be adopted or an action taken.

You should also review the logical fallacies presented in Chapter 4. These are persuasive techniques that use faulty reasoning or misleading methods. The Readers on the AP English exam will certainly recognize these methods and penalize you for using them.

Literary and Rhetorical Tools and Strategies

As a writer you should be aware of all the rhetorical tools at your disposal. Here is a list of literary and rhetorical tools you can use in your essays.

Abstract Language

Language describing ideas and qualities rather than observable or physical things, people, or places.

Examples: love, honor, integrity, evil.

Alliteration

Repetition of initial sounds of words in close proximity to each other.

Examples: the drab and dreary evening

TEST TIP

Fancy rhetorical effects such as alliteration or verbal irony should be used sparingly if at all in your essays for the AP English exam. Don't try to impress the Readers with clever word-play or poetic effects. It is better to concentrate on writing with force and clarity.

Allusion

Indirect reference to something (usually a literary text, mythology, folklore, fairy tales, the Bible, etc.) with which the reader is supposed to be familiar. Allusion is used with humorous intent, to establish a connection between writer and reader or to make a subtle point.

Examples: Like Goldilocks, they had found the solution that was "just right."

Ambiguity

Language that may be interpreted in more than one way. Artful language may be ambiguous, but unintentional ambiguity (or vagueness) is to be avoided.

DIDYOUKNOW?

The English word *ambiguity* dates from about 1400, and comes from the Middle Latin word *ambiguitatem*, which meant "double meaning."

Analogy

A comparison to a directly parallel case. A writer uses an analogy to argue that a claim reasonable for one case is reasonable for the analogous case.

Anecdote

Short narrative used to illustrate a point.

Antithesis

Balancing of two opposite or contrasting words, phrases, or clauses.

Examples: To err is human; to forgive, divine. — Alexander Pope

Assonance

Repetition of a vowel sound within two or more words in close proximity.

> Examples: That solitude that suits abstruser musings — Samuel Taylor Coleridge

Authority

Arguments that draw on recognized experts or persons with highly relevant experience are said to rest on authoritative backing or authority. Readers are expected to accept claims if they are in agreement with an authority's view.

Balance

Construction in which both halves of the sentence are of about the same length and importance.

> Examples: The truth lies in between, or so authorities insist.

Concrete Language

Language that describes specific, observable things, people or places, rather than ideas or qualities.

Connotation

Rather than the dictionary definition, the associations suggested by a word. A *shack* and a *mansion* are both houses, but the words have different connotations.

Consonance

Repetition of an ending consonant sound within two or more words in close proximity.

> Examples: a poor player, that *struts and frets* his hour upon the stage — Shakespeare

Cumulative Sentence

Sentence that begins with the main idea and then expands on that idea with a series of details or other particulars.

> Examples: The ballpark was old, with paint flaking on the dugout walls, boards warping on the bullpen benches, and holes widening in the sagging mesh of the backstop.

Diction

Word choice, particularly as an element of style. Different types and arrangements of words have significant effects on meaning. An essay written in academic diction would be much less colorful, but perhaps more precise than street slang.

Emotional Appeal

When a writer appeals to readers' emotions (often through pathos) to excite and involve them in the argument.

Ethical Appeal

When a writer tries to persuade the audience to respect and believe him or her based on a presentation of image of self through the text. Reputation is sometimes a factor in ethical appeals, but in all cases the aim is to gain the audience's confidence.

Euphemism

Pleasant or sanitized expression used to describe something unpleasant or negative.

Examples: "Passed away" is a euphemism for "died."

Figurative Language

Words that have a special meaning or effect that is different from their literal meaning. Figurative language includes simile, metaphor, imagery, hyperbole, personification, and many other tropes.

Examples: Shakespeare's "All the world's a stage" is an example of non-literal, figurative language (metaphor, specifically).

Hyperbole

Conscious exaggeration used to heighten effect. Not intended literally, hyperbole is often humorous.

Examples: I wandered about town questioning everybody, boring everybody, and finding out that nobody knew anything. — Mark Twain

Hypothetical Example

Example that is not specifically factual but is a possible situation to support the writer's purpose.

Idiom

Common expression that has acquired a meaning different from its literal meaning.

Examples: Things were still *up in the air.* (meaning things were still unsettled)

Imagery

Figurative language that is written to appeal to one or more of the senses — sight, hearing, smell, taste, touch.

Example: That was all he could do, in spite of the size of the downs, the width of the sky, the far-off smoke of houses, and the romantic voice, now and then, of a steamer out at sea. — Virginia Woolf

Implication

A hint given but not stated explicitly.

Example: Certain neighborhoods barely exist where loan officers are concerned.

Incongruity

Juxtaposition of ideas or images that seem inconsistent, incompatible, or out of place.

Example: Of all the wonders of nature, a tree in summer is perhaps the most remarkable, with the possible exception of a moose singing "Embrace-able You" in spats. — Woody Allen

Imperative Sentence

Sentence making a call to action or command where the understood "you" is the subject.

Example: Go forth and multiply.

Inverted Sentence

Variation of the normal word order (subject first, then verb, then complement) that puts a modifier or the verb as first in the sentence. The element that appears first is emphasized more than the subject.

Example: Never have so many people been concerned about their economic future.

Irony

Dramatic irony is when a reader is aware of a reality that differs from a character's perception of reality. Situational irony is when the actual result of a situation is completely different from the expected result. Verbal irony is writing or saying one thing and meaning another.

> Example of verbal irony: It is a wonderful thing that our legislators can waste so much money each year and still get reelected.

Jargon

Technical language of a profession or skill, not typically understood or used by other people.

> Example: The doctor explained that I had a "bilateral probital hematoma," which is a fancy way of saying a "black eye."

DIDYOUKNOW?

The computer field has seen a large increase in jargon in recent years. Do you know what a "killer poke" is? (It's a way of causing physical damage to computer hardware by inserting invalid values.) Or how about a "Frankenmachine"? (This is jargon for a computer that has been assembled from various old and new components, like Frankenstein's monster.) No doubt there will be many more examples in the years to come.

Juxtaposition

Purposeful placement of ideas, images, or language (often incongruous) to heighten their effect.

Metaphor

Comparison of two things, often unrelated, without using the words "like" or "as."

An extended metaphor carries that comparison beyond the initial statement and extends it further. A mixed metaphor is a metaphor that presents an inconsistent comparison and should be avoided.

> Example of metaphor: Life is a journey, but don't worry, you'll find a parking spot at the end. — Isaac Asimov

> Example of mixed metaphor: We were drowning in an avalanche of paper.

Mood

Atmosphere created by a writer's word choice (diction) and the details selected. Syntax is also a determiner of mood because sentence strength, length, and complexity affect pacing.

Non sequitur

Latin for "it does not follow." When one statement isn't logically connected to another.

TEST TIP

To avoid non-sequiturs or sentences that don't fit in logically with those around them, try to read your essay from another person's point of view. Your meaning might be obvious to you but not to someone with a different viewpoint or frame of reference. Avoid obscure references or allusions that might be confusing.

Objectivity

Writer's attempt to remove himself or herself from any subjective, personal involvement in a story. Hard-news journalism is frequently prized for its objectivity.

Onomatopoeia

Use of a word whose pronunciation suggests the sound that it describes.

> **Examples:** buzz, hiss, pop, meow

Oxymoron

Paradoxical construction juxtaposing two contradictory terms.

> **Examples:** wise fool, deafening silence

Paradox

Seemingly contradictory statement that is actually true. This rhetorical device is often used for emphasis or simply to make a humorous point.

> **Example:** I can resist anything but temptation. — Oscar Wilde

Parallel Structure

Sentence construction that places in close proximity two or more equal grammatical constructions. Parallel structure may be as simple as listing two or three modifiers in a row to describe the same noun or verb; it may take the form of two or more of the same type of phrases (prepositional, participial, gerund, appositive) that modify the same noun or verb; it may also take the form of two or more subordinate clauses that modify the same noun or verb. Or, parallel structure may be a complex blend of single-word, phrase, and clause parallelism all in the same sentence.

> **Example:** Rebecca developed an interest in, a respect for, and a fascination with the classical laws of mathematics.

Parody

Exaggerated imitation of a serious work for humorous purposes. The writer of a parody uses the quirks of style of the imitated piece in extreme or ridiculous ways.

Periodic Sentence

Sentence that places the main idea at the end of the sentence, after all introductory elements.

> **Example:** Should the rain stop, the winds abate, and the sun emerge, it would be a lovely day after all.

Personification

Figurative language in which inanimate objects, animals, ideas, or abstractions are endowed with human traits or human form.

> **Example:** The old house sagged with the knowledge that it was about to be abandoned.

Point of View

Perspective from which a work of fiction or nonfiction is presented. Can be first-person, second-person, third-person, or third-person omniscient.

Pun

Play on words that exploits the similarity in sound between two words with different meanings, usually for a humorous effect.

> **Example:** Successful acupuncture is a jab well done.

Qualification

Condition, limitation, or restraint placed on an idea or argument. A qualified argument takes a position somewhere between the two opposing sides.

Repetition

Word or phrase used two or more times in close proximity.

> Example: We shall fight on the beaches, we shall fight on the landing grounds, we shall fight in the fields and in the streets, we shall fight in the hills, and we shall never surrender. — Winston Churchill

Rhetoric

Art of effective communication, especially persuasive discourse. Rhetoric focuses on the interrelationship of invention, arrangement, and style in order to create appealing and appropriate discourse.

Rhetorical Device

Any characteristic of language used to achieve the writer or speaker's purpose.

Rhetorical Question

Question with an obvious, understood answer.

> Example: If you prick us do we not bleed? — Shakespeare

Satire

Work that reveals a critical attitude toward some element of human behavior by portraying it in an extreme way. Satire doesn't simply abuse (as in invective) or get personal (as in sarcasm). Satire targets groups or large concepts rather than individuals.

Sarcasm

Type of verbal irony, the purpose of which is to denigrate the subject.

> Example: The whole world is holding its breath waiting for your decision.

Simile

Figurative comparison of two things, often dissimilar, using the connecting words "like" or "as."

> Example: He had stood among the Forresters one day, like an ash sapling among giant oaks. — Marjorie Kinnan Rawlings

Slang

Very informal or course language, to be avoided in formal writing.

> Example: That job is so cushy that he only has to work four hours a day.

Style

A writer's method of expression, including choices in diction, tone, and syntax.

Subjectivity

Opinions based on personal preference or prejudice and not completely on objective fact.

Symbol

Person, thing, or event that represents or stands for some larger idea or meaning.

> *Example:* The Statue of Liberty is a symbol of freedom for Americans everywhere.

Syntactic Fluency

Ability to create a variety of sentence structures, appropriately complex or simple and varied in length.

Theme

Central idea of a work of fiction or nonfiction revealed and developed in the course of a story or explored through argument.

Thesis

Central argument an author makes in a work of nonfiction, sometimes stated explicitly and sometimes implied.

Tone

Writer's attitude toward his or her subject matter revealed through diction, figurative language, and selection of details, imagery, and organization.

Understatement

An expression that deliberately has less force that would be expected, usually used for comic effect.

> *Example:* Should the world end tomorrow, most of us would not be pleased.

A Few Final Rhetorical Dos and Don'ts

- **Use higher-level vocabulary throughout your essays.** This doesn't mean to always choose a larger or more difficult word, but rather to maintain a formal, sophisticated tone in your writing.

- **Write with subjects and verbs.** Don't depend too much on adjectives, adverbs, and modifying phrases to get your meaning across. Concentrate on using precise nouns for subjects and strong, vivid verbs in the predicate. This will give your writing clarity and forcefulness.

TEST TIP

Practice using strong action verbs in your writing instead of linking or being verbs. As you read published essays or articles, notice how the authors convey meaning with precisely chosen action verbs.

- **Write in the active voice.**

  Passive voice: These changes are being made by many private companies already.

  Active voice: Many private companies are already making these changes.

- **Elaborate on your meaning whenever possible.**

  Vague: The book about restaurants and chefs is interesting.

  Stronger: The book delves into a world of master chefs, chefs' assistants, and kitchen hands that is as stratified as a medieval dukedom.

- **Avoid empty or meaningless words and phrases.** Some of these you might use often in speech but they should be limited or avoided in writing, such as *very, really, totally, interesting, wonderful, fantastic,* or *awesome.*

- **Don't say that a writer or a passage "talks about" something.** Say "The writer shows, reveals, indicates," or "The passage discusses, analyzes," etc.

- **Avoid clichés.** These include such overused phrases as "a fish out of water," "build a better mousetrap," "wrack your brains," and "easy as pie."

- **Don't use ambiguous pronouns.** Make sure that every pronoun has a clear antecedent.

- **Don't use words you do not understand.** Misusing a word will distort your meaning and lower your score.

- **Don't quote too much of the sources or passages.** The Readers also have the passages in front of them, so brief quotes are sufficient.

DIDYOU**KNOW?**

Using words that you don't understand may lead you to commit a "malapropism." This term comes from a character named Mrs. Malaprop in Richard Brinsley Sheridan's 1775 play *The Rivals.* She frequently uses a long word incorrectly, as when she refers to another character as "the pineapple of perfection," rather than *pinnacle.*

Approaching the Essay Questions: The Style-Analysis Essay

In the next three chapters, we will look at each type of essay question you will encounter on the AP English Language and Composition exam. First, let's examine the style-analysis essay.

The style-analysis (or rhetorical-analysis) essay question asks you to analyze the language used in a passage and explain how the language helps achieve the author's purpose. In recent years, this has been statistically the most difficult essay for students on the exam because it is different from most of the writing they have done in school to this point. The style-analysis essay is closely aligned with the skills in the multiple-choice section of the exam, except that on the style-analysis essay you must analyze the author's purpose and use of language in the passage without the benefit of questions to guide you.

Do not oversimplify the author's position or attitude. Even if the essay is satirical in tone, take care not to exaggerate the tone and classify it as "bitter" or "biting" unless you are certain this is the author's intention. Remember, the creators of the test are looking for subtle gradations of analysis in your answer, and subtlety would be difficult to achieve if you were stuck with analyzing a simplistic piece of writing, one with an obvious, one-sided, or "cut-and-dried" approach or tone. Expect and look for a more nuanced approach in the passage or passages.

TEST TIP

For more practice, check out a book of classic essays from the public library. Read one of the essays carefully and then write an analysis of the author's use of style, tone, and rhetorical devices. You might follow this procedure for three or four of the essays in the book.

Sometimes this question takes the form of two passages on the same topic but written in different styles and with different attitudes. Again, if you are asked to discuss the differences between two passages, do not oversimplify or exaggerate the differences.

This question expects you to analyze the style of a passage. The prompt directs you to read the passage carefully. Then, you are instructed to write an essay that (1) analyzes the effect of the passage on the reader; or (2) defines the author's attitude toward his or her topic (usually, the AP test question will name the topic of the passage for you); or, (3) describes the rhetorical purpose of the passage; or (4) identifies the author's purpose or views and how he or she achieves that purpose or conveys those views. Remember that this essay calls for many of the same skills of analysis you used to answer the "writing style" questions in the multiple-choice section — except here you will be generating your own ideas about the rhetorical effects writers use.

DID YOU KNOW?

One of the best guides to style in the English language is *The Elements of Style* by William Strunk, Jr. and E. B. White. Professor Strunk's original guide was published in 1918; White, a writer at the *New Yorker* magazine and a former pupil of Strunk's, revised and updated the guide in 1959. Since then, *The Elements of Style* has sold more than ten million copies and helped countless students and professionals write more effectively. For example, one of the many pithy instructions in the book is "Omit needless words."

A List of Typical Style-Analysis Instructions

Below, you will find a list of the most common directions for writing the style-analysis essay. Become familiar with these directions, since they have been used frequently on past exams.

- Analyze how the author crafts the text to reveal [his or her] view of —.

- Analyze the methods that the author uses to persuade —.

- Analyze the language and rhetorical devices; consider such elements as narrative structure, selection of detail, manipulation of language, and tone.

- Analyze how the author uses juxtaposition of ideas, choice of details, and other aspects of style.

- Analyze stylistic, narrative, and persuasive devices.

- Analyze the figures of speech and syntax.

- Consider word choice, manipulation of sentences, imagery, and use of allusions.

- Consider the rhetorical devices such as arguments, assumptions, attitudes, and diction

Don't let the wording of the questions intimidate you. In Chapter 10, we reviewed several of these terms: "rhetoric" and "rhetorical devices" refer to style, tone, word choice, and poetic devices (figures of speech, imagery, alliteration, etc.); "diction" also refers to word choice, particularly as an element of style; "syntax" refers to sentence structure and placement of words within the sentence; "juxtaposition" refers to unlike ideas or details that are placed side-by-side or in close proximity to create a certain effect.

TEST TIP

The tone of a passage becomes apparent in how the writing makes you feel. Do you sense an overall feeling of playfulness, gloom, or anger when you read the piece? Once you have identified the overall tone, you can look for word choices and poetic devices that the author used to create that tone.

Basically, the style-analysis question asks you to examine (with close attention to nuance) these stylistic devices:

- **Word choice or diction:** How would you characterize the language that the author uses? What unusual words appear? How is the language used to persuade the reader?

- **Imagery:** How does the author use imagery in the passage? What senses does the imagery appeal to? What emotions are evoked in the imagery?

- **Figures of speech:** What figures of speech are used? How do the author's figures of speech contribute to the overall effect of the passage? (Figures of speech may also be referred to as poetic devices or rhetorical devices.)

- **Selection of detail:** What details does the author emphasize? Which details are most effective in helping the author achieve his or her purpose?

- **Tone:** What is the overall tone of the passage? What strategies help the author create and maintain this tone? What words contribute to the tone? Why is the tone appropriate for the author's purpose?

- **Sentence structure:** What unusual sentence structures do you find in the passage? What effect does this syntax have on the reader? Is the passage easy or difficult to read?

- **Text structure:** Does the passage employ a familiar structure such as cause/effect, problem/solution, or illustration? Does it have a narrative or chronological structure? How does the structure help the passage achieve its purpose?

- **Persuasive mode:** Does the author basically appeal to reason, authority, or emotion in the passage? What facts and details are marshaled to support the argument? Are any logical fallacies employed?

Things to Keep in Mind

While you don't want your head swirling with advice and warnings during the test, the following are a few tips that will improve your performance on the style-analysis essay question:

- Misreading the passage is impossible to recover from on this essay, so you must read carefully, bringing all your critical reading skills to the task. If you are a weak reader, you need to address this issue through focused practice using the approaches discussed in the earlier chapters as a guideline.

- Discuss what's important. Don't treat this prompt as a scavenger hunt for literary terms. You need to pick out the rhetorical devices that are playing an important role in the support of the author's purpose. For example, if the piece is built around an extended metaphor or lush imagery, you need to concentrate on those things.

- Don't define the rhetorical devices. The AP Readers know what figurative language and parallel syntax are. Instead, show how the rhetorical devices support the author's purpose. For example, in *Walden,* Henry David Thoreau says, "If a man does not keep pace with his companion, perhaps it is because he hears a different drummer. Let him step to the music which he hears, however measured or far away." Show how Thoreau uses this metaphor to justify his own life choices and, more importantly, to express his larger views on the autonomy of the individual.

- Don't offer any discussion of language unless you connect it back to the author's purpose — *no exceptions.* The author's purpose should be identified in your thesis statement at the beginning of your essay. Your thesis statement should be similar to this formula:

title of work + author's name + subject + devices + author's purpose.

Example:

In "The Gettysburg Address," Abraham Lincoln honors the Union war dead

    [title of work]   [author]   [subject]

by referring to the setting of the Gettysburg cemetery and using the patriotic diction of

    [device]   [device]

democratic ideals to promote the idea of a Union victory that will lead to a rebirth of

                        [author's purpose]

liberty in the United States.

TEST TIP

The elements of the formula for writing a "style-analysis" thesis statement can be rearranged in another order if you wish, but leaving out one of the elements is not advisable unless you are an advanced writer. Beginning with a thesis statement as in the example shown helps you focus on the essential task and gives your essay a specific focus.

- In your essay answer it is useful but not necessary to name the specific rhetorical terms ("metaphor," "inverted sentence," "parallelism," etc.) to which you refer. Superior essay writers will, of course, recognize and discuss the basic devices of style in an easy, confident manner. However, remember that your essay answer must include specific examples in the form of short, direct quotations that illustrate your thesis about the author's rhetorical choices.

Approaching a Sample Style-Analysis Essay Question

Now let's examine a typical style-analysis essay question that might appear on the AP English exam. Read the question and look for the task it gives you.

The following passage comes from the 1845 autobiography *Narrative of the Life of Frederick Douglass, an American Slave*. Aside from its power as a memoir, it is also considered one of the key documents of the abolitionist movement in the first half of the nineteenth century. Read the passage carefully. Then write an essay in which you analyze the rhetorical strategies that Douglass uses to convey his attitudes toward slavery and his yearning for freedom.

DIDYOUKNOW?

Frederick Douglass (1818–1895) lived a remarkably full life, encompassing his early years in slavery, his leadership in the abolition movement, his writing career, his success as a speechmaker, and his time in public office. Douglass not only worked for equality for African Americans but also supported causes such as women's right to vote.

Notice that the passage comes from an 1845 source, so you can expect the diction to be somewhat more difficult to understand than a modern text. Also, notice what you must do to satisfy the prompt: "analyze the rhetorical strategies that Douglass uses to convey his attitudes toward slavery and his yearning for freedom." Underline the words "analyze the rhetorical strategies that Douglass uses." Now you are ready to read the passage.

If at any one time of my life more than another, I was made to drink the bitterest dregs of slavery, that time was during the first six months of my stay with Mr. Covey. We were worked in all weathers. It was never too hot or too cold; it could never rain, blow, hail, or snow, too hard for us to work in the field. Work, work, work, was scarcely more the order of the day than of the night. The longest days were too short for him, and the shortest nights too long for him. I was somewhat unmanageable when I first went there, but a few months of this discipline tamed me. I was broken in body, soul, and spirit. My natural elasticity was crushed, my intellect languished, the disposition to read departed, the cheerful spark that lingered about my eye died; the dark night of slavery closed in upon me; and behold a man transformed into a brute!…

Our house stood within a few rods of the Chesapeake Bay, whose broad bosom was ever white with sails from every quarter of the habitable globe. Those beautiful vessels, robed in purest white, so delightful to the eye of freemen, were to me so many shrouded ghosts, to terrify and torment me with thoughts of my wretched condition. I have often, in the deep stillness of a summer's Sabbath, stood all alone upon the lofty banks of that noble bay, and traced, with saddened heart and tearful eye, the countless number of sails moving off to the mighty ocean. The sight of these always affected me powerfully. My thoughts would compel utterance; and there, with no audience by the Almighty, I would pour out my soul's complaint, in my rude way, with an apostrophe to the moving multitude of ships: —

"You are loosed from your moorings, and are free; I am fast in my chains, and am a slave! You move merrily before the gentle gale, and I sadly before the bloody whip! You are freedom's swift-winged angels, that fly round the world; I am confined in bands of Iron! O that I were free!

O, that I were on one of your gallant decks, and under your protecting wing! Alas! Betwixt me and you, the turbid waters roll. Go on, go on. O that I could also go! Could I but swim! If I could fly! O, why was I born a man, of whom to make a brute! The glad ship is gone; she hides in the dim distance. I am left in the hottest hell of unending slavery. O God, save me! God deliver me! Let me be free! Is there any God? Why am I a slave? I will run away, I will not stand it. Get caught, or get clear, I'll try it. I had as well die with ague as the fever. I have only one life to lose. I had as well be killed running as die standing. Only think of it; one hundred miles straight north, and I am free! Try it? Yes! God helping me, I will. It cannot be that I shall live and die a slave. I will take to the water. This very bay shall bear me into freedom. The steamboats steered in a north-east course from North Point. I will do the same; and when I get to head of the bay, I will turn my canoe adrift, and walk straight through Delaware into Pennsylvania. When I get there, I shall not be required to have a pass; I can travel without being disturbed. Let but the first opportunity offer, and, come what will, I am off. Meanwhile, I will try to bear up under the yoke. I am not the only slave in the world. Why should I fret? I can bear as much as any of them. Besides, I am but a boy and all boys are bound to some one. It may be that my misery in slavery will only increase my happiness when I get free. There is a better day coming."

Thus I used to think, and thus I used to speak to myself; goaded almost to madness at one moment, and at the next reconciling myself to my wretched lot.

After you have read the passage, ask yourself these questions:

- What examples of imagery does Douglass employ? What rhetorical purpose do these have?

- How does the style of rhetoric change in the third paragraph of the passage? Why is this so?

- What rhetorical strategies are most effective in the passage? Why?

Now read a sample response to the style-analysis essay question. Notice how it accomplishes the task that was assigned.

Racial prejudice persists as an issue in society today. Slavery was one of the biggest acts of national discrimination in United States history. In Frederick Douglass's Narrative of the Life of Frederick Douglass, an American Slave, the speaker uses syntax, diction, and metaphor to distinguish the hopeful third paragraph from the rest of the sad, discouraging passage.

Douglass uses syntax to differentiate the third paragraph from the rest of the passage with a passionate outburst to explain his desire to be free. For example, the paragraph opens with: "You are loosed from your mooring, and are free; I am fast in my chains, and am a slave!" Here Douglass uses coordination and parallel structure to connect the freedom that the ship has to the antithesis of the enslaved boy's bondage. The speaker uses this comparison to emphasize the boy's despair and desire by comparing his slavery to the freedom he longs for. In the fourth paragraph, Douglass uses a series of short sentences and repetitive structures that are like outcries expressing his yearning for freedom: "O God, save me! God deliver me! Let me be free!" The dire situation calls his core beliefs into question. He uses an exclamatory sentence when he says, "Only think of it; one hundred miles straight north, and I am free!" This emotional statement shows the urgency of his desire to be a free man. Without modern conveniences of transportation, one hundred miles is quite a long distance. He is willing to do whatever it takes to shake off the chains of slavery. Douglass expresses hope here instead of despairing about his wretched conditions as he does in the first two paragraphs. Near the end of the passage, Douglass employs a sentence that balances his misery and potential happiness: "It may be that my misery in slavery will only increase my happiness when I get free."

The speaker's word choice also distinguishes the optimistic third paragraph from the pessimistic opening. He emphasizes his depression by comparing himself to a brute at the end of the first paragraph. The use of "brute" indicates his feelings of worthlessness as a human being. When white men look at him, they see only a work animal needing to be tamed and harnessed, not the valuable member of society he wishes to be. He juxtaposes the movements of the free ship with those of the slave by saying, "You move merrily before the gentle gale, and I sadly before the bloody whip." The adverbs "merrily" and "sadly" show the stark contrast of one who is free and one who is enslaved.

Finally, Douglass uses metaphors to compare the freedom he desires to the position in which he currently finds himself. He describes freedom in the passage with this metaphor: "You are freedom's swift-winged angels, that fly around the world." The angels represent the peace and happiness available to all free men — a state for which Douglass desperately is striving. Yet he knows of no other description for his current state than that of "the hottest hell of unending slavery." He is treated as one who is damned for all eternity. His spirit is almost broken, but his desires are still strong.

Douglass emphasizes his desire to be a free man through the hopefulness that emerges in the third and fourth paragraphs as opposed to the sad, melancholy tone of the rest of the passage.

Notice how this essay effectively analyzes how Frederick Douglass changes his style to reinforce the rhetorical effect of hope emerging from despair. The essay carefully examines the stylistic elements that distinguish paragraphs 3 and 4 from the rest of the passage. The response points out how Douglass's syntax, figurative language, and selection of detail shift in paragraph 3 and how the shift strengthens Douglass's overall message. The essay also refers to the passage both directly and indirectly to support the thesis that the hopeful and optimistic tone that begins with the third paragraph is meant to contrast with the melancholy and pessimistic tone of the first and second paragraphs. The essay also moves beyond summary into analysis of the rhetorical devices. It employs a variety of sentence structures and a mature vocabulary. The prose, while not perfect, demonstrates an ability to control a wide range of elements for effective writing.

DIDYOU**KNOW?**

In 1838 Frederick Douglass escaped to the safe house of an abolitionist in New York. Douglass said of the life-changing episode: "I have often been asked, how I felt when first I found myself on free soil. And my readers may share the same curiosity. There is scarcely anything in my experience about which I could not give a more satisfactory answer. A new world had opened upon me. . . . Anguish and grief, like darkness and rain, may be depicted; but gladness and joy, like the rainbow, defy the skill of pen or pencil."

Time for a quiz
- Review strategies in Chapter 2
- Take Quiz 5 at the REA Study Center
  (www.rea.com/studycenter)

hing the
estions:
sive

...on is similar to the question for the syn-
...ake a position on a topic of controversy. It differs
...at you will not necessarily be provided with a source on
w...argument. Persuasive essay questions with no reading passage tend
to ...er, taking into account the variety of background information students bring
to the exam. Recent topics for the persuasive essay have included the following:

- academic honesty

- the ethics of offering incentives for charitable acts

- the role adversity plays in the creation of a person's character

You might even be asked to choose a contemporary local, national, or global issue
and argue persuasively for a certain solution or compromise. You are unlikely to get
a question that requires specialized knowledge of a subject. That being said, students
who bring to the table more knowledge and understanding of the world (i.e., history,
literature, current events, science, economics, etc.) generally do better because they
have a deeper pool of facts and examples to draw from. Well-informed writers can find
something interesting to say on almost any topic.

TEST TIP

Try to anticipate counter arguments and objections in your persuasive essay. You might include your rebuttal to these points towards the end of your essay.

The Value — and Limits — of Personal Experience

Try not to depend too much on personal experience in your persuasive essay. While personal experience is a valid method of support, it needs to be augmented with examples from your reading and media sources. The list of potential topics is endless, and very few students your age have enough life experience to speak to every issue intelligently. Also, most life experience is anecdotal. Such stories can be emotionally compelling, but they are still just your own experience and not necessarily relevant to others. If you can connect your experience to broader, more objective evidence, you will present a more convincing and sophisticated argument and earn a higher score. Of course, there are exceptions: if the question is about the homeless and you have spent time living or working in a homeless shelter, you will clearly have the authority to say a great deal about that issue, and you should write your essay accordingly. But most teens, on most topics, need to reach beyond their immediate world.

The good news is you know more than you think you do. As you practice writing these essays, take time to consider books you have read, interesting places you have visited, and subjects you have learned about in school. In addition, get into the habit of following the news. Newspapers and news magazines are great ways to practice and improve your critical reading skills for this exam. Editorials, op-ed articles, and television news commentary provide models of professional argument. Also, try listening to the news on the car radio or watch it on television when you exercise. This commitment is guaranteed to make you a smarter, better-informed person — the kind of student most colleges are looking for. This learning may also come in handy on that other College Board writing assignment: the persuasive essay on the writing section of the SAT.

DIDYOU**KNOW?**

Writing persuasive essays may give you a taste for organized debate. Many schools have debate teams that compete against teams from other schools. Organized debates feature controversial issues from current events, and the competition is governed by detailed rules. Usually a judge or team of judges decides which side has won the debate.

The Persuasive Essay Question

What will the persuasive question look like? This type of question may be in one of two forms:

- You are asked to take a position on an issue.

- You are asked to defend, refute, or qualify the position taken by another writer in a quoted paragraph or passage.

In the first type of question, you might simply be asked to express your views about a controversial issue. Or you might be provided with a few paragraphs of text to help frame the issue and place it in context. Read this material carefully — actually, you should read it twice! — prior to framing your response.

TEST TIP

Remember, qualified responses that attempt to reconcile opposing viewpoints can be tricky. Look for examples of this kind of writing in editorials or blogs, and then practice the skill before you try it on the actual test. Presenting a compromise solution in your summation (and you may be asked to do just that) can show that you understand the complexity of the issue as well as providing an effective way to close your essay.

The other type of question asks you to read a passage from a particular writer and then "refute, support, or qualify" the writer's argument. Again you should read the passage twice before you begin writing. Make sure you understand the writer's viewpoint; underline any phrase or sentence that encapsulates that viewpoint. This question can also contain elements of the rhetorical-analysis essay. As you dissect the writer's position in the passage, you will also analyze and evaluate how the writer tries to persuade his or her readers. If you like debating, you should enjoy writing your response to this question. Jot down the most important points you want to make and use them to organize your essay.

Regardless of which form of persuasive question you get, make sure you write a strong, focused thesis statement. It should cover every aspect of the question and make your position clear from the start.

Things to Keep in Mind

- Address the prompt clearly and thoroughly.

- No matter how strongly you feel about the issue in the question, present your argument in a reasonable manner with the support of solid evidence. This is an essay, not a diatribe. Don't be inflammatory and don't resort to heavy sarcasm or name-calling, no matter how emotional the subject is for you. In fact, addressing the viewpoints of the opposing side in your response will show that you have a sophisticated understanding of how complex the issue is and will help you earn a higher score.

- If you don't have a strong opinion about the topic, just choose the side you can support in the most compelling and interesting way, and proceed from there. Remember, this is a test of your reading, writing, and thinking skills — you will not be judged on your personal views. That being said, AP Readers are human beings: silly, outrageous, or overtly cruel views will be difficult to effectively support and will not earn you a good score.

DIDYOUKNOW?

Many well-known authors have made their living writing opinion pieces for a large readership. H. L. Mencken (1880–1956) became known as "the sage of Baltimore" for his stylish yet controversial editorials for newspapers and magazines. More recently, Anna Quindlen (1952–) built a loyal following with her columns for the *New York Times* and *Newsweek* magazine.

- Avoid hypothetical examples. Some very good writers can use them to good effect, but most students cannot. In addition, hypothetical examples often lead to the dreaded "generic you," a characteristic of weak style. Good writing is specific writing. One exception would be the use of the hypothetical example in order to make an analogy, but that analogy should lead to more specific support.

- Of all the essays, this is the one where your personal voice and distinctive writing style are on display. You will be writing in the first-person point of view, and using humor and imaginative comparisons is perfectly appropriate for the situation. Nevertheless, keep in mind that this is not your Facebook page; you are writing for an audience of adult English teachers, not your peers, and your purpose is to impress them as a student who is already thinking and writing at the level of a college sophomore.

TEST TIP

Don't pad your essay with lots of unnecessary verbiage just to make it longer. The AP Readers are looking for logic, organization, and fluent writing, not for length. If your response is relatively brief but reasoned and written well, you will receive a good score.

Approaching a Sample Persuasive Essay Question

Next we will examine a typical persuasive essay question you might see on the AP English Language and Composition exam. This prompt includes a brief reading passage that frames the issue. Look for your writing task at the end of the prompt.

In 1983, the D.A.R.E. (Drug Abuse Resistance Education) program, a school-based substance abuse prevention program, began a nationwide effort to "teach students good decision-making skills to help them lead safe and healthy lives." The D.A.R.E. program provides police officers with 80 hours of special training in areas such as child development, classroom management, teaching techniques, and communication skills. The officers then visit schools to deliver their anti-drug message and answer questions from students. D.A.R.E.'s goal is to teach students to see police officers as friends and helpers rather than only as enforcers of the law.

Supporters argue that D.A.R.E. effectively helps millions of kids find alternatives to drug abuse in ways beyond what schools and families can provide. Proponents contend that kids and parents like the program, and that it fosters valuable relationships between police, family, and schools.

Critics argue that scientific evidence shows no significant difference between future drug use in kids who have "graduated" from the costly D.A.R.E. program and those who have not. They contend that the program is misleading and can actually increase drug use by students.

> Think about the effectiveness of this program. Then, write an essay that defends, refutes, or qualifies the claim that the D.A.R.E. program is an effective method of preventing teenage drug abuse. Use specific, appropriate evidence to develop your position.
>
> *Source: "D.A.R.E. Home." http//:dare.procon.org. Accessed September 14, 2012.*

You should read the four paragraphs of the prompt at least twice. Then ask yourself these questions:

- What is D.A.R.E.? (It is "a school-based substance abuse prevention program." You should underline those words. The organization trains police officers to speak with students at school about how to avoid drug abuse.)

- What is the main argument in support of D.A.R.E.? (It helps millions of kids avoid drug abuse with methods that are beyond what schools and families can provide.)

- What is the main argument against D.A.R.E.? (Evidence indicates that kids who take the program are no less likely to abuse drugs than those who don't take it. Critics say the program can actually increase student drug use.)

- What is your task for this prompt? ("Write an essay that defends, refutes, or qualifies the claim that the D.A.R.E. program is an effective method of preventing teenage drug use." You should underline those words.)

Now you are ready to jot down the key points you want to make or to write a quick outline of your argument. (If you are a more experienced writer, you might be able to organize the main ideas in your head.) Then you can draft your response. Below is a sample response to this persuasive essay question. Notice how it addressed the task that was assigned.

For close to thirty years, the DARE program has been seeking to teach children the skills needed to make good, responsible decisions. While the program's goals are lofty, they are not feasible. The DARE program is not an effective method of preventing teenage drug abuse.

According to critics, a cost-benefit analysis of DARE "shows no significant difference between future drug use in kids who have 'graduated' " from the program. Certainly the program has been around long enough to produce results. Keeping DARE in schools just because "kids and parents like the program" is not a responsible decision. If officials see that this program is not working, then they should rethink their motives. One resource that education always needs is more money. It's time for those who hold to tradition to let go of the nostalgia they feel for an ineffective program. The money used to fund DARE could be better spent on integrating more technology, hiring more teachers, or building more schools.

In addition to the costs, this program has not been shown to decrease drug use among teenagers. In fact, DARE introduces the subject of drugs to elementary and middle school children at a time when they may not even be thinking of using these substances. Parents should be the ones held responsible for teaching their children decision-making skills in all areas, not just for drugs. Because each child is unique, it is the parents who are best equipped to know when the conversation about drugs should take place. The "Just Say No" campaigns have been around longer than DARE, do not rely on community resources, and teach kids to avoid drugs altogether.

While proponents of the DARE program argue that it "fosters valuable relationships between police, family, and schools," I believe these relationships would exist without DARE. Most schools (like mine) have at least one school resource officer (SRO) to assist with campus security. Even with an increased police presence, students are still dealing and doing drugs on high school campuses. Every day I have to cross through crowds of students smoking in the student parking lot. Although I've reported this behavior to the administration, the smoking hasn't stopped. The students just find another location to smoke. If a student is found to be intoxicated or under the influence of a drug, the administrator will usually send the student home with no other consequence. As long as a student is not in possession of the illegal substance, the SRO has no recourse in pursuing the incident. While students should not be so afraid of a police officer that they wouldn't approach one if in need of assistance, they need to maintain an impersonal respect for police officers and their dangerous duties. A program like DARE encourages students to think of police officers as all-purpose counselors, which is not their proper job or responsibility. Children should not think of police officers — nor parents, teachers, and principals — primarily as friends, like many do.

Oftentimes, letting go of a fondly remembered tradition is difficult. Adults need to recognize that the DARE program is not fulfilling its promises to children, schools, and communities. It's time for parents to take the responsibility of drug education away from DARE.

This essay is an example of taking an unusual position — in this case, *against* the DARE program. While most students would probably write in support of the popular program, this student's essay stands out by taking the negative position. The student presents a succinct thesis that makes the focus of the essay clear. The evidence is organized effectively, with clear transitions between the proponents of the DARE program and the critics. In addition, the student uses a *logos* or logical appeal in presenting the negative aspects of DARE as counter arguments to the proponent's claims. For example, the student writes in the fourth paragraph, "While proponents of the DARE program argue that it 'fosters valuable relationships between police, family, and schools,' I believe these relationships would exist without DARE." While many of the examples come from personal experience, the student presents the evidence with logic and in-depth details. Overall, the essay presents an effective — if somewhat unusual — argument supported by sufficient evidence and the use of a mature prose style.

DIDYOU**KNOW?**

D.A.R.E., which has its headquarters in Inglewood, California, has grown into an international education program that deals not only with drug abuse issues but questions of gang membership and violent behavior. Students who join the program sign a pledge not to use drugs or join a gang.

Chapter 13

Approaching the Essay Questions: The Synthesis Essay

The third type of essay question you will face on the AP English Language and Composition exam requires you to synthesize ideas from various sources to either support an argument or analyze an issue. To "synthesize" means to combine various components into a new whole; for the synthesis prompt, you will be asked to read and cull information from five to eight brief sources on a topic of some controversy in which differing sides will be presented. At least one of the sources will be visual: a photograph, chart, editorial cartoon, graph, advertisement, etc. Essentially, the AP English synthesis essay is meant to be a facsimile of a research paper (without the actual research since you are provided with the sources). A 15-minute reading period is provided for you to read the sources for this prompt.

TEST TIP

If you check sample student essays from the AP Central website, notice how top-scoring writers incorporate quotes and evidence seamlessly in their writing to make persuasive points. Remember that you will be scored on your essay's fluency and clarity in the use of sources.

The Prompt for the Synthesis Essay

The synthesis prompt can run the entire content-area gamut, so be prepared for just about any topic that might be controversial. Recent topics have included the following:

- the funding of space exploration

- the proposed abolishment of the penny

- the use of information technologies in schools

DIDYOUKNOW?

The word *synthesis* comes from a Greek word that means "a composition or a putting together." The first use of *synthesis* in English occurred around 1589.

The question for the synthesis essay will be one of two basic types. The first type is primarily persuasive: you will be asked to defend, challenge, or offer a qualified position on an argument. A qualified position is one that falls somewhere in between the two extremes, pointing out the merits and problems with both sides and offering a compromise stance. Arguing for a qualified position shows off your ability to understand the complexity of an issue. However, it can also be tricky. If not handled skillfully, a qualified response can sound weak and ambivalent rather than nuanced. It's essential to begin with a strong thesis statement that establishes your intent to pursue a compromise position. Here is an example of the persuasive type of synthesis essay prompt:

> In most states, the legal age for obtaining a driver's license is sixteen, but in response to a recent increase in accidents caused by teen drivers, some state legislatures are looking at raising the minimum driving age to eighteen.
>
> Carefully read the following sources, including the introductory information for each source. Then synthesize information from at least three of the sources and incorporate it into a coherent, well-developed essay that defends, challenges, or qualifies the claim that the legal driving age should be raised to eighteen.

The second type of question for the synthesis essay asks you to analyze and/or evaluate the issues surrounding a controversy. A sample prompt would look something like this:

In most states, the legal age for obtaining a driver's license is sixteen, but in response to a recent increase in accidents caused by teen drivers, some state legislatures are looking at raising the minimum driving age to eighteen.

Carefully read the following sources, including the introductory information for each source. Then synthesize information from at least three of the sources and incorporate it into a coherent, well-reasoned essay that develops a position about what issues are most important in making a decision about raising the legal driving age to eighteen.

Notice that we have the same topic but a very different kind of prompt. In the second prompt, your task is not to take a position but *to discuss what considerations are most important in making a decision on the controversy.* Since your number one objective is to address the prompt, you have to notice this distinction. If you are asked to do B but instead you do A, you have no chance of scoring well regardless of how inspired your essay is.

DIDYOU**KNOW?**

In the 1920s the widespread use of automobiles led to state laws that arbitrarily set the minimum age for getting a driver's license. Connecticut was the first state to allow sixteen-year-olds to drive, albeit with a licensed driver along. By the 1940s, most states had set the minimum driving age at 16.

Finally, each prompt for the synthesis essay will contain a final paragraph similar to the following:

Make sure that your argument is central. Use the sources to illustrate and support your reasoning. Avoid merely summarizing the sources. Indicate clearly which sources you are drawing from, whether by direct quotation, paraphrase, or summary. You may cite the sources as Source A, Source B, etc., or by using the descriptions in parentheses.

Source A (The American Highway Safety Task Force)
Source B (Photo)
Source C (Collins)
Source D (Denis)
Source E (U.S. Department of Transportation)

This part of the prompt alludes to another trap students can fall into: merely summarizing the sources rather than using them to support a position. Don't take your reader on a tour of the sources — use them as tools to make your argument or develop your position. Also, you are instructed on how to refer to your sources in your essay.

TEST TIP

Be sure to put quotation marks around each section of material quoted from one of the sources, even if it is only a few words. Part of your score will reflect your careful use of sources.

Writing the Synthesis Essay

The more experienced you are as a writer, the less you must rely on a schematic approach to writing a fairly complex essay like the one required for the synthesis prompt. Nevertheless, it might help you to follow this basic approach. (This example addresses the prompt about the legal age for obtaining a driving license.)

- **Introduction:** Present your thesis statement.

  "While concern for public safety is a compelling reason to consider raising the driving age from sixteen to eighteen, we should keep the law the way it is because raising the driving age is unlikely to ultimately reduce the number of serious accidents on the road."

- **First Body Paragraph:** Briefly discuss motivation for the discussion — probably the number of sixteen- and seventeen-year-olds involved in accidents as well as the injuries to innocent people and damage to property. Be sure, however, to not overdo it. Just show that you understand why the public is concerned.

- **Second Body Paragraph and Beyond:** Discuss the reasons why raising the driving age won't improve safety. Choose your examples from the sources and document your use of each one.

- **Conclusion:** Offer a compromise, perhaps. For example: Don't change the driving age but improve driver education and place more restrictions on young drivers.

Should you refer to the sources that contradict your opinion? Higher-scoring papers usually acknowledge the complexity of the issue by including some discussion of the opposing viewpoint. The danger, however, is that less mature writers can produce papers that appear indecisive and unfocused rather than nuanced and sophisticated. Thus, you should acknowledge the contrary sources only if you have practiced this skill and are confident you can do it well. Try this approach:

- Make sure the thesis statement is strong and emphatic, keeping your main point in the independent clause and the acknowledgment of the other side in the subordinate clause.

- Emphasize the shift to your main point with a strong topic sentence in the third paragraph. For example: "Despite these legitimate concerns for public safety, the evidence shows that raising the driving age is not the answer."

- Make sure you spend significantly more time on your main point that on the opposing side.

- Stay focused on the task at hand. If you decide to go in a particular direction, you are restricted in the evidence you can use. For example, with this particular thesis statement, you need to focus on the safety issue. While the argument that teens need to drive to get to after-school jobs supports your preference to keep the law the same, it muddies your safety argument, so it doesn't really fit. In fact, this evidence implies that teens really are problematic drivers, but that the benefits outweigh the risks. If you want to use this evidence, make sure your thesis statement supports its inclusion in your essay.

Things to Keep in Mind

The synthesis essay causes some trepidation among students who are about to take the AP English exam, but generally it is easier for them to deal with than the style-analysis essay. Read the prompt and the sources carefully and follow these tips to do well on the synthesis essay.

- Make sure you address the synthesis essay prompt clearly and thoroughly. Decide if you must take a position on a controversy or discuss which considerations are most important in developing a position.

- Remember to use at least three of the sources provided for the synthesis essay. You can use more if you choose, but you don't need to. Discussing fewer sources well is better than taking a cursory glance at all of them. Also, time is a factor as well. You have three essays to write and only 135 minutes to write them. Don't worry about doing more than is required.

- You can draw on your own knowledge and experience in your essay as long as you still cite at least three of the sources. You might consider using a personal experience, local issue, or historical or literary example as an interesting introduction to your essay if the perfect one comes to you. If not, don't worry about it; you'll still get a high score if you do a good job with the sources you have on the exam.

DIDYOUKNOW?

Historians divide the sources they use into the categories of primary and secondary. A primary source is a firsthand account written by a participant or eyewitness to an event. A secondary source is written by someone who did not witness the original event, but relied on interviews or research for information.

- Don't just read the sources that support the position you want to take. Read all the sources carefully, reserving judgment until you have completed your reading. The College Board recommends this procedure, and it makes sense for two reasons. First, you likely will not know enough about the topic to have an informed position beforehand, so you will need the sources to develop one — as much as you can in the limited time available. Second, the sources provided might not be the best for the position that you want to take. Given your limited time to read, think, and respond, it is safer to go where the sources lead you. Remember, this essay is essentially an exercise — it is not a measure of your value system, nor is it a forum for your political or social views, so it is perfectly acceptable to formulate an argument that you might not necessarily endorse in this context. Unlike the people who read your college admissions essay, the AP Readers are not trying to get to know you here. Rather, they are evaluating your ability to read, think, and write critically.

- Regarding style, remember that this is an academic essay, so write in an academic style. That means no first-person singular (unless briefly for a personal anecdote), slang, abbreviations, or other kinds of casual language.

- Document any material you have taken from the sources through direct quotation or paraphrasing. It's better to document too much rather than too little.

The directions in the prompt tell you how to document the sources you use. Remember, a source never "talks about" something — it "shows," "indicates," or "suggests." Here are some options for documentation:

> The American Highway Safety Task Force data shows . . .
>
> Source B asserts . . .
>
> There is a strong causal relationship between accidents and inexperience that applies to drivers regardless of age (Source C). In fact, eighteen-year-old new drivers are involved in accidents at almost identical rates as sixteen-year-old new drivers. The increased risk of accidents subsides after three years, and goes away completely after five years (Source E). Thus, we can conclude that raising the driving age will only delay the spike in accident statistics for eighteen-year-old new drivers.

Notice also that the third example does not merely paraphrase the sources, but also discusses their broader implications as they apply to your thesis.

- Use your time wisely when answering the synthesis essay question. You are allotted 135 minutes to complete all three essays; that means 40 minutes for each essay plus an extra 15 minutes to read the sources for the synthesis essay. You may find that using some of that 15 minutes of reading time on the style-analysis essay is your best strategy. This is where practice to determine your own capabilities is key. Find out which type of essay is easiest for you and which type gives you the most difficulty. Then you can allot your writing time accordingly. Familiarity with each kind of prompt will allow you to develop a rhythm for maximum success: reading time, planning time, writing time, editing time.

To practice writing synthesis essays, you can find sample prompts from past AP English Language and Composition exams at *http://apcentral.collegeboard.org*. Sample student responses are also provided at the site.

TEST TIP

The best way to train yourself to write an incisive essay in 40 minutes is to practice and practice some more. This work will give you confidence and make you familiar with your strengths and weaknesses as a writer.

Approaching the Essay Questions: Strategy and Preparation

Now you've reviewed how to organize and write an essay as well as how to approach each type of essay on the AP English Language and Composition exam. You are almost ready to tackle the essay questions. Here are a few final reminders regarding the essay portion of the test.

Strategies for Responding to the Essay Questions

1. Read the prompt carefully before you read the passage or sources. As you read the prompt, underline the specific task required. Make sure you understand what you are looking for as you read. In the passage, underline significant details, words with connotative meaning, reasons, logical structure, notable sentence beginnings or endings, unusual sentence structures, sentences that are noticeably short or long, vivid imagery, figures of speech, and words or phrases that may indicate the author's attitude or point of view.

2. Plan your response before you start writing. The English Language and Composition essay answers are graded as "first draft" papers. You are not given enough time to do prewriting, rough draft, and final copy — prewriting and one rapid draft are all you have time for in roughly 40 minutes per essay. Therefore, whatever prewriting you can do — organizing before you begin to write by deciding on content and order of ideas — is critical to your success. Give yourself about 5–10 minutes to read the essay question, write a working thesis sentence, and

list 3–5 points in order of importance or logical development. The remaining time (30–35 minutes) should be spent writing. If you're particularly efficient, you may have 5 minutes to proofread and make a few revisions.

DIDYOUKNOW?

Nearly 444,000 students took the AP English Language and Composition Exam in 2012, according to the College Board. It currently is the most frequently taken AP exam.

3. Since you are pressed for time, you should avoid long introductory or long concluding remarks. Lengthy openings and conclusions take valuable time away from your main argument. Remember that you have only about 40 minutes to read the question, read the passage, plan your strategy, write your answer, and proofread and revise. Another argument against lengthy openings and conclusions is that your central development will be shorter, and therefore probably weaker in development. One or two sentences of introduction and conclusion are adequate. If you have a *eureka!* moment and a great idea for a punchy introduction just comes to you, go for it — but don't labor over it or you won't have time to write the paper. Also, a silly introduction that says nothing is worse than nothing. (For example: "Rhetorical strategies are an important part of writing." Ugh!) Some students like to leave a little space at the top of the page above the thesis. Then, if a good idea for an introduction comes to you later and you have time, you can add it. If not, the important part of the essay, the part that earns points for you on the rubric, is written. The same applies to conclusions.

4. Your ideas should lead from one to the other in a smooth, logical progression. Organization of ideas in prewriting and composing will depend on the type of essay, but organize before you write. Decide if a particular rhetorical structure (compare/contrast, cause/effect, problem/solution, etc.) would be suitable for the essay and allow it to guide you. The multi-paragraph, thesis and support essay structure is adequate for answering many of the AP essay prompts as long as you make sure to shorten the introduction and conclusion.

5. It is often a good idea to start your essay by answering the prompt in the first or second sentence you write. The AP Readers will be reading your essays rapidly, and it is critical to show them right away that you are performing the

task set forth in the prompt. In addition, as mentioned before, the longer you spend writing an introduction, the less time you'll have to write a convincing body of the essay.

6. Use strong transition topic sentences to emphasize your progression of thought. Each one can present the specific aspect of the thesis statement to be discussed in the rest of the paragraph. *Never start a body paragraph with a quotation or example.* Quotations and examples support points. You cannot introduce support unless you have first made an assertion. Also, make sure the quotations and examples you choose are apt and relate clearly to the point you're making. Vague or confusing references to the passage or sources will usually limit your score to the mediocre range at best.

TEST TIP

Don't use too many quotes from the passage or sources in your essays. You don't want your writing to look like a strung-together line of quotations. Include only the quoted words that you need.

7. Each quotation or example should be followed by interpretation and analysis that connects it back to the thesis statement. Always ask yourself "Why is this significant?" It is essential that your reader understand this significance after each point of support in your essay. For examples of fluent use of source material in an essay, consult the sample essays on the AP website.

8. Though won't be time for much revision of your essay, and lots of cross-outs would be impractical anyway. Nonetheless, try to set aside a few minutes to skim each of your responses. As you read, look for awkward sentences, run-ons and fragments, and any hurried errors in spelling and punctuation. You know your writing tendencies better than anyone. If you have chronic issues with pronoun/antecedent agreement or apostrophes, assume that you might have made some of these errors and check for them. Flawless first drafts — for your essays are first drafts — are rare indeed.

9. Don't fret if you run out of time on an essay. While it's best to write some sort of conclusion, you may not have that opportunity if the proctor is waiting for you to hand over your test. Overall the introduction and the body of the essay are most important anyway, and if done well will earn a good score.

Preparing for the Essay Questions

1. As suggested in the previous chapter, you should research essay prompts from previous years. The College Board website offers you many past questions along with scored sample student essays (called anchor papers) with explanations of the scoring *(http://apcentral. collegeboard.com/)*. Spend time reading these questions and responses and develop an understanding of how they were scored. Learn what the graders expect on the different types of questions and motivate yourself to satisfy these standards.

2. Practice writing essays for the sample prompts on the website. Then, read the anchor papers and try to score your essays according to how the rubric aligns with the student examples. Does yours read more like a "2" paper, a "5" paper, or an "8" paper? If you are unsure, ask a teacher to help you evaluate your papers or work with a friend who is also taking the test.

3. At first, write your practice papers in one sitting but don't otherwise apply any time constraint. Take as long as you need to do a good job. Then, as you gain more confidence, begin timing yourself. Also, always write your practice papers in longhand. You won't have a keyboard available for the test.

DIDYOU KNOW?

Long before the invention of the fountain pen and ballpoint pen, people wrote with quill pens. A quill is a feather from the wing of a large bird such as a goose. When the quill is dipped in ink, the hollow shaft of the feather holds the ink as in a reservoir and the ink then flows to the tip. Imagine all the feathers that a writer like Shakespeare went through!

4. Good writers use this trick to improve their fluency: read your essays out loud, with expression, and listen to your prose. If you are stumbling over your own words or your meaning seems ambiguous, there is a problem. Do this test for everything you write and your style will improve.

5. Build your skills and confidence by writing "skeleton" papers. Take a question from the website and allow yourself 5–10 minutes to write a thesis statement and plan out your response — the skeleton of a final essay. You can do several of these in the weeks leading up to the exam!

TEST TIP

Avoid redundant phrases in your essays. Instead of "plan ahead," simply write "plan." Instead of "looking back in retrospect," write "in retrospect."

6. If you have issues with basic grammar and spelling, put yourself on a self-improvement plan. The AP Readers understand the limitations of timed, first-draft writing and expect a few mistakes on even the "9" papers, but if you are still confusing *your* and *you're* and are unsure when to use *they* or *them*, it is time to address these problems. Make sure you know how to spell the words you probably will need to use on the AP English Language and Composition exam — *imagery, parallel syntax, simile, rhetorical,* and *persuasive* — to name a few.

7. Read, read, and read some more. A great way to improve your writing is to read voraciously, especially good contemporary prose. Reading examples of the kind of persuasive writing you will be asked to do on the exam will also help.

Time for a quiz
- Review strategies in Chapter 2
- Take Quiz 6 at the REA Study Center
  (www.rea.com/studycenter)

Take Mini-Test 2
on Chapters 8–14
Go to the REA Study Center
(www.rea.com/studycenter)

Practice Exam

Also available at the REA Study Center (*www.rea.com/studycenter*)

This practice exam is available at the REA Study Center. Although AP exams are administered in paper-and-pencil format, we recommend that you take the online version of the practice exam for the benefits of:

- Instant scoring
- Enforced time conditions
- Detailed score report of your strengths and weaknesses

Practice Exam
Section I

(Answer sheets appear in the back of the book.)

TIME: 1 Hour
52 Questions

Directions: This section of the test consists of selections from nonfiction works and questions on their use of language. After reading each passage, choose the best answer to each question and blacken the corresponding oval on the answer sheet.

Questions 1–10 are based on the following passage. Read the passage carefully before choosing your answers.

The following letter was published in The Freedmen's Book, a collection of African American writings compiled by the abolitionist Lydia Marie Child in 1865. The letter is a response to a slave owner who has written to his former slave at the war's end, asking him to return to work in Tennessee.

To my old Master, Colonel P.H. Anderson, Big Spring, Tennessee.

Sir. I got your letter, and was glad to find that you had not forgotten Jourdan, and that you wanted me to come back and live with you again, promising to do better for me than anybody else can. I have often felt uneasy about you. I thought the
(5) Yankees would have hung you long before this, for harbouring Rebs they found at your house. I suppose they never heard about your going to Colonel Martin's to kill the Union soldier that was left by his company in their stable. Although you shot at me twice before I left you, I did not hear of your being hurt, and am glad you are still living. It would do me good to go back to the dear old home again, and see Miss
(10) Mary and Miss Martha and Allen, Ester, Green, and Lee. Give my love to them all, and tell them I hope we will meet in the better world, if not in this. I would have gone back to see you all when I was working in Nashville Hospital, but one of the neighbors told me that Henry intended to shoot me if he ever got a chance.

I want to know particularly what the good chance is you propose to give
(15) me. I am doing tolerably well here. I get twenty-five dollars a month, with victuals and clothing; have a comfortable home for Mandy, — the folks call her Mrs. Anderson, — and the children — Milly, Jane, and Grundy — go to school and are learning well....we are kindly treated. Sometimes we overhear others saying, "Them colored people were slaves" down in Tennessee. The children feel hurt when
(20) they hear such remarks; but I tell them it was no disgrace in Tennessee to belong to

Colonel Anderson. Many darkeys would have been proud, as I used to be, to call you master. Now if you will write and say what wages you will give me, I will be better able to decide whether it would be to my advantage to move back again.

(25) As to my freedom, which you say I can have, there is nothing to be gained on that score, as I got my free papers in 1864 from the Provost-Marshall-General of the Department of Nashville. Mandy says she would be afraid to go back without some proof that you were disposed to treat us justly and kindly; and we have concluded to test your sincerity by asking you to send us our wages for the time we served you. This will make us forget and forgive old scores, and rely on your justice and friend-
(30) ship in the future. I served you faithfully for thirty-two years, and Mandy twenty years. At twenty-five dollars a month for me, and two dollars a week for Mandy, our earnings would amount to eleven thousand six hundred and eighty dollars. Add to this the interest for the time our wages have been kept back, and deduct what you paid for our clothing, and three doctors visits for me, and pulling a tooth for Mandy,
(35) and the balance will show what justice we are entitled. Please send the money by Adam's Express, in the care of V. Winters, Esq., Dayton, Ohio. If you fail to pay us for faithful labors in the past, we can have little faith in your promises in the future. We trust the good Maker has opened your eyes to the wrongs which you and your fathers have done to me and my fathers, in making us toil for you for generations
(40) without recompense….Surely there will be a day of reckoning for those who defraud the laborer of his hire.

In answering this letter, please state if there would be any safety for my Milly and Jane, who are now grown up, and both good-looking girls. You know how it was with poor Matilda and Catherine. I would rather stay here and starve — and die, if it came
(45) to that — than have my girls brought to shame by the violence and wickedness of their young masters. You will also please state that if there has been any schools opened for the colored children in your neighborhood. The great desire of my life now is to give my children an education, and have them form virtuous habits.

Say howdy to George Carter, and thank him for taking the pistol from you when
(50) you were shooting at me.

From your old servant,
Jourdan Anderson

1. Read the following sentence from paragraph 3 of the passage.

   If you fail to pay us for faithful labors in the past, we can have little faith in your promises in the future.

   This sentence is an example of

   (A) oxymoron

   (B) subordinate clause

   (C) balanced sentence

   (D) metaphor

   (E) antithesis

2. In paragraph 4, what does Jourdan Anderson imply about Matilda and Catherine?

   (A) They were sold by Colonel P. H. Anderson.

   (B) Colonel P. H. Anderson's sons sexually assaulted them.

   (C) Colonel P. H. Anderson did not feed or clothe them.

   (D) Colonel P. H. Anderson's sons killed them.

   (E) Colonel P. H. Anderson sexually assaulted them when he was younger.

3. Jourdan Anderson uses all of the following rhetorical techniques to convince Colonel P. H. Anderson of his "sincere" desire to return to work for him EXCEPT

   (A) irony

   (B) anecdote

   (C) sarcasm

   (D) logos

   (E) apostrophe

4. In paragraph 1, the sentence "I have often felt uneasy about you" (line 4) is an example of which rhetorical device?

   (A) metaphor

   (B) understatement

   (C) ethos

   (D) hyperbole

   (E) euphemism

5. Jourdan Anderson's attitude toward his old master is best described as

   (A) reverential and laudatory

   (B) pedantic and didactic

   (C) candid and colloquial

   (D) arrogant and moralistic

   (E) condescending and sardonic

6. In paragraph 2, "the folks here call her Mrs. Anderson" (lines 16–17) implies which of the following?

   (A) Jourdan Anderson's wife was not married to him when he worked for Colonel P. H. Anderson.

   (B) Slaves were not called by their names at Colonel P. H. Anderson's plantation.

   (C) Jourdan Anderson's wife is respected where she now lives, unlike when she worked for Colonel P. H. Anderson.

   (D) Slaves preferred to use only their first names on a plantation.

   (E) Slaves were not allowed to use a title such as "Mrs." on a plantation.

7. Jourdan Anderson's primary purpose in writing a response to Colonel P. H. Anderson is to

    (A) work for him again and see his old friends

    (B) forgive Colonel P. H. Anderson and make amends

    (C) collect his wages from working for Colonel P. H. Anderson in the past

    (D) seek restitution for wrongs committed against him

    (E) assert ironically how ludicrous Colonel P. H. Anderson's offer is

8. Since Colonel P. H. Anderson wrote to Jourdan Anderson first, all of the following can be inferred about the Colonel's letter and the resulting response from his former slave EXCEPT

    (A) Colonel P. H. Anderson believed that he was offering Jourdan Anderson a good opportunity.

    (B) Colonel P. H. Anderson did not feel that he had wronged Jourdan Anderson at all.

    (C) Colonel P. H. Anderson believed that payment for Jourdan's services in the future would erase all of the Colonel's past debts.

    (D) Colonel P. H. Anderson offered to pay Jourdan Anderson all the money he owed him, so he asked his former slave to send him the bill for services rendered.

    (E) Colonel P. H. Anderson did not apologize to his former slave for the wrongs from his past in his letter to his former slave.

9. Read the following excerpt from lines 38–41.

    We trust the good Maker has opened your eyes to the wrongs which you and your fathers have done to me and my fathers, in making us toil for you for generations without recompense. . . . Surely there will be a day of reckoning for those who defraud the laborer of his hire.

    This excerpt is an example of which rhetorical device?

    (A) Biblical allusion

    (B) antithesis

    (C) anecdote

    (D) personification

    (E) hypothetical example

10. Paragraph 5 is a short sentence: "Say howdy to George Carter, and thank him for taking the pistol from you when you were shooting at me." What is this sentence's function in the letter?

    (A) a summary of views previously established

    (B) a final diatribe against Colonel P. H. Anderson

    (C) an authorial judgment on how Colonel P. H. Anderson treated him

    (D) a frivolous conclusion to an otherwise deadly serious letter

    (E) a satirical remark to show why Jourdan Anderson would never trust his old master

Questions 11–24 are based on the following passage. Read the passage carefully before choosing your answers.

Unjust laws exist: shall we be content to obey them, or shall we endeavor to amend them, and obey them until we have succeeded, or shall we transgress them at once? Men generally, under such a government as this, think that they ought to wait until they have persuaded the majority to alter them. They think that, if they should
(5) resist, the remedy would be worse than the evil. But it is the fault of the government itself that the remedy *is* worse than the evil. *It* makes it worse. Why is it not more apt to anticipate and provide for reform? Why does it not cherish its wise minority? Why does it cry and resist before it is hurt? Why does it not encourage its citizens to be on the alert to point out its faults, and *do* better than it would have them? Why does it
(10) always crucify Christ, and excommunicate Copernicus and Luther, and pronounce Washington and Franklin rebels?

If the injustice is part of the necessary friction of the machine of government, let it go, let it go: perchance it will wear smooth — certainly the machine will wear out. If the injustice has a spring, or a pulley, or a rope, or a crank, exclusively for
(15) itself, then perhaps you may consider whether the remedy will not be worse than the evil; but if it is of such a nature that it requires you to be the agent of injustice to another, then, I say, break the law. Let your life be a counter-friction to stop the machine. What I have to do is to see, at any rate, that I do not lend myself to the wrong which I condemn.

(20) Under a government which imprisons any unjustly, the true place for a just man is also a prison. The proper place today, the only place which Massachusetts has provided for her freer and less desponding spirits, is in her prisons, to be put out and locked out of the State by her own act, as they have already put themselves out by their principles. It is there that the fugitive slave, and the Mexican prisoner on
(25) parole, and the Indian come to plead the wrongs of his race should find them; on that separate, but more free and honorable, ground, where the State places those who are not *with* her, but *against* her — the only house in a slave State in which a free man can abide with honor. If any think that their influence would be lost there, and their voices no longer afflict the ear of the State, that they would not be as an enemy
(30) within its walls, they do not know by how much more eloquently and effectively he can combat injustice who has experienced a little in his own person. Cast your whole vote, not a strip of paper merely, but your whole influence. A minority is powerless while it conforms to the majority; it is not even a minority then; but it is irresistible when it clogs by its whole weight. If the alternative is to keep all just men in prison,
(35) or give up war and slavery, the State will not hesitate which to choose. If a thousand men were not to pay their tax-bills this year, that would not be a violent and bloody measure, as it would be to pay them, and enable the State to commit violence and shed innocent blood. This is, in fact, the definition of a peaceable revolution, if any such is possible. If the tax-gatherer, or any other public officer, asks me, as one has
(40) done, 'But what shall I do?' my answer is, 'If you really wish to do anything, resign

your office.' When the subject has refused allegiance, and the officer has resigned his office, then the revolution is accomplished. But even suppose blood should flow. Is there not a sort of blood shed when the conscience is wounded? Through this wound a man's real manhood and immortality flow out, and he bleeds to an everlasting
(45) death. I see this blood flowing now.

11. In paragraph 2, the author refers to "the machine of government" (line 12). As the author uses it, how does this metaphor characterize the government?

(A) efficient and reliable

(B) noisy and polluting

(C) single-minded and unfeeling

(D) reparable and industrious

(E) labor-saving and cost-effective

12. The opening paragraph features a series of questions. What is the author's purpose in posing these questions?

(A) He states the topics to be covered in the essay as questions.

(B) He expects the government officials to provide the reasons he seeks.

(C) He is satirically posing the questions to those with whom he disagrees.

(D) He is rhetorically criticizing what the government does and should not do.

(E) He aims to polarize his readers between those who agree with him and those who do not.

13. In the passage, one goal of the author is to

(A) arouse the moral responsibility of the reader

(B) encourage an armed rebellion

(C) attract persecuted minorities to Massachusetts

(D) promote a political party

(E) reduce the tax burden

14. The passage contains all of the following EXCEPT

(A) proposal for a peaceful protest

(B) historical reference to other governments

(C) criticism of specific persons

(D) justification of bloodshed

(E) unanswered questions

15. Which location is the word "there" referring to in line 24?

(A) Massachusetts

(B) the prison

(C) a legislative building

(D) a church

(E) the grave

16. Lines 32–34 are best restated as which of the following?

    (A) A minority must maintain a difference from the majority, so it can disable the majority.

    (B) A minority is an important part of the majority; without the minority, the majority would collapse under its own weight.

    (C) A majority exists only by actively contrasting itself with the minority and it is unconquerable when it acts in unison.

    (D) A minority remaining in silence brings injustice upon itself; the minority could make a stand against the majority with a strong voice and unified action.

    (E) A minority that complies with the will of the majority ceases to exist, but a minority that fully commits itself to impeding the unjust action of the majority is unconquerable.

17. According to the passage, what should the tax-gatherer do?

    (A) steal the state's funds

    (B) submit counterfeit money

    (C) quit his job

    (D) expect gunshots for greetings

    (E) be wary of a surprise attack

18. In lines 7–11 of the passage, what is the antecedent of "it" and "its"?

    (A) the electorate

    (B) the minority

    (C) law

    (D) Congress

    (E) government

19. Which of the following correctly contrasts lines 18–19 with lines 20–21?

    (A) In lines 18–19, the author is content not to participate in injustice; but in lines 20–21, the existence of an injustice compels the author to surrender his freedom in protest.

    (B) Lines 18–19 imply the author needs only react to what he sees; but lines 20–21 imply the author must react to all he knows.

    (C) Lines 18–19 advise one to condemn neither a borrower nor a lender; but lines 20–21 advise one to give up one's freedom for a man unjustly imprisoned.

    (D) In lines 18–19, the author implies it is enough to condemn injustice; but in lines 20–21, the author says the only place for an honest man under a dishonest government is prison.

    (E) Lines 18–19 advise a man to circumvent the wrongs of his state; but lines 20–21 advise him to oppose them even at the cost of his own freedom.

20. What does the author mean by "cast your whole vote" (lines 31–32)?

    (A) Vote in every election, whether local or national.

    (B) Vote for the same party in every election.

    (C) Run for office yourself.

    (D) Do everything possible to influence lawmaking.

    (E) Vote with a conscience.

21. It can be inferred from lines 21–24 that

(A) the author has been unjustly imprisoned

(B) the author has a loved one who is unjustly imprisoned

(C) the author is either in prison or not in Massachusetts

(D) Massachusetts' prisons are overcrowded

(E) Massachusetts has banished citizens that the author feels are principled

22. In lines 10–11, the author refers to Christ, Copernicus, Luther, Washington, and Franklin for their roles as

(A) religious figures

(B) iconoclasts

(C) political philosophers

(D) geniuses

(E) leaders

23. Identify the stage of the discussion through the passage.

(A) Question, answer, enact

(B) Goad, insult, attack

(C) Taunt, imply, condemn

(D) Criticize, suggest, inspire

(E) Argue, reason, propose

24. The tone of the passage is best described as

(A) hopeful and uplifting

(B) acerbic and cynical

(C) superior and dismissive

(D) prodding and impassioned

(E) cautious and logical

Questions 25–38 are based on the following passage. Read the passage carefully before you choose your answers. This passage is excerpted from an article in a biology journal published on April 5, 2006.

Born on July 5, 1904, in Kempten in southern Germany, Ernst Mayr passed away peacefully at the Methuselah-like age of 100 on February 3, 2005, in Bedford near Cambridge, Massachusetts. Mayr was, by the accounts of his Harvard colleagues the late Stephen Jay Gould and Edward O. Wilson, not only the greatest

(5) evolutionary biologist of the 20th century, but even its greatest biologist overall. . . . Ernst Mayr has been called "Darwin's apostle" or the "Darwin of the 20th century" for promoting and dispersing Darwin's hypotheses throughout the past century. . . .

Ernst Mayr had many fundamental insights into evolutionary biology, and almost every topic of importance in evolution was advanced by his ideas. Perhaps

(10) his most widely known contribution is to the current notion of what constitutes a species. Darwin did not think that species were real in the philosophical sense, but rather that they were the result of the human predilection to perceive discontinuity among continuously varying individuals. Most biologists nowadays disagree with

Darwin's view of species, largely because of Mayr's "biological species concept."
(15)   Together with [population geneticist] Dobzhansky, Mayr developed this definition of
species "as groups of interbreeding populations in nature, unable to exchange genes
with other such groups living in the same area."[1,2] Barriers to gene flow between species — termed reproductive isolating mechanisms — keep biological species distinct
through processes such as species-specific mate choice and hybrid sterility. Although
(20)   there are theoretical and operational problems with the biological species concept
(e.g., it does not apply to asexually reproducing organisms such as bacteria), it is still,
by far, the most widely used species concept among the 20 or so competing definitions that have been proposed in the past several decades. Students of biology all over
the world have memorized Mayr's definition of species for more than half a century.

(25)   . . . Mayr's understanding of the biogeographic distributions of bird species, overlaid with extensive knowledge about variation in morphology, led him
to develop concepts about the geographic mechanisms of speciation — cornerstones for those studying speciation today. The geographic separation of
populations, such as by rivers or valleys, he argued, prohibits homogenizing gene
(30)   flow between them. If such isolated (termed allopatric) populations accumu-
late mutations over time, this might lead to the divergence of such populations from
each other, and reproductive isolation might arise as a simple byproduct of these
separate evolutionary histories. Mayr staunchly defended this idea during sometimes
heated debates and further developed it and other hypotheses regarding geographic
(35)   mechanisms of speciation over many decades (outlined in depth in the 797 pages of
Animal Species and Evolution[3]) . . . .

Clearly, Ernst Mayr felt very strongly that he had something of importance to
say to the world. . . . Although Ernst Mayr lived only about a tenth of the 969 years
that Methuselah is purported to have lived, he still accomplished much more than
(40)   one might expect to get done, even in 100 years. . . . On the occasion of his 100th
birthday Mayr published an article in *Science*[4] looking back over eight decades of
research in evolution that he closed with the following words: "The new research
has one most encouraging message for the active evolutionist: it is that evolutionary
biology is an endless frontier and there is still plenty to be discovered. I only regret
(45)   that I won't be present to enjoy these future developments."

[1.] T. Dobzhansky, *Genetics and the Origin of Species* (New York: Columbia University Press, 1937), p. 364

[2.] E. Mayr, *Systematics and the Origin of Species* (New York: Columbia University Press, 1942) p. 334

[3.] E. Mayr, *Animal Species and Evolution.* (Cambridge, Massachusetts: Belknap Press, 1963)

[4.] E. Mayr, "Happy Birthday: 80 Years of Watching the Evolutionary Scenery." *Science* 305, 46–47 (2004).

25. The purpose of footnotes 1 and 2 is to inform the reader that the quotation in lines 15–17

    (A) was Mayr's own original creation, copied by Dobzhansky

    (B) was used by both Mayr and Dobzhansky in their books on the origin of species

    (C) Mayr needed Dobzhansky's help in developing this definition

    (D) was Dobzhansky's own original creation, copied by Mayr

    (E) was the definition that students memorized for many years

26. The use of the word "Methuselah-like" in line 2 of the passage is an example of

    (A) allusion

    (B) understatement

    (C) satire

    (D) metaphor

    (E) personification

27. The audience for this article is assumed to be

    (A) general readers

    (B) acquaintances of Mayr's

    (C) scholars

    (D) Harvard colleagues

    (E) geneticists

28. In lines 1–2, the term "passed away" is an example of which rhetorical device?

    (A) imagery

    (B) emotional appeal

    (C) antithesis

    (D) oxymoron

    (E) euphemism

29. In line 30, the pronoun "them" refers to

    (A) gene flow

    (B) rivers or valleys

    (C) separation

    (D) mutations

    (E) populations

30. Based on the information in lines 35–36 and footnote 3, which of the following statements is accurate?

    (A) Mayr's explanation of animal species and evolution appears on page 797 of his book.

    (B) The author of the book *Animal Species and Evolution* quotes Mayr on page 797.

    (C) An outline of Mayr's hypotheses appears in the book *Animal Species and Evolution*.

    (D) Mayr wrote a 797-page book for Belknap Press titled *Animal Species and Evolution*.

    (E) In 1942, the Columbia University Press published a book about Mayr's theories on animal species and evolution.

31. This article compares Mayr to

    (A) Dobzhansky

    (B) Darwin

    (C) Darwin and Dobzhansky

    (D) Wilson and Gould

    (E) Wilson and Darwin

32. The structure of lines 11–17 can best be described as

    (A) moving from general to specific

    (B) moving from specific to general

    (C) focusing on the general

    (D) focusing on specifics

    (E) contrasting conflicting ideas

33. A look at the footnotes informs the reader that

    (A) both Dobzhansky and Mayr wrote about Mayr's life

    (B) Dobzhansky had a longer writing career than Mayr

    (C) Dobzhansky relied heavily on the works of Mayr regarding evolutionary biology

    (D) Mayr's writing career lasted at least sixty years

    (E) Mayr often liked to write about himself

34. The main purpose of the passage can be characterized as

    (A) expository

    (B) analytical

    (C) eulogistic

    (D) investigative

    (E) persuasive

35. The quote taken from Mayr's *Science* article (lines 40–42) implies that

    (A) Mayr believed evolutionary biology had unveiled many intriguing mysteries

    (B) Mayr believed that evolutionary biologists will continue to make new discoveries

    (C) advances in evolutionary biology were likely to end with Mayr's death

    (D) Mayr was worried that he would die soon

    (E) Mayr had made tremendous contributions to the field of evolutionary biology

36. Read the following excerpt.

    Mayr's understanding of the biogeographic distributions of bird species, overlaid with extensive knowledge about variation in morphology, led him to develop concepts about the geographic mechanisms of speciation — cornerstones for those studying speciation today.

    This excerpt contains examples of which of the following?

    I. jargon

    II. appositive

    III. analogy

    (A) I only

    (B) II only

    (C) I and II only

    (D) I and III only

    (E) I, II and III

37. The word "heated" in line 34 means which of the following?

    (A) intense

    (B) disruptive

    (C) violent

    (D) wreckless

    (E) magnified

38. Which of the following is the best description of the author's tone in this passage?

    (A) envy

    (B) gratitude

    (C) admiration

    (D) pomposity

    (E) skepticism

Questions 39–52 are based on the following passage. Read the passage carefully before you choose your answers.

Prohibition was the world's first enactment, written by the finger of God in the Garden of Eden to keep the way of life, to preserve the innocence and character of man. But under the cover of the first night, "in the cool of the day," there crept into the Garden a brewer by the name of Beelzebub, who told the first man that God was a liar; that he
(5)   could sin and not die; that the prohibition law upon the tree of life was an infringement upon his personal liberty and that the law had no right to dictate what a man should eat or drink or wear. The devil induced Adam to go into rebellion against the law of God in the name of personal liberty, and from that hour dates the fall of man.

We are hearing something of that same argument in this campaign against the
(10) serpent drink, and not only on the part of the enemy. There are many good men who look upon prohibition as an assault upon the personal liberty of the citizen; but it seems to us they do not keep clear the issues involved in this fight. They are not personal at all.

Personal liberty is a matter of personal choice, of personal right to eat or to
(15) drink. No prohibitory law ever adopted or proposed attempts to interfere with that right. It does not seek to compel a man to abstain; it does not say that he ought not, must not, or dare not drink. It passes only upon the social right of trade, traffic and sale. Whether a man drinks or abstains is entirely his own affair, so long as he does not poison himself, compel society to cure him, support him when he is unable to
(20) take care of himself, lock him up when he is dangerous to be at large, bury him at the public expense when he is a corpse, or interfere with the personal liberty of others when he is exercising his own.

Men do not properly discriminate between a personal right and a social act. Personal liberty relates to private conduct. If a man signs the temperance pledge he
(25) surrenders his personal liberty or personal privilege to drink; when he votes dry — to prohibit liquor traffic — it has nothing to do with the ques-tion of personal liberty.

You have a personal right to eat putrid meat; I have no right to sell it. If your hog dies a natural death, or with the cholera, you have a personal right to grind it

up into a sausage and eat it, but you have no right to offer it for public sale. A man
(30) has a personal right to corn his dead mule and serve it on his own table. You have as
good a right to eat your cat as I have my chicken, or your dog as I have my pig. The
Chinese in New York have a dog feast at their New Year's celebration and the police
have never interfered with their personal right. But if you opened a meat market and
skinned dogs and cats or exposed horse sausage for public sale, the meat inspector
(35) would confiscate the entire supply, close up the place as a public nuisance and arrest
you for selling what you had a personal right to eat.

To abstain is a personal act; to market, traffic and trade is a social act, limited by
the social effect of the thing sold and the place where it is kept for sale. This distinction between total abstinence, which relates to personal liberty or personal conduct,
(40) and prohibition, which relates to social conduct and the State, is perfectly clear. The
one is the act of the individual; the other is the act of the State.

Total abstinence is the voluntary act of one man; it recognizes the right of choice
of personal liberty. Prohibition is the act of the community, the State, the majority,
which is the State, and is a matter of public policy, to conserve social and civic liberty
(45) by denying to an immoral and dangerous traffic the right of public sale.

39. Which of the following does the author use as a synonym for "the majority"?

(A) the Right

(B) the God-fearing populace

(C) Society

(D) the State

(E) Men

40. What does the author believe about "personal rights"?

(A) Personal rights must be agreed upon by society.

(B) Personal rights are confined to the privacy of the home.

(C) Personal rights are a fiction — societies have only personal privileges.

(D) Personal rights are granted by the state.

(E) Personal rights do not justify all social acts.

41. What means of argument is used in paragraph 5?

(A) a series of distinct metaphors

(B) a sustained analogy

(C) repetitious legal examples

(D) satirical pseudo-legal examples

(E) point-by-point counter-examples

42. The first sentence of the fifth paragraph (line 27) is distinct from others in the paragraph in that it

(A) distinguishes between personal rights and public acts

(B) associates liquor with putrid meat

(C) emphasizes the differences between reader and author

(D) associates the author with the Prohibition movement

(E) implicates the reader in the Prohibition movement

43. Read the following sentence from lines 18–22.

Whether a man drinks or abstains is entirely his own affair, so long as he does not poison himself, compel society to cure him, support him when he is unable to take care of himself, lock him up when he is dangerous to be at large, bury him at the public expense when he is a corpse, or interfere with the personal liberty of others when he is exercising his own.

This sentence is an example of

(A) a balanced sentence

(B) antithesis

(C) a run-on sentence

(D) parallelism

(E) faulty parallelism

44. In lines 9–10, the phrase "the serpent drink" is an allusion to

(A) the Garden of Eden story

(B) the tales about sea monsters

(C) the "bite" of hard liquor

(D) the "snakes in the grass" who sell liquor

(E) the entangling effects of alcohol addiction

45. The author uses all the following to refer to Satan EXCEPT

(A) Beelzebub

(B) a liar

(C) the devil

(D) the enemy

(E) a brewer

46. The last two paragraphs primarily contrast which of the following?

(A) abstinence and personal liberty

(B) the state and personal liberty

(C) the individual and Prohibition

(D) the individual's act and the state's act

(E) the state's authority and Prohibition

47. According to the passage, the ultimate purpose of prohibition is to

(A) conserve social and civic liberty

(B) limit hazardous personal liberties

(C) deny public sale to immoral and dangerous traffic

(D) enforce the will of God on weak men

(E) eliminate the profit from liquor consumption

48. In paragraph 1, the author implies that

(A) Satan is a lawyer

(B) Satan was correct

(C) the Eden story is historical fact

(D) the forbidden fruit is analogous to alcohol

(E) abstinence is Eden

49. In context, the word "dry" (line 25) is best interpreted as having which of the following meanings?

    (A) to be sober

    (B) to have signed a temperance pledge

    (C) to not offer alcohol

    (D) to outlaw the sale of alcohol

    (E) to thirst for alcohol

50. What does the last paragraph imply about the speaker?

    (A) His principal concern is the safety of the public.

    (B) He has a strong belief in God.

    (C) He believes laws should uphold morality.

    (D) He wants drinkers to brew their own intoxicants.

    (E) He maintains that the majority is always right.

51. With which of the following statements would the author of this passage most likely agree?

    (A) "What people do in the privacy of their own homes is their own business."

    (B) "Your liberty to swing your fist ends just where my nose begins."

    (C) "Disobedience is the true foundation of liberty. The obedient must be slaves."

    (D) "The people never give up their liberties, but under some delusion."

    (E) "The spirit of liberty is the spirit that is not too sure that it is right."

52. The tone of this passage is best described as

    (A) lyrical and sentimental

    (B) contemplative and conciliatory

    (C) stern and strident

    (D) informal and cajoling

    (E) earnest and pontificating

Section II

TIME: 2 hours
3 essay questions

Question 1

(Suggested time — 40 minutes. This question counts for one-third of the total essay section score.)

As technology has advanced, the curricula in American schools have changed. Schools increasingly use technology as a means of educating students today. Not only are schools focusing more on teaching computer skills, they also are including the use of such technology as video games, iPods, and podcasts as part of ordinary class

(5) work. Not surprisingly, school districts vary widely in their ability to provide technological aids for all students. Yet incorporating new technologies into the average classroom remains a priority for school districts across the country. What is the effect of this changing approach to education? Is it a clear improvement over traditional education, or is it merely a compromise?

(10) Carefully read the following six sources, including the introductory information for each source. Then synthesize information from at least three of the sources and incorporate it into a coherent, well-developed essay taking a clear position that defends, refutes, or qualifies the claim that schools that are embracing the new technological approach to education are effectively teaching students the skills they

(15) need in today's world.

Make sure your argument is central; use the sources to illustrate and support your reasoning. Avoid merely summarizing the sources. Indicate clearly which sources you are drawing from, whether through direct quotation, paraphrase, or summary. You may cite the sources as Source A, Source B, etc., or by using the

(20) descriptions in parentheses.

Source A (Empire High School)

Source B (U.S. Department of Education)

Source C (Cartoon)

Source D (Johnson)

Source E (Miller)

Source F (National Education Association)

Source A

"Arizona High School Chooses Laptops Over Textbooks." *VOANews.com.* Voice of America, 20 Oct. 2005. Web. 15 Oct. 2010.

The following passage is excerpted from an article about a new educational approach adopted by Empire High School in Vail, Arizona.

A new high school opened in Vail, Arizona, this past July with all the resources you would expect to find in classrooms these days — except textbooks. Instead, every student received an Apple laptop computer . . . making Empire High School a pioneer in the growing use of technology in American education.

. . . a committee visited classrooms that were making partial use of laptops, and came away with two distinct impressions. "One was that students in schools where laptops were being used were clearly more engaged," Mr. Baker says. "And the other impression was that we felt we could do more with laptops. Because we had the opportunity here of opening a new school, we could make them an integral part of what we do, and actually change the way we do things. And we sort of forced that issue by not buying any textbooks."

Teachers helped plan the school's wireless curriculum, often experimenting with different ideas in classrooms where they taught before. . . .

Michael Frank teaches a first-year biology course, where students use their laptops to access instructions for their lab work, organize data, and graph the results. . . . "[Students] will be putting together all the results from this experiment in a Power Point presentation for the class later. . . . And I know I can just give them an address for a website that has information and they can go look at it there. A lot of times with science, we use it because you can get immediate access to the most recent information. You don't have to wait 5 or 6 years for it to get into a textbook. So there's much more access to just a huge amount of data about things."

. . . There was a surprise once classes got under way as well. . . . "We thought the kids would be better at computing than they actually are. Being able to drive your X-box or your iPod is not the same thing as being able to take a computer, use it, create a document, save it with a file name, put it in a particular location and retrieve it. And that has been a real challenge."

But administrators say the system is working well overall, and students seem to agree. . . .

Calvin Baker also stresses that he is not trying to make Empire High a technology school. And he says quality education still has to be about things like hard work, self-discipline and outstanding teaching — with laptops becoming a natural part of the classroom, just as they have become a natural part of workplaces across America.

Source B

"Archived: Educational Technology Fact Sheet." *Ed.Gov.* U.S. Department of Education, 29 Mar. 2006. Web. 15 Oct. 2010.

The following information is excerpted from the Department of Education's "Educational Fact Sheet" regarding the availability of technology to students in the United States. Today's technology allows distance learning courses; in these courses, students work on their own from home or another off-site location, communicating with teachers and other students by using such technology as e-mail, video-conferencing, and instant messaging.

Statistics:

- In 2003, the ratio of students to computers in all public schools was 4.4 to 1.

- 48 states included technology standards for students in 2004–2005.

- In 2003, 8 percent of public schools lent laptop computers to students. . . .

- Schools in rural areas (12 percent) were more likely than city schools (5 percent) and urban fringe schools (7 percent) to lend laptops.

- In 2003, 10 percent of public schools provided a handheld computer to students or teachers.

- 16 states had at least one cyber-charter school operating in 2004–2005.

- 22 states had established virtual schools in 2004–2005.

- 56 percent of 2- and 4-year degree-granting institutions offer distance education courses, with 90 percent of public institutions offering distance education courses. . . .

Distance Learning

- 36% of school districts and 9% of all public schools have students enrolled in distance education courses.

- There were an estimated 328,000 enrollments in distance education courses by K-12 students during the 2001–2002 school year.

- 68% of the enrollments were in high school with an additional 29% in combined or ungraded schools.

- 45,300 enrollments in distance education were Advanced Placement or college-level courses.

- A greater proportion of rural area districts had students enrolled in distance education courses than did urban and suburban districts.

- 42% of districts that have students enrolled in distance-education courses are high poverty districts.

- When small districts offer distance learning, they are more likely to involve a greater proportion of schools.

- 80% of public school districts offering online courses said that offering courses not available at their schools is one of the most important reasons for having distance education.

- 50% of public school districts offering online courses cited distance learning as very important in making Advanced Placement or college-level courses available to all students.

- 92% of districts enrolled in online distance education courses had students access online courses from school.

- 24% of districts with students accessing online courses from home provided or paid for a computer for all students, while an additional 8% did so for some students.

Friendship Through Education

- Using the Internet to connect students in the U.S. and Arab nations to develop mutual understandings of one another's cultures.

Source C

Rosandich, Dan. "EDUCATION CARTOONS." *Danscartoons.com*. Web. 16 Oct. 2010. *(Reprinted with permission.)*

"What a school day! The computers broke down and we had to LISTEN!"

> ## Source D
>
> Johnson, Doug. "School Media Services for the "Net Generation" Part One." *Doug Johnson Website*. 1 Jan. 2007. Web. 15 Oct. 2010.

This passage is excerpted from an article by Doug Johnson who has been director of media and technology for the Mankato (Minnesota) Public Schools since 1991.

. . . kids expect fast communication responses, tune out when things aren't interesting, and may be more visually than verbally literate. For them, technology is a tool for learning on any topic they choose. (Are you reading anything you don't already know from the media or from personal observation?)

. . . Our current crop of students believes "teachers are vital," "computers can't replace humans," and motivation is critical in learning. They like group activities, believing building social skills is a part of schooling. They identify with their parents' values. And they are achievement oriented, feeling it is "cool to be smart." And although they are fascinated with new technologies, their knowledge of them is often "shallow."

(Who actually maintains the computers in your home or school?)

Finally, the studies point to how this generation learns — or likes to learn. Our current crop of students with their hypertext minds like inductive discovery rather than being told what they should know. In other words, they want to learn by doing rather than simply listening or reading. They enjoy working in teams, on "things that matter," often informally, and not just during school hours. And given their quick response requirements, they need to be encouraged to reflect.

It is my firm belief that schools will be more productive if educators acknowledge the unique attributes and preferences of the Net Generation and adapt educational environments to suit students instead of trying to change their basic natures. So what are some implications for NG (Net Generation) library media centers?

To a large degree, media centers may be the most NG-oriented places in schools. . . . Given their preference to work in groups, the NG media center should provide spaces for collaboration on school projects and socialization. It should contain the tools necessary for the production of information, not just its consumption — computers with the processing power and software to edit digital movies and photographs, scanners, and high-quality printers and projection devices — and, of course, assistance in the use of these tools.

. . . It should have comfy chairs, and be a friendly atmosphere, low-stress, safe, and forgiving — and yes, in high schools, an in-house coffee shop. Spaces for story times, puppetry, plays, and games along with computer stations with age-appropriate software and Web sites are just as important in elementary schools. If the "room" is not a wonderful place to be, students and teachers will stay on the Internet or in the classroom. Period. (And given the rise in online schools, is there a lesson here for classrooms as well?)

Source E

Miller, Ed, and Joan Almon. "Child Advocates Challenge Current Ed Tech Standards" (press release). Alliance for Childhood. 30 Sept. 2004. Retrieved 21 Jan. 2011 at *http://drupal6.allianceforchildhood.org*. Reprinted by permission.

The following passage has been excerpted from a press release from the Alliance for Childhood, a non-profit organization concerned with healthy child development.

The high-tech, screen-centered life style of today's children — at home and at school — is a health hazard and the polar opposite of the education they need to take part in making ethical choices in a high-tech democracy, according to a new report released today by the Alliance for Childhood.

Tech Tonic: Towards a New Literacy of Technology challenges education standards and industry assertions that all teachers and children, from preschool up, should use computers in the classroom to develop technology literacy. That expensive agenda ignores evidence that high-tech classrooms have done little if anything to improve student achievement, the report says.

The report strongly criticizes the extensive financial and political connections between education officials and school technology vendors. It urges citizens to wake up to the increasing influence of corporations in policymaking for public education.

"The lack of evidence or an expert consensus that computers will improve student achievement — despite years of efforts by high-tech companies and government agencies to demonstrate otherwise — is itself compelling evidence of the need for change," *Tech Tonic* states. "It's time to scrap...national, state, and local policies that require all students and all teachers to use computers in every grade, and that eliminate even the possibility of alternatives."

At the same time, the Alliance suggests, high-tech childhood is making children sick — promoting a sedentary life at a time when childhood obesity is at epidemic levels

Today's children will inherit social and ecological crises that involve tough moral choices and awesome technological power, *Tech Tonic* warns. To confront problems like the proliferation of devastating weapons and global warming, children will need all the "wisdom, compassion, courage, and creative energy" they can muster, it adds. Blind faith in technology will not suffice.

"A new approach to technology literacy, calibrated for the 21st century, requires us to help children develop the habits of mind, heart, and action that can, over time, mature into the adult capacities for moral reflection, ethical restraint, and compassionate service," the report states.

The Alliance for Childhood is a nonprofit partnership of educators, researchers, health professionals, and other advocates for children, based in Maryland. *Tech Tonic* is a follow-up to the Alliance's widely noted 2000 report *Fool's Gold*. In *Tech Tonic* the Alliance proposes a new definition of technology literacy as "the mature capacity to participate creatively, critically, and responsibly in making technological choices that serve democracy, ecological sustainability, and a just society."

Tech Tonic proposes seven reforms in education and family life. These will free children from a passive attachment to screen-based entertainment and teach them about their "technological heritage" in a new way, rooted in the study and practice of technology "as social ethics in action" and in a renewed respect for nature.

The seven reforms:

- Make human relationships and a commitment to strong communities a top priority at home and school.

- Color childhood green to refocus education on children's relationships with the rest of the living world.

- Foster creativity every day, with time for the arts and play.

- Put community-based research and action at the heart of the science and technology curriculum.

- Declare one day a week an electronic entertainment-free zone.

- End marketing aimed at children.

- Shift spending from unproven high-tech products in the classroom to children's unmet basic needs.

"To expect our teachers, our schools, and our nation to strive to educate all of our children, leaving none behind, is a worthy goal," *Tech Tonic* says. "To insist that they must at the same time spend huge amounts of money and time trying to integrate unproven classroom technologies into their teaching, across the curriculum with preschoolers on up, is an unwise and costly diversion from that goal. It comes at the expense of our neediest children and schools, for whom the goal is most distant."

The report proposes 10 guiding principles for the new technology literacy and offers examples of each. It also includes suggestions for educators, parents, and other citizens to develop their own technology literacy, with a similar emphasis on social ethics in action.

"Today's children will face complex and daunting choices, in a future of biotechnology, robotics, and microchips, for which we are doing very little to prepare them," says Joan Almon, head of the Alliance. "We immerse them in a virtual, high-tech world and expect them to navigate the information superhighway with little guidance and few boundaries. It is time for a new definition of technology literacy that supports educational and family habits that are healthy both for children and for the survival of the Earth."

"It is within the context of relationships that children learn best," adds Dr. Marilyn Benoit, past president of the American Academy of Child and Adolescent Psychiatry and vice president of the Alliance Board of Trustees. "As we shift more towards the impersonal use of high technology as a major tool for teaching young children, we will lose that critical context of interactive relationship that so reinforces early learning."

Source F

"NEA's policy recommendations" from "Technology in Schools: The Ongoing Challenge of Access, Adequacy and Equity," An NEA policy brief, 2008, http://www.nea.org.

The following information is excerpted from a policy brief released by the National Education Association.

1. **Improve access to technology**

    Educators have been remarkably creative with limited computer access, but if technology is to be integrated into instruction, more computers must be made available for students' use, whether that is through stand-alone computers or portable and wireless technologies. States and school districts should pay more attention to building wireless infrastructures that can support increased access to technology.

2. **Increase Internet access, address software issues, and expand technical support**

    Programs designed to close the achievement gaps must begin addressing equity issues related to Internet access, software, and technical support. Educators across the board should have greater access to computer software for planning and instruction. Educators in urban schools, in particular, need better instructional software, and more instructional staff should be involved in making decisions about software purchases for their schools. Educators in elementary schools should have more age-appropriate software for students, but, just as importantly, they need more high-speed Internet services.

    Maintenance support for computers must be adequate to ensure that computers function properly and reliably. Quality technical support for computers and other technologies should be available in every school. Particular attention should be given to senior high schools, as well as to schools located in urban areas, where maintenance and technical support are less likely to be provided. One option is for districts or schools to make use of their students' technical expertise by formally arranging for qualified students to provide technical assistance where needed. Another important point is separating the instructional support role of paraprofessionals from that of providing maintenance and technical support.

3. **Expand professional development in technology**

    Technology training, most commonly offered for administration, communications, and research, should focus more on applications for instruction. And those entering the profession, as well as experienced educators, should have access to high-quality professional development in technology. Particular attention should be paid to training opportunities provided for educators working in schools located in urban and rural areas, where educators believe the technology training in their schools has not been adequate.

4. Capitalize on teachers' and students' enthusiasm about technology

Schools should seek more ways to use technology for the greatest gain in student achievement, particularly in urban and rural/small-town schools. State and district leaders should encourage schools to use technology in more creative ways by permitting more flexibility in instruction and by providing incentives that support technology-enriched programs. More ways should be found to motivate the most experienced educators to use technology through better training and more curriculum-related opportunities.

5. Involve educators as advocates

Teacher organizations, such as NEA and its state affiliates, can be a valuable ally in the goal of fully integrating technology into education. State and local Associations can also help educate parents and the business community about the benefits of better integrating technology into teaching and learning. They can actively support district and state efforts to secure more funding for school technology by lobbying stage legislatures, establishing partnerships with commercial and private enterprises, and seeking federal and private grants.

Question 2

(Suggested time — 40 minutes. This question counts for one-third of the total essay section score.)

The passage below is an excerpt from Pauline Kael's 1967 essay "Movies on Television." The essay examines how old movies, "the worst with the mediocre and the best," found a new life on television. Read the passage carefully. Then write an essay in which you analyze how Kael crafts the text to express her view of popular culture and its ironies. Support your analysis with specific references to the text.

So much of what formed our tastes and shaped our experiences, and so much of the garbage of our youth that we never thought we'd see again — preserved and exposed to eyes and minds that might well want not to believe that this was an important part of our past. Now these movies are there for new generations, to
(5) whom they cannot possibly have the same impact or meaning, because they are all jumbled together, out of historical sequence. Even what may deserve an honorable position in movie history is somehow dishonored by being so available, so meaninglessly present. Everything is in hopeless disorder, and that is the way new generations experience our movie past. In the other arts, something like natural selection
(10) takes place: only the best or the most significant or influential or successful works compete for our attention. Moreover, those from the past are likely to be touched up to accord with the taste of the present. . . . By contrast, movies, through the accidents of commerce, are sold in blocks or packages to television, the worst with the mediocre and the best, the successes with the failures, the forgotten with the
(15) half forgotten, the ones so dreary you don't know whether you ever saw them or just others like them with some so famous you can't be sure whether you actually saw them or only imagined what they were like. A lot of this stuff never really made it with any audience; it played in small towns or it was used to soak up the time just the way TV in bars does.

(20) There are so many things that we, having lived through them, or passed over them, never want to think about again. But in movies nothing is cleaned away, sorted out, purposefully discarded. . . . There's a kind of hopelessness about it: what does not deserve to last lasts, and so it all begins to seem one big pile of junk, and some people say, "Movies never really were any good — except maybe the Bogarts."[1]
(25) If the same thing had happened in literature or music or painting — if we were constantly surrounded by the piled-up inventory of the past — it's conceivable that modern man's notions of culture and civilization would be very different. Movies, most of them produced as fodder to satisfy the appetite for pleasure and relaxation, turned out to have magical properties — indeed, to be magical properties. This
(30) fodder can be fed to people over and over again. Yet, not altogether strangely, as the

---

[1] Kael is referring to old movies starring Humphrey Bogart, such as *The Maltese Falcon* (1941) and *Casablanca* (1942).

years wear on it doesn't please their palates, though many will go on swallowing it, just because nothing tastier is easily accessible. Watching old movies is like spending an evening with those people next door. They bore us, and we wouldn't go out of our way to see them; we drop in on them because they're so close. If it took some effort

(35) to see old movies, we might try to find out which were the good ones, and if people saw only the good ones maybe they would still respect old movies. As it is, people sit and watch movies that audiences walked out on thirty years ago. Like Lot's wife, we are tempted to take another look, attracted not by evil but by something that seems much more shameful — our own innocence. We don't try to reread the girls' and

(40) boys' "series" books of our adolescence — the very look of them is dismaying. The textbooks we studied in grammar school are probably more "dated" than the movies we saw then, but we never look at the old schoolbooks, whereas we keep seeing on TV the movies that represent the same stage in our lives and played much the same part in them — as things we learned from and, in spite of, went beyond.

Question 3

(Suggested time — 40 minutes. This question counts for one-third of the total essay section score.)

Consider the distinct perspectives expressed in the following statements.

Advice is seldom welcome; and those who want it the most always like it the least.

Philip Dormer Stanhope, Earl of Chesterfield (1694–1773)

I have lived some thirty years on this planet, and I have yet to hear the first syllable of valuable or even earnest advice from my seniors.

Henry David Thoreau (1817–1862)

In a well-organized essay, take a position on the importance of advice, using the above quotes as a starting point. Support your argument with appropriate examples.

Answer Key

Section I

1. (C)	18. (E)	35. (A)
2. (B)	19. (A)	36. (C)
3. (E)	20. (D)	37. (A)
4. (B)	21. (C)	38. (C)
5. (E)	22. (B)	39. (D)
6. (C)	23. (D)	40. (E)
7. (E)	24. (D)	41. (C)
8. (D)	25. (B)	42. (B)
9. (A)	26. (A)	43. (E)
10. (E)	27. (C)	44. (A)
11. (C)	28. (E)	45. (B)
12. (D)	29. (E)	46. (D)
13. (A)	30. (D)	47. (A)
14. (C)	31. (B)	48. (D)
15. (B)	32. (A)	49. (D)
16. (E)	33. (D)	50. (C)
17. (C)	34. (C)	51. (B)
		52. (E)

```
┌─────────────────────────────────────────────────────┐
│                                                       │
│         Detailed Explanations of Answers              │
│                                                       │
└─────────────────────────────────────────────────────┘
```

Section I

1. **(C)**

    The sentence is an example of a balanced sentence, in which both halves of the sentence are of about the same length and importance. Jourdan Anderson uses this structure to explain in well-reasoned language why he cannot believe in his old master. The sentence does not juxtapose contradictory terms (A). Since it is a complete sentence, it is not a subordinate clause (B). It is not a metaphor (D), nor does it balance two opposite words or phrases (E).

2. **(B)**

    The letter says that the "girls were brought to shame by the violence and wickedness of their young masters," inferring that Colonel Anderson's young sons took advantage of Jourdan Anderson's daughters. This interpretation is made even more likely because Jourdan states that he would rather die than have something happen to his other children. It is not clear if the girls survived the attacks, so (D) is not correct. Answers (A), (C), and (E) are not supported by the text.

3. **(E)**

    Jourdan Anderson does not use apostrophe by addressing an inanimate object or one that is considered dead in his letter to Colonel Anderson. Answer (E) is correct. Answer (A) is not correct; throughout the letter, he is very sarcastic and uses a delightful educated irony that may trick the reader into thinking otherwise. Anderson tells anecdotes to prove why he was a good worker for Colonel Anderson, so (B) is not correct. As pointed out here, he uses sarcasm, a heavy form of irony, throughout the letter, so (C) is not correct. Also, Jourdan Anderson uses facts or logos to demonstrate a type of ironic good will for his old employer; therefore, (D) is not correct as well.

4. **(B)**

    The sentence is an example of understatement because Anderson says he has often "felt uneasy" about the Colonel, instead of expressing his more obvious hatred and horror toward a man who enslaved him and tried to kill him. Answer (B) is correct. The sentence is not comparing two unlike things without using comparison words so it is not a metaphor (A). The reader does not feel ethically compelled to do anything, so (C) is incorrect. The sentence is the opposite of hyperbole, so answer (D) is not correct. Answer (E) is not correct because the sentence, while in a sense shying away from the truth, is not intended as a more delicate way of saying something.

5. (E)

To be condescending is to patronize someone or assume an air of superiority, while a sardonic attitude is derisively mocking. These describe Jourdan Anderson's attitude toward his old master, although he is so polite and seemingly respectful that the careless reader may miss his true meaning. Answer choice (E) is correct. Jourdan is certainly not reverential and laudatory (A) toward the man who mistreated him and his family so horribly. Jourdan is not pedantic in his language and he is not teaching anything directly, so (B) is not correct. He is being ironic, not candid, and his style is more formal than colloquial, so (C) is incorrect. He is not arrogant and moralistic (D), but rather calmly confident in his new life and position.

6. (C)

It is obvious that Jourdan includes this detail in his letter to convey that his wife is now respected by her employers. The other answer choices are not supported by the information in the letter.

7. (E)

Jourdan wants his former master to see how ridiculous is the idea that Jourdan would ever return to work for him. He uses irony to make this point throughout the letter. Answer (E) is correct. Jourdan has no intention of working for his old master again (A) or forgiving him and making amends (B). He is only mockingly suggesting that he should collect past wages (C) or get any sort of restitution for past wrongs (D).

8. (D)

Colonel Anderson certainly did not offer to pay Jourdan for his work in the past. Jourdan's letter reads as though the Colonel must pay, but of course this is Jourdan's playful conceit. All the other answers are in fact true or likely inferences.

9. (A)

The words "the Good Maker" and "day of reckoning" make it clear that this is a biblical allusion to the deity and to the Christian idea of Judgment Day. Answer (A) is correct. There are not two opposing viewpoints to create an antithesis (B), and this is not a brief story, or anecdote (C). There is no personification (D) used. The passage does not feature a hypothetical example (E).

10. (E)

The author wants to show unmistakably the distrust and contempt that he feels for his old master. The correct answer is (E). The rest of the answers are incorrect assertions that do not apply.

11. (C)

The author suggests that "injustice is part of the necessary friction" of government, implying that government does not react to the injustices it encounters. This gives the impression of a lack of awareness and concern. The idea that your life should "be a counter-friction to stop the machine" implies that the machine cannot be diverted, that it is going about its purpose and can only be sabotaged. For these reasons, the correct answer is (C). The passage says nothing favorable about the "machine," so answers (A) and (E) are incorrect. Nowhere does the author complain literally about machines, so (B) is not correct. Answer (D) is incorrect because the author is not optimistic about the machine being "reparable."

12. (D)

A quick scan of these questions will tell you that these are not "topics to be covered in the essay," so (A) is incorrect. Also, one will note that these are the legitimate concerns of the author, so (C) is incorrect. At no point in the essay does the author antagonize his reading audience, so (E) is incorrect. The idea of (B), that the author "expects…the reasons," seems possible at first with the beginning questions, but the last question, "Why does it always crucify Christ,…pronounce Washington and Franklin rebels?" obviously is accosting different governments of different centuries. These questions of the author are rhetorical questions — they have no addressee and expect no answers. The author is criticizing the government for its actions and inactions. Answer (D) is correct.

13. (A)

As shown in lines 20–21, "Under a government which imprisons any unjustly, the true place for a just man is also a prison," the author seeks to arouse the reader's moral responsibility. Answer (A) is correct. The speaker would obviously prefer a simple tax revolt, so (B) is incorrect. And the idea of a tax revolt is a means, not an end, so reducing the tax burden (E) is also incorrect. He would certainly not "attract persecuted minorities to Massachusetts" (C), nor is he promoting a political party (D).

14. (C)

The passage suggests that men not pay their taxes, which is "a proposal of peaceful protest" (A). The passage refers to the governments of Christ, Copernicus, and Washington, which are "historical references to other governments" (B). The passage states, "But even suppose blood should flow. Is there not a sort of bloodshed when the conscience is wounded?" or "justification for bloodshed" (D). The passage opens with a series of rhetorical questions, which are "unanswered questions" (E). By elimination, the answer is "criticism of specific persons" (C), which never occurs in the passage.

15. (B)

The passage reads "…in her prisons…It is there that…," so the correct answer is (B) "prison." The same paragraph refers to "Massachusetts, (A)" but at best you would have to say "Massachusetts prisons" to capture the same meaning. Neither "legislative building," (C) "church," (D) nor "the grave" (E) occurs in the paragraph and thus cannot be potential antecedents.

16. (E)

The lines being paraphrased are "A minority is powerless while it conforms to the majority; it is not even a minority then; but it is irresistible when it clogs by its whole weight" (A). "A minority…so it can disable the majority" is an inaccurate paraphrase because the minority should clog the "machine" of government, not assault the majority. "A minority is an important part of the majority…" (B) is obviously wrong. The minority is an important part of the people, but, by definition, not any part of the majority. "A majority exists…" (C) is incorrect because it transposes "minority" and "majority." "A minority…brings injustice upon itself" (D) is incorrect because lines 32–34 say nothing of the kind. The answer is "A minority that complies to the will of the majority ceases to exist, but a minority that fully commits itself to impeding the unjust action of the majority is unconquerable" (E), because it accurately hits all the points of the original.

17. (C)

The author says to the tax-gatherer "if you really wish to do anything, resign your office," which is (C), "quit his job." The author never suggests "steal the state's funds" (A) or "submit counterfeit money" (B). Nor does the author threaten the officer, as the phrases "expect gunshots for greetings" (D) and "be cautious of a surprise attack" (E) suggest.

18. (E)

Lines 5–6 contain the antecedent "government": "But it is the fault of the government itself that the remedy is worse than the evil." The author uses the pronouns *it* and *its* in his accusatory questions about government's role and responsibilities. The correct answer is (E).

19. **(A)**

The question asks to contrast "What I have to do is to see, at any rate, that I do not lend myself to the wrong which I condemn" with "Under a government which imprisons any unjustly, the true place for a just man is also a prison." "...only react to what he sees..." (B) takes "to see" from the original in the too literal sense of vision when the author meant "to see" as in "to make sure." Similarly, "...neither borrower nor lender be..." (C) takes "lend" too literally when the author used "lend myself" to mean "aid." "...it is enough to condemn justice..." (D) is incorrect because, in the original, the author insists that beyond condemning injustice, he must not assist its function. "... advise a man to circumvent the wrongs of his state..." (E) is incorrect because the author nowhere advises avoidance of problems — he always advises protesting to them, whether by strike or opposition. "In lines 18–19, the author is content not to participate in injustice; but in lines 20–21, the existence of an injustice compels the author to give up his freedom in protest." (A) accurately paraphrases the conflict of the original lines.

20. **(D)**

The entire sentence referred to in this question is "Cast your whole vote, not a strip of paper merely, but your whole influence." The key word is "influence," which helps to identify (D), "do everything you can to influence lawmaking" as the correct answer. "Vote in every election..." (A) does not convey the "whole influence" of a person, and neither does (B), "vote...across the board," or (E), "vote...your conscience." "Run for office" (C) suggests one's whole influence is given, but nowhere does the passage imply that the author is suggesting everyone run for office.

21. **(C)**

While "the author has been unjustly imprisoned" (A) or "the author has a loved one...imprisoned" (B) are conceivable, they are not inferred by lines 21–24. Nowhere is it suggested that "Massachusetts' prisons are overcrowded" (D). When the passage says the state "put out and locked out" some citizens, it is metaphorically referring to imprisonment (note line 22 "in her prisons"), not the banishment suggested by (E), "... banished citizens..." While one may argue that imprisonment is a form of banishment, the correct answer must reflect most precisely what the passage's lines imply. These lines say the principled men in Massachusetts should be in prison; thus, the answer is (C), "the author is either in prison or not in Massachusetts."

22. **(B)**

The author alludes to these historical figures for their roles as iconoclasts, or rebels, that governments felt the need to punish or banish. The author even writes "pronounce Washington and Franklin rebels." The names alluded to are not all religious (A) or political

(C). The historical figures were not persecuted mainly for their genius (D) or their leadership skills (E).

23. (D)

Because the questions of the opening paragraph are never answered, "question, answer, enact" (A) is incorrect. Because the opening paragraph does not intend to address the government, it cannot be said to prod anyone or anything into action; so "goad, insult, attack" (B) is incorrect. Similarly, (C), "taunt, imply, condemn," is incorrect because the government must be addressed to be taunted. "Argue, reason, propose" (E) is a reasonable answer; but (D) is better and correct because the opening of the passage is best described as criticizing. Also, the passage does more than merely "suggest" and "propose." It follows through to "inspire" action.

24. (D)

The author's overall tone is "prodding" in its attempt to awaken the conscience of citizens and inspire them to oppose unjust government. It is also "impassioned" in its fervor, as in the fiery rhetorical questions at the beginning of the passage. Answer (D) is correct. The author's tone is not one of hopelessness, but it certainly is not blandly "hopeful and uplifting" (A). While he is "acerbic" in places, he does not display overt cynicism (B). He can be "dismissive" of government's crimes, but his tone is not one of superiority (C). He is anything but cautious in his approach, so (E) is incorrect.

25. (B)

The fact that both sources are cited tells the reader that this quote appears in both sources. One source is by Dobzhansky and one is by Mayr; each has the words "the origin of species" in the title. Therefore, (B) is the correct answer. The passage specifically says "together with Dobzhansky, Mayr developed this definition"; it does not say that the definition is (A) Mayr's or (D) Dobzhansky's own creation. And although it does say that the two men developed the definition together, nowhere does it say that (C) Mayr needed Dobzhansky's help. The question specifically asks about the purpose of footnotes 1 and 2. These footnotes have nothing to do with the fact that "students of biology . . . memorized Mayr's definition of species for more than half a century," which appears at the end of the paragraph; therefore, (E) is incorrect.

26. (A)

The word alludes to the Biblical character Methuselah, who (as the author states later in the passage) is purported to have lived 969 years. Answer (A) is correct. The word is more of an exaggeration than an understatement (B). There is no satirical intention (C), metaphor (D), or personification (E).

27. (C)

    With its academic language about evolutionary biology, the article seems written to appeal to a scholarly audience. Answer choice (C) is correct. It is too technical in its details to appeal to general readers (A). It would be impractical to write a journal article only for Mayr's acquaintances (B) or Harvard colleagues (D). While the article contains much technical language, it also contains more general information ("Students of biology all over the world have memorized Mayr's definition of species for more than half a century"), so it seems unlikely to have been written strictly for specialists such as "geneticists" (E).

28. (E)

    "Passed away" is an example of a euphemism, or a pleasant or sanitized expression used to describe something unpleasant or negative — i.e., death. The correct answer is (E).

29. (E)

    This question requires a close reading of the sentence in lines 28–30. To simplify it: The separation of populations prohibits gene flow between *the populations*. One way to determine the correct answer is to replace the pronoun "them" with each of the answers to see which one makes sense. Answer (E) is correct.

30. (D)

    Lines 35–36 refers to "the 797 pages of *Animal Species and Evolution*" and footnote 3 lists the publisher of the book as Belknap Press, so (D) is correct. The "797" reference is to total pages in the book, not a specific page, so (A) and (B) are incorrect. The phrase "outlined in depth" means described thoroughly, not literally written as an outline, so (C) is incorrect. (E) does not fit the passage or the footnote.

31. (B)

    The first paragraph states that "Ernst Mayr has been called 'Darwin's apostle' or the 'Darwin of the 20th century' " because of his work in evolutionary biology. But Mayr is not compared to Dobzhansky, who he worked with to develop his definition of species. Nor is he compared to Wilson and Gould, who are mentioned as his colleagues at Harvard. Answer (B) is correct.

32. (A)

    The sentence that starts with line 8 offers the general idea that "Mayr had many fundamental insights into evolutionary biology." The next sentence becomes a little more specific, presenting "his most widely known contribution." The next sentence is more specific still, explaining the particular "notion" mentioned in the preceding statement. Therefore, the structure is clearly moving from a general idea to more specific information about it. The correct answer is (A).

33. **(D)**

Three of the sources cited in the footnotes are by Mayr. The earliest was published in 1942, and the latest was published in 2004—a span of 62 years. So without any information other than these three footnotes, it is reasonable to assume that Mayr's writing career lasted at least sixty years. Answer (D) is correct. Only the first footnote cites a work by Dobzhansky, and nothing implies that this work discussed Mayr's life. Likewise, the second and third footnotes do not cite works that appear to be about Mayr's life; thus, (A) is not a reasonable choice. A look at the footnotes tells us only that Dobzhansky wrote one book — not how long his writing career was; so (B) is incorrect. And although footnote 1 tells us that Dobzhansky wrote about the origin of the species, just as Mayr did, it does not tell us whether or not (C) he relied on Mayr's works. Footnote 4 reveals that Mayr wrote at least one article about himself, but we have no way of knowing if (E) is true.

34. **(C)**

The passage is eulogistic (C), praising an accomplished man who has recently died. It is not merely expository (A). It is not really analytical (A), since it only skims over the details of Mayr's career. It is not investigative (D), since it does not seek to uncover or reveal new information. And it is not persuasive (E), since it does not try to convince the reader of any position.

35. **(A)**

The passage quotes Mayr as referring to evolutionary biology as "an endless frontier" with "still plenty to be discovered," implying that he believed that evolutionary biologists would continue making new discoveries. Therefore, answer (B) is correct. (A) and (E) are not correct; note that the question focuses specifically on Mayr's comments quoted in lines 40–42. Although Mayr may have believed evolutionary biology had unveiled many intriguing mysteries, nothing in the quote indicated this belief; thus, (A) is incorrect. Likewise, although Mayr did make tremendous contributions to the field of evolutionary biology, nothing in lines 40–42 relates to that fact; thus, (E) is not the correct choice. Mayr was 100 years old when he made these comments. And although Mayr expressed his regret that he would not be present to enjoy the future accomplishments of active evolutionists, nothing in his statement implies that he was worried that he would die soon (D).

36. (C)

The excerpt contains scientific jargon, or specialized technical language, such as "biogeographic distributions of bird species," and "variation in morphology." It also contains an appositive, in which a noun or noun phrase is used to rename another noun nearby. The noun phrase "cornerstones for those studying speciation today" renames the nearby noun "concepts." There is no analogy in the excerpt, so I and II are the correct examples. Answer (C) is correct.

37. (A)

The "heated" debates concerned ideas about the origin of species, so they were conducted among scientists, probably in the pages of journals like *Science*. Therefore, "heated" here means *intense* rather than "disruptive (B), violent (C), or wreckless (D). The correct answer is (A). There is no mention of whether the debates were "magnified" in some way, so (E) is not correct.

38. (C)

References to Mayr as "the greatest evolutionary biologist of the 20th century," "greatest biologist overall," "Darwin's apostle," and "Darwin of the 20th century" all convey the author's admiration, as does the comment that "he accomplished much more than one might expect to get done, even in 100 years." The correct answer is (C).

39. (D)

In lines 43-45, the passage says, "Prohibition is the act of the community, the State, the majority, which is the State...." Thus the correct answer is (D). The passage does not use the words "the right" (A) or "the God-fearing populace" (B). "[S]ociety" (C) is never used as a synonym for the majority. While the passage tends toward gender bias, the author does not go so far as to equate the majority with "men" (E).

40. (E)

The author never goes so far as to question the provenance, existence, or legitimacy of personal rights. He simply asserts that personal rights do not justify any and all social acts, such as the sale of rotting meat. Answer (E) is correct.

41. (C)

Paragraph 5 uses examples, not metaphors or an analogy, eliminating (A) and (B). The examples are in earnest, not "satirical" (D). However, they are not "point by point counter-examples" (E). The examples in paragraph 5, while numerous, make the same point repeatedly. They are "repetitious legal examples." Answer (C) is correct.

42. (B)

The sentence at the beginning of paragraph 5 is unlike the others in the paragraph because it tries to associate the idea of liquor (the overall topic) with putrid meat. Answer (B) is correct. The sentence is like the others, not different from them, in its distinction between personal rights and public acts (A). The author does not emphasize the difference between himself and the reader (C) nor does he implicate the reader in Prohibition (E). His use of "you" and "I" are examples, not distinctions of roles. The sentence also does less to associate the author with Prohibition than many other sentences in the passage, so (D) is incorrect.

43. (E)

The sentence is an attempt to use parallel construction, in which parallel grammatical elements appear close together or in a series. The parallel elements are the verbs *poison, compel, support,* etc. However, the parallelism is faulty because the subject of some of the verbs is "a man" while the subject of others is "society." Answer (E) is correct.

44. (A)

The author is alluding to the serpent's temptation of Eve in the Garden of Eden. He is intimating the alcohol is similarly tempting and dangerous like the apple. He is also continuing the allusion he resorted to in the first paragraph. Answer (A) is correct.

45. (B)

The first paragraph alternately refers to Satan as "Beelzebub" (A), "the devil" (C) and "a brewer" (E). Paragraph 2 refers to those against prohibition as (D), "the enemy," but there is a secondary meaning implying that "the enemy" is Satan and that he is also against prohibition. The correct answer is (B), "a liar," which occurs in the first paragraph but is Satan's reference to God.

46. (D)

The contrast is drawn in each paragraph between the act of the individual and the act of the state. From the sixth paragraph: "The one (i.e., total abstinence) is the act of the individual; the other (i.e., prohibition) is the act of the State." From the last paragraph: "Total abstinence is the voluntary act of one man . . . Prohibition is the act of the community, the State . . ." The correct answer is (D).

47. (A)

The purpose of prohibition, at least according to the passage and as stated in line 44, is to "conserve social and civic liberty." Answer (A) is correct. The passage never claims that the law should or does "limit hazardous personal liberties," so (B) is incorrect. While allowing people to drink, but not allowing the sale of liquor, may seem to intend (E), the passage never makes that contention. Nor does the passage overtly make the claim in (D), that prohibition "enforce(s) the will of God on weak men." The passage does claim that prohibition "den[ies] public sale to immoral and dangerous traffic," but this statement (C) is a definition, not its purpose.

48. (D)

In the first paragraph, the author definitely implies that "the forbidden fruit is analogous to alcohol," that drinking alcohol is another Fall, when he refers to the devil as "a brewer" (line 4). Answer (D) is correct. While the author describes Satan as advising the first man about his "rights," he never implies that "Satan is a lawyer" (A). The concessions of later paragraphs may suggest (B), but the first paragraph does not. The author uses the Eden story as a form of truth without necessarily implying that "the Eden story is historic fact" (C). While it emphasizes that the Fall was connected to eating and drinking whatever was desired, paragraph 1 falls short of implying that paradise can be regained by avoiding alcohol, that "abstinence is Eden" (E).

49. (D)

Lines 25–26 state, "when he votes dry — to prohibit liquor traffic." The correct answer is (D), "to outlaw the sale of alcohol." The passage does not define *dry* as "…sober" (A) or as "to thirst for alcohol" (E). The passage specifically distinguishes between "[having] signed a temperance pledge" (B) and "dry" in paragraph 4. Also, the passage never mentions "to not offer alcohol" (C).

50. (C)

Line 45 refers to "an immoral and dangerous traffic," which implies that the immorality of the product is a reason to restrain it from public sale. The correct answer is (C). The author's belief or disbelief in God is not referred to in the closing lines of the passage, eliminating (B), "He has a strong belief in God." Nowhere does the passage suggest that the author "…wants drinkers to brew their own intoxicants" (D). In the closing lines, the author uses the will of the majority to justify prohibition, but does not "…maint[ain that] the majority is always right" (E). The author expresses "…concern…[for] the safety of the public" (A), but this concern is not implied to be primary.

51. (B)

The author emphasizes his belief that "personal liberty relates to private conduct" and has its limitations when it conflicts with society as when a person "is dangerous to be at large." The author would most likely agree with (B). While (A) accords with the author's overt idea that "personal liberty is a matter of personal choice," he probably would want some restrictions on what people can actually do even in their own homes. He would not be in favor of disobedience (C). He would argue that Prohibition is *not* a delusion that makes people give up their liberties (D), but a good idea for society as a whole. His absolute certainty that he is right about Prohibition and personal liberty would make him disagree with (E).

52. **(E)**

The author is overwhelmingly earnest in his defense of Prohibition as the justified action of the community, and his tone is often "pontificating," or preachy, in his assured pronouncements of what is right and wrong and in his biblical references. Answer (E) is correct. He is not at all lyrical and sentimental (A). He is more forceful than contemplative and never conciliatory, or accommodating, in his views (B). While his style is certainly stern, it doesn't cross over to stridency, or a harsh and grating tone (C). His writing is more formal than informal, and he asserts his opinions bluntly rather than cajoling the reader (D).

Section II

Model Student Response to Essay Question 1

Technology has become an important part of our lives in today's world. One can hardly get through a day without encountering laptop computers, videogames, smartphones, iPods, iPads, and many other forms of technology. So it is not surprising that such technology should be found in our schools as they seek to prepare students for today's world. An examination of the issue of technology in education predictably reveals both benefits and drawbacks.

For all the wonders of the digital revolution, there is still more to life than tapping out a text message on a smartphone or downloading a video. Even at the college level, where students today may have the convenience of listening to a lecture on an iPod, there is still the question of how much those same students miss from not interacting face-to-face with the professor and their peers. As Miller (Source E) asserts, reforms may be needed to free children from "a passive attachment to screen-based entertainment." And although Source B may encourage friendships via the Internet, one can learn so much more with face-to-face friendships. As Source D points out, humans and social skills are important and necessary in our schools.

Clearly, technology should not replace human interaction at school or anywhere else. However, it definitely has a place in today's education. Empire High School in Arizona successfully uses computers instead of textbooks in every classroom and every subject (Source A). Because of technological advances, education is no longer physically confined to a classroom or even a building. The many students who are enrolled in distance learning courses (Source B) may complete courses without ever actually meeting their instructors or classmates.

Schools are responsible for preparing students for the world of work, and it is difficult to be a productive worker today without possessing certain technological skills. While many students are familiar with videogame technology, many do not have the skills to complete basic word processing and presentation tasks (Source A). Utilizing technology in classes other than computer labs helps students gain real-world computer skills. Also, an inviting school media center that offers adequate or better technology can encourage teamwork among students (Source D). As Source B points out, a growing number of schools provide computers to students and offer "distance learning" or online courses. Certainly that fact underscores the NEA's concerns about providing computer technology and Internet access to school districts that lack them, such as urban and rural schools (Source F). The importance of technological know-how to future success in the workplace makes learning these skills at school more important than ever.

Careful examination of the issue reveals that technology in the schools can be both detrimental and beneficial. Employing computers, iPods, tablets, and videogames as educational tools may encourage the individual to become isolated from teachers and other students. However, these devices obviously have entered the educational world and the workplace, and they are certainly not going away. So it is the responsibility of the individual — young or old — not to use technology as a substitute for interaction with teachers and peers. And it is the school's responsibility to allow time and activities to encourage students to develop imagination and creativity, to make sure students learn adequate technology skills, and to focus on enhancing students' learning experiences and preparation for work and for life in the 21st century.

Analysis of Student Response to Essay Question 1

The student's response effectively addresses the challenge of the question (taking a clear position that defends, refutes, or qualifies the claim that schools that are embracing the new technological approach to education are effectively teaching students the skills they need in today's world). The first paragraph introduces the general topic of technology in today's world, gradually narrowing to the specific idea of the essay. In this essay, the writer has chosen to present both positive and negative effects ("benefits and drawbacks") of the use of technology in schools. The writer synthesizes — combines information from chosen sources with a reasoned opinion to form a cohesive argument — rather than simply paraphrasing or quoting the sources. Each source is clearly attributed. The second paragraph focuses on the negative aspects of schools' use of technology as an educational tool, citing specific examples from the sources. For example, the writer cites the expert opinion in Source E that reforms may be needed to free children from "a passive attachment to screen-based entertainment." The next two paragraphs cite sources that support the positive aspects of technology in the classroom — for example, "an inviting school media center that offers adequate technology can encourage teamwork among students (Source D)." The writer also includes concerns from the National Education Association (Source F) "about providing computer technology and Internet access to school districts that lack them," — an important issue related to technology use in schools. The conclusion summarizes the essay's main ideas. The essay's language and development are effective, and the writer's position is supported with well-chosen examples. Overall, this is an effective response to the prompt.

Model Student Response to Essay Question 2

In the essay, Pauline Kael expresses her view that old movies, unlike most other art forms today, have not been winnowed down to a few timeless classics but instead live on perpetually on television (and now on DVD), regardless of quality. To portray this (to her) unfortunate state of affairs, she resorts to images that show just what she thinks of bad old movies.

As she puts it, "in the other arts, something like natural selection takes place," meaning that survival of the fittest keeps only the best works in the public eye. However, with television's voracious need for programming, old movies — "the successes and the failures," "the piled-up inventory of the past" — found a new audience on the small screen. The result is that "there's a kind of hopelessness about it," and the new audience sees movie history as "one big pile of junk" — a devastating metaphor. Kael makes it plain what she thinks of most of these movies, describing them as "fodder to satisfy the appetite for pleasure," or like spending an evening with "those people next door," who are boring but "we drop in on them because they're so close." Her forceful, no-nonsense style is perfect for making the point that "people sit and watch movies that audiences walked out on thirty years ago." With this, the reader understands the irony of an art form whose worst examples live on like cultural zombies.

Kael also contends that the datedness of old movies makes them difficult for a new audience to comprehend, even when they are fairly good. These movies "are there for new generations, to whom they cannot possibly have the same impact or meaning because they are all jumbled together, out of historical sequence." (Today's viewers of Turner Classic Movies can attest to this jumbled effect.)

Overall, Kael leaves the impression that old movies are like an overstocked junk shop, where "nothing is cleaned away, sorted out, purposefully discarded." She presents her passionate belief (for she seems extremely passionate about movies) that if people saw only the best old movies, they would have more respect for them. As she sadly notes toward the end of the passage, viewing most old movies is like rereading our old schoolbooks: "the very look of them is dismaying." Alluding to the biblical Lot's wife, she sees us as almost punished for looking back. Kael has effectively portrayed how a form of popular culture — and its audience — can lose its innocence.

Analysis of Student Response to Essay Question 2

The student's response is alert not only to Kael's use of a "forceful, no-nonsense style" to express her thoughts about old movies, but also identifies the overall impression that the passage leaves: "that old movies are like an overstocked junk shop." The student points out that Kael carefully uses images like "the piled-up inventory of the past" and "one big pile of junk" to portray the hopeless jumble of the movie past as it appears on television. The student points out that the latter image is "a devastating metaphor." Throughout the essay, the student chooses appropriate quotations to make a point. In the third paragraph, the student explains an idea about "the datedness of old movies" with a quote that explains how this would affect new audiences. This is followed with a parenthetical remark about Turner Classic Movies that emphasizes the point. In the final paragraph, the student summarizes the impression that Kael leaves with the reader (close to "her view of popular culture" as the prompt required) and points out (rather late) a biblical allusion. In general, the student has effectively analyzed Kael's stylish tirade about old movies that never go away.

Model Student Response to Essay Question 3

"Take my advice." You hear it from your elders from childhood on. The idea that you are in dire need of their wisdom and experience can be irritating, particularly if you are an independent, headstrong person. However, it is best to listen closely to the advice you are given. If experience is the best teacher, certainly you can learn from someone else's experience and the advice that comes out of it.

Most people like to think for themselves, make their own decisions, learn from their own mistakes. As Chesterfield asserts, "advice is seldom welcome." Young people in particular tend to believe that they know what is best for themselves, and they chafe at following the advice of some busybody or know-it-all. Yet as Chesterfield also observes, the people who need advice the most like it the least. It is precisely the headstrong, overconfident person who could use a bit of wise counsel, who blunders ahead despite what anyone advises. A moment's reflection on some helpful advice might lead that person to make a life-improving decision. In junior high, I had my heart set on making the basketball team, but my uncle suggested that my small size and agility were better suited to soccer. After some long nights of thinking (and some choice words for my uncle's unwanted advice), I finally decided to give soccer a try. The result was a fun career in a sport I still enjoy.

Thoreau's quote is the perfect encapsulation of the headstrong attitude many young people have. Thoreau claims to have never heard "the first syllable of valuable or earnest advice" from his elders. In this way, he seems to be one of the very people that Chesterfield is describing in his quote. And apparently Thoreau still held his view about advice at the relatively advanced age of thirty. Nevertheless, most young people, lacking the genius of Thoreau, could surely benefit from the advice of older, wiser people. Even Thoreau must have learned something from reading older writers or following the example of some admired person. You could say that much classical literature is a form of advice from the past, from our "seniors."

Human nature being what it is, young people will doubtless go on ignoring or despising advice from their elders. But that doesn't mean that advice isn't necessary. Like a dose of bitter medicine, a piece of helpful advice can prevent much worse consequences in the future.

Analysis of Student Response to Essay Question 3

The student's response to the prompt makes good use of the opposed quotes on advice from Chesterfield and Thoreau. First, the student sets out a viewpoint on the importance of advice in the first paragraph: "However, it is best to listen closely to the advice you are given." Next, the student organizes the second paragraph around the two parts of Chesterfield's quote — that "advice is seldom welcome" and that the people who need it the most like it the least. The student points out that helpful advice can lead to a life-changing decision for the better, and then the student offers an example from his own experience that reinforces the point. In the third paragraph, the student examines the Thoreau quote and criticizes the idea that advice from elders is not valuable. The student makes the canny point that "much classical literature is a form of advice from the past, from our 'seniors.'" In the final paragraph, the student briefly summarizes the main idea that advice can be helpful. Overall the essay is forcefully argued and well organized.

Answer Sheet

Section I

1. Ⓐ Ⓑ Ⓒ Ⓓ Ⓔ
2. Ⓐ Ⓑ Ⓒ Ⓓ Ⓔ
3. Ⓐ Ⓑ Ⓒ Ⓓ Ⓔ
4. Ⓐ Ⓑ Ⓒ Ⓓ Ⓔ
5. Ⓐ Ⓑ Ⓒ Ⓓ Ⓔ
6. Ⓐ Ⓑ Ⓒ Ⓓ Ⓔ
7. Ⓐ Ⓑ Ⓒ Ⓓ Ⓔ
8. Ⓐ Ⓑ Ⓒ Ⓓ Ⓔ
9. Ⓐ Ⓑ Ⓒ Ⓓ Ⓔ
10. Ⓐ Ⓑ Ⓒ Ⓓ Ⓔ
11. Ⓐ Ⓑ Ⓒ Ⓓ Ⓔ
12. Ⓐ Ⓑ Ⓒ Ⓓ Ⓔ
13. Ⓐ Ⓑ Ⓒ Ⓓ Ⓔ
14. Ⓐ Ⓑ Ⓒ Ⓓ Ⓔ
15. Ⓐ Ⓑ Ⓒ Ⓓ Ⓔ
16. Ⓐ Ⓑ Ⓒ Ⓓ Ⓔ
17. Ⓐ Ⓑ Ⓒ Ⓓ Ⓔ
18. Ⓐ Ⓑ Ⓒ Ⓓ Ⓔ

19. Ⓐ Ⓑ Ⓒ Ⓓ Ⓔ
20. Ⓐ Ⓑ Ⓒ Ⓓ Ⓔ
21. Ⓐ Ⓑ Ⓒ Ⓓ Ⓔ
22. Ⓐ Ⓑ Ⓒ Ⓓ Ⓔ
23. Ⓐ Ⓑ Ⓒ Ⓓ Ⓔ
24. Ⓐ Ⓑ Ⓒ Ⓓ Ⓔ
25. Ⓐ Ⓑ Ⓒ Ⓓ Ⓔ
26. Ⓐ Ⓑ Ⓒ Ⓓ Ⓔ
27. Ⓐ Ⓑ Ⓒ Ⓓ Ⓔ
28. Ⓐ Ⓑ Ⓒ Ⓓ Ⓔ
29. Ⓐ Ⓑ Ⓒ Ⓓ Ⓔ
30. Ⓐ Ⓑ Ⓒ Ⓓ Ⓔ
31. Ⓐ Ⓑ Ⓒ Ⓓ Ⓔ
32. Ⓐ Ⓑ Ⓒ Ⓓ Ⓔ
33. Ⓐ Ⓑ Ⓒ Ⓓ Ⓔ
34. Ⓐ Ⓑ Ⓒ Ⓓ Ⓔ
35. Ⓐ Ⓑ Ⓒ Ⓓ Ⓔ
36. Ⓐ Ⓑ Ⓒ Ⓓ Ⓔ

37. Ⓐ Ⓑ Ⓒ Ⓓ Ⓔ
38. Ⓐ Ⓑ Ⓒ Ⓓ Ⓔ
39. Ⓐ Ⓑ Ⓒ Ⓓ Ⓔ
40. Ⓐ Ⓑ Ⓒ Ⓓ Ⓔ
41. Ⓐ Ⓑ Ⓒ Ⓓ Ⓔ
42. Ⓐ Ⓑ Ⓒ Ⓓ Ⓔ
43. Ⓐ Ⓑ Ⓒ Ⓓ Ⓔ
44. Ⓐ Ⓑ Ⓒ Ⓓ Ⓔ
45. Ⓐ Ⓑ Ⓒ Ⓓ Ⓔ
46. Ⓐ Ⓑ Ⓒ Ⓓ Ⓔ
47. Ⓐ Ⓑ Ⓒ Ⓓ Ⓔ
48. Ⓐ Ⓑ Ⓒ Ⓓ Ⓔ
49. Ⓐ Ⓑ Ⓒ Ⓓ Ⓔ
50. Ⓐ Ⓑ Ⓒ Ⓓ Ⓔ
51. Ⓐ Ⓑ Ⓒ Ⓓ Ⓔ
52. Ⓐ Ⓑ Ⓒ Ⓓ Ⓔ

Glossary

absolute phrase A word group that modifies an entire sentence and consists of a noun plus at least one other word.

abstract language Language describing ideas and qualities rather than observable or physical things, people, or places.

academic style A style of writing in formal Standard English, as used in an academic setting.

active voice Writing in which the emphasis is on a subject doing something, instead of something being done to it. Writing in the active voice tends to sound more forceful and assured.

address A formal speech presented to a group of listeners; i.e., "the Gettysburg Address."

ad hominem Latin for "against the man;" this argument is an attack on a person's character instead of on the person's ideas or opinions.

adjective A word that modifies a noun or pronoun and answers such questions as "What kind? Which one? How many?"

ad populum See *common knowledge*.

adverb A word that modifies a verb, adjective, or another adverb and answers such questions as "How? When? Where? How often? To what extent?"

alliteration Repetition of initial sounds of words in close proximity to each other.

allusion Indirect reference to something (usually a literary text, mythology, folklore, fairy tales, the Bible, etc.) with which the reader is supposed to be familiar. Allusion is used with humorous intent, to establish a connection between writer and reader or to make a subtle point.

ambiguity Language that may be interpreted in more than one way. Artful language may be ambiguous, but unintentional ambiguity (or vagueness) is to be avoided.

ambiguous pronoun A pronoun without a clear antecedent.

analogy A comparison to a directly parallel case. A writer uses an analogy to argue that a claim reasonable for one case is reasonable for the analogous case.

analysis Breaking something down or studying it closely to see how the parts fit together to form the whole.

anecdote Short narrative used to illustrate a point.

annotation Information about a source that is keyed to each mention of the source in a passage or article.

anonymous source A passage for which the author is unknown or which is presented without the author's name.

anthology A collection of articles or essays on a particular subject or by a particular group of writers.

antithesis Balancing of two opposite or contrasting words, phrases, or clauses.

annotation Explanatory notes added to a text to explain, cite sources, or give bibliographical data.

antecedent A noun, clause, or phrase to which a pronoun or other part of speech refers.

apostrophe Direct address to an absent or imaginary person or to an object, quality, or idea.

appeal to emotion A persuasive writing technique in which the author uses an emotional argument designed to engage a reader's sympathies, values, and compassion.

appeal to morality A persuasive writing technique in which the author tries to garner moral support for an argument by linking it to a value that is widely accepted.

appeal to reason A persuasive writing technique in which the author employs logic to make an argument.

appeal to tradition A persuasive writing technique in which the writer suggests that a course of action is proper or necessary simply because things have always been done that way.

appositive A noun or noun phrase that renames another noun nearby.

archaic vocabulary Words that are rarely or never used in modern English or that have a different meaning from contemporary usage. Shakespeare often uses what we consider archaic vocabulary in his plays and poems.

archive A collection of source material such as public records or historical documents.

assonance Repetition of a vowel sound within two or more words in close proximity.

audience Readers or listeners addressed by a piece of writing or a speech.

author's purpose The reason that an author is writing a passage, such as to persuade, to inform, to instruct, or to entertain.

authority Arguments that draw on recognized experts or persons with highly relevant experience are said to rest on authoritative backing or authority. Readers are expected to accept claims if they are in agreement with an authority's view.

autobiography A person's life story written by the person her- or himself. An autobiography is usually a chronological presentation of the events in the writer's life with her or his thoughts about those events.

backing Support or evidence for a claim in an argument.

balanced sentence Construction in which both halves of the sentence are of about the same length and importance.

bandwagon appeal An argument that taps into people's desire to be like the group or to hold the trendy opinion. Similarly to ad populum, it argues that "everyone is doing this" or "the hip people believe this."

begging the question An argument that assumes as evidence the very conclusion it is trying to prove. Also called Circular Reasoning.

bibliography A list of the sources used in a piece of writing.

biography The story of a person's life written by another person.

body paragraph A paragraph between the opening and conclusion of an essay in which the author develops the main argument or theme.

brainstorming Listing ideas at random that could be of use in an essay or passage.

capitalization Beginning a word with an upper-case letter to denote the beginning of a sentence, a proper noun, a word in a title, etc.

causal relationship An assertion that a particular result was brought about by a certain action or policy. Showing how an action produces an outcome is often relevant in establishing a logical argument.

cause/effect An organizational pattern in which the writer shows how actions or events and their results are related.

Chicago Manual of Style A guide to style for American English that also provides a uniform standard for citing source material in research publications.

Chronological An organizational pattern in which the writer presents facts or events in time order.

circular reasoning See *begging the question*.

circumlocution Indirect, wordy language used to avoid stating something simply and directly.

classification An organizational pattern in which the writer explains how concepts or terms are related.

clause Group of words containing a subject and a verb. An independent (or main) clause can stand alone grammatically as a complete sentence. A subordinate (or independent) clause begins with a subordinating conjunction and is considered a sentence fragment unless attached to an independent clause.

clausal modifier A clause that acts like an adjective or adverb in the structure of a sentence.

cliché A hackneyed, overused, or trite expression, such as "a fish out of water" or "build a better mousetrap."

colloquial language Language that is informal and conversational as opposed to formal.

comma splice A sentence in which two independent clauses are joined with only a comma.

commentary A writer's or reporter's opinions about a current news story or controversy.

common knowledge An argument that appeals to the opinion of the masses, as if the agreement of large numbers of people makes it unnecessary to offer any more evidence for a contention. Also called *ad populum*.

compare/contrast An organizational pattern in which the writer shows how two or more people, things, or ideas are alike and how they are different.

complex sentence A sentence made up of an independent clause and one or more dependent clauses joined by subordinating conjunctions.

compound sentence A sentence formed by joining two independent clauses using a coordinating conjunction, a semicolon, or a conjunctive adverb.

compound-complex sentence A sentence formed from two or more independent clauses and one or more dependent clauses joined by one of a variety of conjunctions or punctuation marks.

concision The elimination of unnecessary words and phrases in writing.

conclusion The last paragraph or section of an essay, in which the writer sums up the main argument, presents a solution to a problem, briefly reviews effects or consequences, or calls for a particular action.

concrete language Language that describes specific, observable things, people or places, rather than ideas or qualities.

conjunction A word that connects words or groups of words.

connotation Rather than the dictionary definition, the associations suggested by a word. A *shack* and a *mansion* are both houses, but the words have different connotations.

consonance Repetition of an ending consonant sound within two or more words in close proximity.

controversy A discussion of an issue or question in which strongly-held opposing views are being expressed.

coordinating conjunction A word such as *and, but, or, nor, for, yet,* and *so* that joins two simple sentences or independent clauses.

criticism The genre of opinion writing about works of art, such as films, novels, plays, paintings, and musical compositions.

cumulative sentence Sentence that begins with the main idea and then expands on that idea with a series of details or other particulars.

debate A formal contest in which two participants or teams present opposing points of view with supporting facts and details.

declarative sentence A sentence that makes a statement and ends with a period.

deconstruct The act of breaking down a text into its constituent parts or elements in order to analyze it more thoroughly.

deductive reasoning A logical appeal in which the author presents a generalization and then applies it to a specific case.

defend a claim Offer an argument in support of a stated position in a writing prompt.

definition An organizational pattern in which the writer defines something by carefully describing what characteristics it has and does not have.

denotation The common dictionary definition of a word.

dependent clause A clause that cannot stand alone as a complete sentence and that may begin with a subordinating conjunction; often called a subordinate clause.

descriptive writing Writing that uses sensory language, rich detail, and figurative language to portray people, places, or things.

detail A subordinate part that contributes to a passage of writing, such as a fact or an instance of description.

development The way in which a writer uses facts, details, and various rhetorical devices to present and add to an argument or theme in an essay.

dialect Word choice, particularly as an element of style. Different types and arrangements of words have significant effects on meaning. An essay written in academic diction would be much less colorful, but perhaps more precise than street slang.

diary A person's daily or frequent account of his or her life and intimate reflections. Each section of writing in a diary is called an "entry."

diction Word choice, particularly as an element of style. Different types and arrangements of words have significant effects on meaning. An essay written in academic diction would be much less colorful, but perhaps more precise than street slang.

direct object A noun or pronoun that follows a verb and answers the question "Whom?" or "What?"

documenting Providing factual source material to support an argument.

drafting The stage of the writing process in which most of the actual writing is done.

editing The stage of the writing process in which a writer polishes the work and correct mistakes.

editorial A brief opinion piece on some current event or topical subject. Most editorials are written for newspapers, magazines, or websites, and they tend to date very quickly.

either/or A logical fallacy that deceptively reduces an argument to two oversimplified alternatives. Also called false dichotomy.

elaboration Adding supporting details, expert opinion, or reasoned analysis to enrich the meaning of a passage.

emotional appeal When a writer appeals to readers' emotions (often through pathos) to excite and involve them in the argument.

encyclopedia A reference work composed of articles on a variety of subjects in alphabetical order.

endnote Citation of a source placed at the end of a article or essay.

essay A text written in the first person and describing or expressing strong opinions about some topic or life experience.

ethical appeal When a writer tries to persuade the audience to respect and believe him or her based on a presentation of image of self through the text. Reputation is sometimes a factor in ethical appeals, but in all cases the aim is to gain the audience's confidence.

euphemism Pleasant or sanitized expression used to describe something unpleasant or negative.

evoke To transmit a particular feeling, emotion, or sensory image.

example An individual instance taken to be representative of a general pattern. Arguing by example is considered reliable if examples are demonstrably true or factual as well as relevant.

excerpt A passage of writing selected from a larger work.

exclamatory sentence A sentence that expresses strong emotion and often ends with an exclamation point.

expectation and surprise Important parts of an author's style, which includes following a pattern, which creates expectation in the reader, and deviating from it, which creates surprise.

explication The act of interpreting or discovering the meaning of a text. Explication usually involves close reading and special attention to figurative language.

expository writing Writing that seeks to inform, explain, instruct, clarify, or define. It generally features a main topic, supporting details and facts, strong organization, and logical transitions.

extrapolation A logical appeal in which areas beyond the area of focus are assumed to be like the focused-on area.

false analogy When two cases or situations are not sufficiently parallel to lead readers to accept a claim of connection between them.

faulty appeal to authority An argument that attempts to justify a claim by misrepresenting the trustworthiness of a supposedly authoritative source, failing to acknowledge that experts disagree on the point, or appealing to a source who is not an expert.

false dichotomy See *either/or*.

first draft A piece of writing as it is first drafted, without revision or editing.

first-person The point of view used by a writer to express her or his own experiences or opinions; characterized by pronouns such as *I*, *me*, and *my*.

flow The presentation in a piece of writing of ideas that are logically connected and lead to a natural conclusion.

footnote Citation of a source placed at the bottom of the page where the reference appears.

formal writing Writing that carefully follows the rules of grammar and syntax and usually avoids slang, dialect, or contractions.

figurative language Words that have a special meaning or effect that is different from their literal meaning. Figurative language includes simile, metaphor, imagery, hyperbole, personification, and many other tropes.

footnote Information provided outside and in addition to the main text of a piece of writing.

generalization When a writer bases a claim upon an isolated example or asserts that a claim is certain rather than probable.

genre A category of writing or art characterized by a certain style, form, or content.

gerund A present participle that always functions as a noun.

glittering generalities An argument that uses "happy words" that sound important but actually have little or no real meaning. The words, such as *wonderful, fair*, and *decent*, are employed in general statements that can't be proved or disproved.

grammar The system of rules that define the structure and correct usage of a language.

graphic organizer A graphic such as a T-chart, Venn diagram, or cluster diagram for use in generating ideas in prewriting.

guilt by association An argument that relies on prejudice instead of careful thought. It seeks to impugn a person because of the actions or reputation of those with whom he or she associates.

hasty generalization An argument based on too few samples to prove the point. Also called "jumping to conclusions."

historical context Background information that helps a reader understand the contemporary circumstances surrounding a piece of writing.

hyperbole Conscious exaggeration used to heighten effect. Not intended literally, hyperbole is often humorous.

hypothesis/support An organizational pattern in which the writer presents a hypothesis or theory and provides details and examples to support it or refute it.

hypothetical example Example that is not specifically factual but is a possible situation to support the writer's purpose.

idiom Common expression that has acquired a meaning different from its literal meaning, as in "Things were still *up in the air*" (meaning things were still unsettled).

idiomatic language Language that conforms to the style and usage of a particular group.

illustration An organizational pattern in which the writer presents a topic and then gives examples to explain it further.

image Word or words, either figurative or literal, used to describe a sensory experience or an object as perceived by the senses.

imagery Figurative language that is written to appeal to one or more of the senses—sight, hearing, smell, taste, touch.

imperative sentence Sentence making a call to action or command where the understood "you" is the subject.

implication A hint given but not stated explicitly.

impressionistic prose Prose writing that is abstract and employs imagery and figurative language to create its effects.

incongruity Juxtaposition of ideas or images that seem inconsistent, incompatible, or out of place.

independent clause A clause that can stand alone as a complete sentence.

indirect object A noun or pronoun that follows a verb and answers the question "To whom?" or "For What?"

inductive reasoning A logical appeal in which the author presents a specific case or example and then draws general conclusions from it.

inference Drawing a conclusion from the available evidence.

infinitive A phrase made up of the word *to* and the base form of a verb (*to love, to decide*). It can function as an adjective, adverb, or noun.

informal writing Writing that is not intended for a formal audience or readership and that follows more relaxed standards of grammar, syntax, and punctuation.

interjection A word or phrase that generally expresses strong emotion, such as surprise or delight.

interrogative pronoun A pronoun that asks which person or thing is meant, such as *who* or *what*.

interrogative sentence A sentence that asks a question and ends with a question mark.

interview A formal question-and-answer session between a writer or reporter and a subject, often transcribed or recorded.

introduction The opening of an essay in which the writer presents the topic or thesis statement.

inverted sentence Variation of the normal word order (subject first, then verb, then complement) that puts a modifier or the verb as first in the sentence. The element that appears first is emphasized more than the subject.

irony Dramatic irony is when a reader is aware of a reality that differs from a character's perception of reality. Situational irony is when the actual result of a situation is completely different from the expected result. Verbal irony is writing or saying one thing and meaning another.

issue A question or controversy of current interest.

jargon Technical language of a profession or skill, not typically understood or used by other people.

journal A person's record of experiences, ideas and reflections written for private use.

juxtaposition Purposeful placement of ideas, images, or language (often incongruous) to heighten their effect.

lecture A formal speech or presentation designed to inform an audience about a particular subject.

letter A written communication to another person, often of an intimate nature.

logic The use of carefully structured reasoning and evidence to make an argument.

logical fallacy An argument that includes one or more common errors in reasoning or assumption.

malapropism The incorrect use of a long word, often to comic effect.

maxim A proverbial saying.

mechanics The functional details of the rules of using the English language.

memoir A narrative that presents experiences and impressions from an author's life. Generally less formal than an autobiography, a memoir is based around a mood or attitude toward a particular section of the author's life.

metaphor Comparison of two things, often unrelated, without using the words "like" or "as." An extended metaphor carries that comparison beyond the initial statement and extends it further. A mixed metaphor is a metaphor that presents an inconsistent comparison and should be avoided.

MLA documentation style System of citing source material, recommended by the Modern Language Association (MLA).

mood Atmosphere created by a writer's word choice (diction) and the details selected. Syntax is also a determiner of mood because sentence strength, length, and complexity affect pacing.

narration The use of the elements of narrative fiction to develop a passage of writing as a story.

narrative writing Writing that tells a story or describes a situation in a (usually) chronological sequence of events.

nonfiction Writing that is based on either documented historical facts or facts as the writer knows them or understands them.

non-sequitur Latin for "it does not follow." When one statement isn't logically connected to another.

noun A word that names a person, place, thing, or idea. Proper nouns naming a particular person or place are capitalized, while common nouns are not.

op-ed article A brief opinion piece for a newspaper that is usually written by someone unaffiliated with the editorial board. The name comes from "opposite the editorial page."

objectivity A writer's attempt to remove himself or herself from any subjective, personal involvement in a story. Hard-news journalism is frequently prized for its objectivity.

online database An organized collection of data on a computer network.

onomatopoeia Use of a word whose pronunciation suggests the sound that it describes.

opinion piece A piece of writing in which an author expresses his or her viewpoint on a current issue.

oration A formal speech delivered in a dignified manner to a gathering of listeners.

organization The presentation of ideas in a smooth, logical progression in a written essay.

outline A list of ideas and facts organized by subject and importance.

oversimplification When a writer obscures or denies the complexity of the issues in an argument.

oxymoron Paradoxical construction juxtaposing two contradictory terms.

paradox Seemingly contradictory statement that is actually true. This rhetorical device is often used for emphasis or simply to make a humorous point.

parallel structure Sentence construction that places in close proximity two or more equal grammatical constructions. Parallel structure may be as simple as listing two or three modifiers in a row to describe the same noun or verb; it may take the form of two or more of the same type of phrases (prepositional, participial, gerund, appositive) that modify the same noun or verb; it may also take the form of two or more subordinate clauses that modify the same noun or verb. Or, parallel structure may be a complex blend of single-word, phrase, and clause parallelism all in the same sentence.

parody Exaggerated imitation of a serious work for humorous purposes. The writer of a parody uses the quirks of style of the imitated piece in extreme or ridiculous ways.

participle A verb form that usually ends in *-ed* or *-ing* and can function as an adjective but with certain characteristics of a verb.

part-to-whole A logical appeal in which the whole is assumed to be like individual parts only larger.

passage A unified excerpt from a nonfiction text presented for analysis.

passive voice Writing in which the emphasis is on something being done to the subject, rather than on the subject doing something. The use of passive voice can make a piece of writing sound vague, weak, or wordy.

periodic sentence Sentence that places the main idea at the end of the sentence, after all introductory elements.

personal experience Information that is drawn from a writer's own life for use in an essay, often in anecdotal form.

personal pronoun A pronoun that substitutes for a noun denoting a person or people, such as *I*, *me*, *you*, *she*, and *they*.

personification Figurative language in which inanimate objects, animals, ideas, or abstractions are endowed with human traits or human form.

persuasive essay An essay that attempts to convince the reader to agree with a point of view or accept the parameters of an argument about a particular problem or controversy.

phrasal modifier A phrase that acts like an adjective or adverb in the structure of a sentence.

phrase A group of words that combine to create meaning but do not have a subject and verb, and therefore cannot stand alone as a sentence. Types of phrases include prepositional, participial, infinitive, gerund, verb, etc.

podcast A neologism combining the words "broadcast" and "pod" and denoting a computer-based form of media that includes academic lectures, interviews, reports, slide shows, and a variety of video and audio clips.

poetic device A use of figurative language such as simile, metaphor, or imagery in a passage of writing.

point of view Perspective from which a work of fiction or nonfiction is presented. Can be first-person, second-person, third-person, or third-person omniscient.

possessive pronoun A word that replaces a noun and shows possession or ownership, such as *mine* and *yours*.

post hoc, ergo propter hoc Latin for "after this, therefore because of this," this argument suggests that because one event precedes another, it also causes it.

predicate A verb that expresses the subject's action or state of being. A simple predicate consists of only a verb or compound verb. A complete predicate consists of the verb and all accompanying modifiers and words that complete the meaning of the sentence.

predicting Using prior knowledge and logic to decide on the probable correct answer to a multiple-choice question before reading the answer choices.

prediction A logical appeal in which the future is assumed to be like the past.

prefix A word part that precedes the root of a word and alters its meaning.

premise A proposition presented as a previously proved statement of fact.

preposition A word such as *at, above*, or *beneath* that expresses position or state.

prepositional phrase A group of words that begins with a preposition that links to an object.

prewriting The steps of the writing process that involve planning and determining purpose before the actual drafting begins.

primary source A source written by or in the subject's own words, such as an autobiography, personal journal, or interview.

problem/solution An organizational pattern in which the writer describes a problem and proposes a solution.

process of elimination The strategy of using logic and reasoned analysis to eliminate incorrect answers and choose the best answer on a multiple-choice question.

prompt The question or situation to which a student essay writer must respond on an essay test.

pronoun A word used in place of a noun or noun phrase.

pronoun agreement The grammatical rule that a pronoun must agree in person, number and gender with its antecedent.

pronoun reference The relationship between a pronoun and the noun, clause, or phrase it refers to.

proofreading Carefully checking a piece of writing for mistakes such as misspelled words, subject-verb disagreement, or punctuation errors.

proper noun A word that names a particular or unique person, place, or thing and is capitalized.

proposition of fact A persuasive writing strategy in which the author seeks to convince the reader that a proposition is true or false.

publishing or sharing The last stage of the writing process when no time constraints exist. The writer decides on the best way to publish or share a piece of writing with an audience.

pun Play on words that exploits the similarity in sound between two words with different meanings, usually for a humorous effect.

punctuation The use of standardized marks to clarify meaning and control the pace and flow of a passage of writing.

qualification Condition, limitation, or restraint placed on an idea or argument. A qualified argument takes a position somewhere between the two opposing sides.

question of policy A persuasive writing strategy in which the author tries to convince the reader that some action should be taken or some policy adopted.

question of value A persuasive writing strategy in which the author seeks to convince the reader that an action or activity is right or wrong, moral or immoral, ethical or unethical, or better or worse than another action or activity.

quotation Insertion of the exact words from a literary or other source into a passage of writing.

red herring An argument that avoids the key issue by introducing a separate issue as a diversion.

refute a claim An argument that opposes or attempts to disprove the points of a statement in a writing prompt.

repetition Use of a word or phrase two or more times in close proximity.

review An article that presents the writer's opinion about a work of art, such as a film, novel, play, or art exhibition.

reviewing Due to the time constraints on the AP writing exam, the last stage of the writing process, in which the writer skims the essay one final time for any errors.

revising The stage of the writing process in which the writer re-reads and reworks a piece of writing for content, structure, and flow.

rhetoric Art of effective communication, especially persuasive discourse. Rhetoric focuses on the interrelationship of invention, arrangement, and style in order to create appealing and appropriate discourse.

rhetorical analysis A systematic and detailed consideration of how an author uses rhetorical devices and strategies to achieve a purpose.

rhetorical device Any characteristic of language used to achieve the writer or speaker's purpose.

rhetorical strategy An author's use of various rhetorical devices to achieve a particular purpose or create an effect.

rhetorical question Question with an obvious, understood answer.

rhyme Repetition of the ending sounds of words to form a verbal pattern.

rhythm The alternation and repetition of strong and weak sound elements in writing.

root The main lexical unit of a word. Also called *root word*.

rubric A detailed description of what is required to earn a particular score on an essay.

run-on sentence A sentence in which two independent clauses are joined together without a coordinating conjunction.

sarcasm Type of verbal irony, the purpose of which is to denigrate the subject.

satire Work that reveals a critical attitude toward some element of human behavior by portraying it in an extreme way. Satire doesn't simply abuse (as in invective) or get personal (as in sarcasm). Satire targets groups or large concepts rather than individuals.

scientific writing A book, article, or essay that presents an aspect of science in order to explain it or debate its legitimacy.

secondary source A source that presents information that originally appeared elsewhere or was generated by someone who was not present at or involved in the events discussed.

sentence A syntactical unit that expresses a statement, question, command, wish, or exclamation. It begins with a capital letter and ends with a punctuation mark.

sentence fragment A flawed sentence that lacks a subject or predicate.

sentence variety An author's use of a number of different sentence lengths and types to create interest or for special emphasis.

simile Figurative comparison of two things, often dissimilar, using the connecting words "like" or "as."

simple sentence An independent clause containing a subject and a verb.

skim Read over a piece of writing very quickly to check for errors or certain points of information.

slang Very informal or course language, to be avoided in formal writing.

slippery slope An argument based on the idea that if a first step is taken, then a second and third step will follow inevitably, until a disaster occurs like a person sliding on a slippery incline until he or she falls to the bottom.

source A documented reference used for information about a certain topic or controversy.

speech A public address usually presented to a large group of people.

standard English The form of the English language accepted as the norm for writing and speaking in a particular Anglophone country.

straw man An argument that creates a "straw man," or misrepresented version of an opponent's position, by exaggerating, overstating, or over-simplifying an opposing point of view.

style A writer's method of expression, including choices in diction, tone, and syntax.

style-analysis essay An essay that analyzes the language used in a passage to explain how the author uses rhetorical devices to achieve an effect or accomplish a purpose Also called *rhetorical-analysis essay*.

subject A noun or pronoun that is partnered with an action verb or being verb. The subject may also be understood as (you), as in the sentence "Come here, please."

subjectivity Opinions based on personal preference or prejudice and not completely on objective fact.

subject-verb agreement Using singular subjects with singular verbs and plural subjects with plural verbs.

subordinate clause A clause that cannot stand alone as a complete sentence; a dependent clause.

subordinating conjunction A word such as *since, when, because,* or *after* that signals a subordinating relationship between a clause and the main part of a sentence.

suffix A word part that is appended to the root of a word and alters its meaning.

summary A brief review of the main points in an essay or passage of writing.

syllogism A stylized deductive argument in which a major premise and a minor premise lead to a logical conclusion. Example: All men are mortal. Socrates is a man. Therefore, Socrates is mortal.

symbol Person, thing, or event that represents or stands for some larger idea or meaning.

syntactic fluency Ability to create a variety of sentence structures, appropriately complex or simple and varied in length.

syntax The arrangement of words in meaningful patterns. An author's use of syntax involves the devices employed to create an emotional or intellectual effect.

synthesis essay An essay in which the student writer culls ideas and supporting facts from various sources to support an argument or analyze an issue.

text structure The organizational plan employed in a passage, such as cause/effect or problem/solution.

theme Central idea of a work of fiction or nonfiction revealed and developed in the course of a story or explored through argument.

thesis Central argument an author makes in a work of nonfiction, sometimes stated explicitly and sometimes implied.

thesis statement A concise presentation of the main argument in an essay, often expressed in a single sentence.

third-person An omniscient or impersonal point of view used by an author and characterized by pronouns such as *he, her, it, they,* and *theirs.*

tone Writer's attitude toward his or her subject matter revealed through diction, figurative language, selection of details, imagery, and organization.

topic sentence The sentence in a paragraph that presents the main idea to be discussed there.

topical subject A subject that is currently interesting or controversial to a large audience.

transition word or phrase Words or phrases that help a reader understand the progression of ideas in a passage.

travel writing Writing that blends sensory detail and personal reactions to describe a place that is foreign to the writer.

understatement An expression that deliberately has less force that would be expected, usually used for comic effect.

unity A quality of a work that relates all the parts to one central idea or organizing principle.

usage The correct way to employ words and phrases in a language.

verb A word that expresses action (action verbs) or state of being (linking or helping verbs).

verbal A verb that also functions as another part of speech.

verbal phrase A phrase made up of a verbal and all of its modifiers and objects.

viewpoint The opinion about or approach to an issue that a writer expresses in a persuasive essay.

visual source A source for the synthesis essay such as a photograph, painting, or chart.

vocabulary An author's store of words or characteristic use of language in writing.

voice An author's distinctive use of language and tone in a piece of writing.

website Any of various unique sites on the Internet featuring web pages with content such as text, video, audio, etc.

word analysis Use of a basic knowledge of the English language, especially familiarity with its numerous prefixes, to help decode unfamiliar words, build vocabulary, and strengthen spelling skills.

word choice The use of words that are strong, clear, and accurate, and that avoid problems such as sexist language.

writing process The steps of composing a piece of writing, from planning to presentation.

writing task What a student writer must do to complete successfully an essay in response to a writing prompt.

Index

NOTES

NOTES

NOTES

NOTES

NOTES

NOTES